# Reading and Learning Across the Disciplines

# Reading and Learning Across the Disciplines

Second Edition

**Mary-Jane McCarthy    Joan Rasool    Caroline Banks**

WADSWORTH PUBLISHING COMPANY

I(T)P® An International Thomson Publishing Company

Belmont • Albany • Bonn • Boston • Cincinnati • Detroit • London • Madrid • Melbourne •
Mexico City • New York • Paris • San Francisco • Singapore • Tokyo • Toronto • Washington

ENGLISH EDITOR: Angela Gantner Wrahtz
EDITORIAL ASSISTANT: Royden Tonomura
PRODUCTION EDITOR: Angela Mann
DESIGNER: Kaelin Chappell and Ann Butler
PRINT BUYER: Barbara Britton
COPY EDITOR: Thomas Briggs
PERMISSIONS EDITOR: Robert Kauser
COVER DESIGNER: Cassandra Chu
COMPOSITOR: Thompson Type
PRINTER: Malloy Lithographing

*This book is printed on
acid-free recycled paper.*

For more information, contact:
Wadsworth Publishing Company
10 Davis Drive
Belmont, California 94002, USA

International Thomson Publishing Europe
Berkshire House 168-173
High Holborn
London, WC1V 7AA, England

Thomas Nelson Australia
102 Dodds Street
South Melbourne 3205
Victoria, Australia

Nelson Canada
1120 Birchmount Road
Scarborough, Ontario
Canada M1K 5G4

International Thomson Editores
Campos Eliseos 385, Piso 7
Col. Polanco
11560 México D. F. México

International Thomson Publishing GmbH
Königswinterer Strasse 418
53227 Bonn, Germany

International Thomson Publishing Asia
221 Henderson Road
#05-10 Henderson Building
Singapore 0315

International Thomson Publishing Japan
Hirakawacho Kyowa Building, 3F
2-2-1 Hirakawacho
Chiyoda-ku, Tokyo 102, Japan

**Library of Congress Cataloging-in-Publication Data**
McCarthy, Mary-Jane
    Reading and learning across the disciplines / Mary-Jane McCarthy,
Joan Rasool, Caroline Banks. — 2nd ed.
        p.    cm.
    Includes bibliographical references and index.
    ISBN 0-534-25722-4 (pbk.)
    1. Reading — Language experience approach.    2. Language experience
approach in education.    3. Critical thinking — Study and teaching.
4. Study skills.    5. Learning.    I. Rasool, Joan.    II. Banks,
Caroline.    III. Title.
LB1050.35.M33   1996
372.4'14 — dc20                                    95-41173

# Brief Contents

**PART I**    *The Foundations*      3

    **CHAPTER 1**    **Understanding Context and Learning Vocabulary 5**
         *with readings on vocabulary*

    **CHAPTER 2**    **Activating Knowledge to Create Context 31**
         *with readings on time*

    **CHAPTER 3**    **Understanding the Main Idea 67**
         *with readings on intelligence and learning*

    **CHAPTER 4**    **Understanding Yourself as a Reader and a Learner 97**
         *with readings on learning strategies*

    **CHAPTER 5**    **Listening and Lecture Notes 141**
         *with a reading from Communications*

**PART II**    *Structures and Strategies*      163

    **CHAPTER 6**    **Problems and Solutions 167**
         *with readings from Psychology*

    **CHAPTER 7**    **Definitions, Examples, and Lists 195**
         *with readings from Sociology*

    **CHAPTER 8**    **Chronological Order and Narration 223**
         *with readings from Health Studies*

    **CHAPTER 9**    **Cause and Effect 251**
         *with readings from Environmental Studies*

    **CHAPTER 10**    **Comparison and Contrast 289**
         *with readings from Business and Economics*

**PART III**  *Critical Thinking and Research*                    **317**

    CHAPTER 11  **Issue and Debate   319**
                *with readings from Criminal Justice*

    CHAPTER 12  **Research Studies and Statistical Data   353**
                *with readings on nature versus nurture*


**PART IV**  *Additional Readings for Review*                    **393**

    APPENDIX A  **Glossary of Reading Vocabulary   463**

    APPENDIX B  **Sample Lecture/Reading Source Materials for Chapter 5 Exercises   473**

    APPENDIX C  **Periodical Indexes   483**

# Detailed Contents

*To the Instructor*   *xxiii*
*To the Student*   *xxviii*


**PART I**   *The Foundations*        **3**

**CHAPTER 1**   **Understanding Context and Learning Vocabulary  5**

Creating Context   7
    *Warm-Up:* Using Context to Establish Meaning   8
    *Exercise 1:* Where Does Comprehension Come From?   9
    *Exercise 2:* Variations in Meaning   10

Using Context to Unlock the Meaning of New Words   12
    *Exercise 3:* Identifying Context Clues   13

**Reading Selection One   14**
    *Prereading Activity:* Using Context to Supply Meaning   14
    **"How to Improve Your Vocabulary"   15**
    *Comprehension Check*   19
    *Comprehension Exercise:* Putting Randall's Five Steps to Work   20

**Reading Selection Two   20**
    *Prereading Activity 1:* Identifying Context Clues   20
    *Prereading Activity 2:* Finding the Meaning of New Words   21
    **"Symbols of Humankind"   22**
    *Comprehension Check*   24
    *Comprehension Exercise:* Using Context to Define New Words   25

Chapter Application   25
    *Prereading Activity:* Identifying Context Clues   26

*Going Beyond:* "Don't Talk Dirty to Me"   27
    *Journal Writing*   29

**CHAPTER 2**   **Activating Knowledge to Create Context**   **31**

Activating Prior Knowledge   33
    *Warm-Up:* Measuring Background Knowledge   33

**Reading Selection One**   **34**
    *Prereading Activity:* What Do You Know About Hypnosis?   34
    **"Hypnosis: Altered Consciousness or Role Playing?"**   **35**
    *Comprehension Check*   38

Previewing by Scanning and Skimming   39
    *Exercise 1:* Skimming for Main Ideas   40

**Reading Selection Two**   **42**
    *Prereading Activity:* Previewing an Article   42
    **"Chronobiology: Finding Your Peak Time of Day"**   **45**
    *Comprehension Check*   50

**Reading Selection Three**   **51**
    *Prereading Activity:* Previewing an Article   51
    **"Sleep as a Biological Rhythm"**   **53**
    *Comprehension Check*   58

Chapter Application 1   59

Chapter Application 2   62

*Going Beyond:* "All Work and Not Enough Play"   63

*Journal Writing*   66

**CHAPTER 3**   **Understanding the Main Idea**   **67**

The Main Idea and the Building Block Approach to Writing   69
    *Warm-Up 1:* Finding the Stated Main Idea of a Paragraph   71
    *Exercise 1:* Finding the Topic Sentence   73
    *Warm-Up 2:* Finding the Implied Main Idea of a Paragraph   78
    *Exercise 2:* Inferring the Main Idea When There Is No Topic
    Sentence   79

**Reading Selection One**   **82**
    *Prereading Activity:* Finding the Topic Sentence   82
    **"Get Smart"**   **83**
    *Comprehension Check*   86

**Reading Selection Two    88**
*Prereading Activity:* Rating Yourself    88
**"Better Late Than Never"    89**
*Comprehension Check*    92

Chapter Application    93

*Going Beyond:* "What Is Intelligence, Anyway?"    93

*Journal Writing*    95


**CHAPTER 4    Understanding Yourself as a Reader
and a Learner    97**

Learning Styles    99
*Warm-Up 1:* Learning Style Inventory    101

Coordinating Your Learning Style with Your Instructor's    103
*Exercise 1:* Adapting Your Learning Style for Tests    104

Coordinating Your Learning Style with the Task    105
*Exercise 2:* Creating a Study Group    106

Metacognition and Reading Comprehension    107
*Warm-Up 2:* Reading Profile    109

Improving Your Reading Through Metacognitive Monitoring    111

**Reading Selection One    114**
*Prereading Activity 1:* Paraphrasing    114
*Prereading Activity 2:* Creating Questions    118
**"Development of Metamemory"    118**
*Comprehension Check*    123

**Reading Selection Two    125**
*Prereading Activity:* Remembering    125
**"How to Improve Your . . . Oh, Yeah, Memory"    126**
*Comprehension Check*    133

Chapter Application    134

*Going Beyond:* "from *Black Boy*"    135

*Journal Writing*    140

**CHAPTER 5   Listening and Lecture Notes   141**

Being an Active Listener   143
   *Warm-Up:* Improving Your Note Taking   143
   *Exercise 1:* How Actively Do You Listen to a Lecture?   145
   *Exercise 2:* The Importance of Active Listening   146

Why Take Notes?   147

The Three Stages of Note Taking   148
   *Exercise 3:* Preparing to Take Lecture Notes   149
   *Exercise 4:* Condensing and Abbreviating   154
   *Exercise 5:* Practicing Note Taking   156
   *Exercise 6:* Monitoring by Summarizing   156

Chapter Application   158

*Going Beyond:* "Can We Talk?"   158

*Journal Writing*   160


**PART II**   *Structures and Strategies*   163


**CHAPTER 6   Problems and Solutions   167**

Questions and Answers   169
   *Warm-Up:* Generating Solutions   170

Viewing Problems as Effects   170

Solving Problems   172
   *Exercise 1:* Solving a Personal Problem   172

**Reading Selection One   173**
   *Prereading Activity:* Previewing the Selection   173
   **"Stress and Its Management"   174**
   *Comprehension Check*   178
   *Comprehension Exercise:* A Stress Management Program   179

**Reading Selection Two   181**
   *Prereading Activity:* Previewing the Selection   181
   **"Reappraisal: Ellis's Rational Thinking"   181**
   *Comprehension Check*   184
   *Comprehension Exercise:* Reappraising a Stress-Inducing Situation   186

**Reading Selection Three    187**
    *Prereading Activity:* Previewing the Selection    187
    **"How Much Stress Can You Survive?"    188**
    *Comprehension Check*    190

Chapter Application    191

*Going Beyond:* "Problems and Pain"    192

*Journal Writing*    193


**CHAPTER 7    Definitions, Examples, and Lists    195**

The Importance of Terminology    197

Definitions    197

Examples and Explanations    199
    *Warm-Up 1:* Definitions and Examples    200

Simple Listing or Enumeration    200
    *Warm-Up 2:* Lists    200

Underlining and Annotating    201
    *Exercise 1:* Underlining and Annotating    202

**Reading Selection One    204**
    *Prereading Activity:* Previewing    204
    **"Types of Groups"    205**
    *Comprehension Check*    207

**Reading Selection Two    208**
    *Prereading Activity:* Previewing    208
    **"Collective Behavior"    208**
    *Comprehension Check*    211

Summarizing    212
    *Exercise 2:* Summarizing    213

**Reading Selection Three    213**
    *Prereading Activity:* Previewing a Magazine Article    213
    **"Going 'Wilding' in the City"    214**
    *Comprehension Check*    216
    *Comprehension Exercise:* Outlining and Summarizing    217

Chapter Application    219

*Going Beyond:* "The Male Response to Rape"    219

*Journal Writing*    222

**CHAPTER 8**  **Chronological Order and Narration**  **223**

Chronologies Versus Narrations  225
  *Warm-Up:* Distinguishing Between Chronologies and Narrations  227
  *Exercise 1:* Previewing for Chronological Sequence  227

Time Lines  228
  *Exercise 2:* Creating a Time Line  228

Narrative Illustrations  229
  *Exercise 3:* Inferring the Main Idea  230

**Reading Selection One**  **232**
  *Prereading Activity:* Note Taking to Get the Facts  232
  **"Using Alcohol and Drugs"**  **232**
  *Comprehension Check*  237

Graphs  238
  *Exercise 4:* Reading Graphs  239

**Reading Selection Two**  **240**
  *Prereading Activity:* Scanning for Time Signals  240
  **"Smoking Tobacco"**  **240**
  *Comprehension Check*  242

Objective Tests  242

Chapter Application 1  245

Chapter Application 2  246

*Going Beyond:* "The Endless Binge"  246

*Journal Writing*  250


**CHAPTER 9**  **Cause and Effect**  **251**

Causal Relationships  253
  *Warm-Up:* Identifying Effects from Causes  255

Chain Reactions and Mapping  256
  *Exercise 1:* Mapping a Chain Reaction  257

**Reading Selection One**  **262**
  *Prereading Activity:* Previewing for Causal Relationships  262
  **"Earthly Belches Perturb the Weather"**  **262**
  *Comprehension Check*  265
  *Comprehension Exercise:* Outlining Cause-and-Effect
  Relationships  267

**Reading Selection Two**   **269**

    *Prereading Activity:* Mapping Cause-and-Effect Relationships   269

    **"The Villain in the Atmosphere"**   **270**

    *Comprehension Check*   274

    *Comprehension Exercise:* Mapping Cause-and-Effect Relationships   276

**Reading Selection Three**   **276**

    *Prereading Activity:* Previewing for and
    Mapping Causal Relationships   276

    **"Where Have All the Dinos Gone?"**   **276**

    *Comprehension Check*   278

Essay Exams   280

    *Exercise 2:* Direction Words and Rhetorical Structures   281

    *Exercise 3:* Direction Words   283

    *Exercise 4:* Creating Essay Questions   283

Chapter Application   285

*Going Beyond:* "Running Cars on Plain $H_2O$"   285

*Journal Writing*   288

**CHAPTER 10**   **Comparison and Contrast**   **289**

Comparing and Contrasting   291

    *Warm-Up:* Charting Similarities and Differences to
    Make Decisions   293

**Reading Selection One**   **296**

    *Prereading Activity:* Previewing for Comparison and Contrast   296

    **"Private Versus Public Goods"**   **296**

    *Comprehension Check*   297

    *Comprehension Exercise:* Taking Comparison-and-Contrast Notes   299

Two Methods of Organizing Comparison and Contrast   300

**Reading Selection Two**   **301**

    *Prereading Activity:* Previewing for the Main Idea   301

    **"The Isms: Socialism, Communism, Capitalism"**   **301**

    *Comprehension Check*   303

    *Comprehension Exercise:* Taking Comparison-and-Contrast Notes   305

**Reading Selection Three**  306

*Prereading Activity:* Comparing Living Costs  306

**"What Is a Less Developed Country?"**  **307**

*Comprehension Check*  309

*Comprehension Exercise:* Outlining for Comparison and Contrast  311

Chapter Application  312

*Going Beyond:* "Minds of States"  312

*Journal Writing*  314

PART III  *Critical Thinking and Research*  317

CHAPTER 11  **Issue and Debate**  **319**

What Is an Issue?  321

*Warm-Up:* Stating an Issue  323

*Exercise 1:* Identifying the Issue  324

*Exercise 2:* Identifying a Writer's Position or Viewpoint  325

*Exercise 3:* Taking a Position or Point of View  326

*Exercise 4:* Fact Versus Opinion  328

**Reading Selection One**  **329**

*Prereading Activity:* Scanning for Signal Words  329

**"Death"**  **330**

*Comprehension Check*  333

*Comprehension Exercise 1:* Mapping the Arguments  334

*Comprehension Exercise 2:* Summarizing the Arguments  335

**Reading Selection Two**  **336**

*Prereading Activity:* Evaluating Arguments  336

**"For the Death Penalty"**  **336**

*Comprehension Check*  338

*Comprehension Exercise 1:* Summarizing and Mapping the Arguments  338

*Comprehension Exercise 2:* Determining Validity  339

**Reading Selection Three**  **342**

*Prereading Activity:* Stating an Opinion  342

**Two Editorials on Vigilantism**  **343**

*Comprehension Check 1*  345

*Comprehension Check 2*  347

Chapter Application 1    348

Chapter Application 2    348

*Going Beyond:* "Getting Away with Murder"    348

*Journal Writing*    352

## CHAPTER 12    Research Studies and Statistical Data    353

The Search for Knowledge    355
    *Warm-Up:* Postulating Theories    356

Research Methods    358
    *Exercise 1:* Choosing a Research Method    359
    *Exercise 2:* Finding Flaws    360
    *Exercise 3:* Constructing Tables and Graphs    361

Locating Information on Research    364
    *Exercise 4:* Previewing Technical Vocabulary    364

**Reading Selection One    365**
    *Prereading Activity:* Previewing Textbook Material    365
    **"Sexual Differentiation"    365**
    *Comprehension Check*    371
    *Comprehension Exercise 1:* Examining the Research    373
    *Comprehension Exercise 2:* Charting Research Data    374

**Reading Selection Two    375**
    *Prereading Activity:* Sex Roles    375
    **"Biology Influences Sex Roles"    375**
    *Comprehension Check*    378
    *Comprehension Exercise:* Examining the Research    380

**Reading Selection Three    381**
    *Prereading Activity:* Your Family    381
    **"When Siblings Are *Unlike* Peas in a Pod"    382**
    *Comprehension Check*    387

Chapter Application 1    388

Chapter Application 2    388

*Going Beyond:* "Where Have All the Smart Girls Gone?"    389

*Journal Writing*    391

**Chapter 1: Practice in Building Vocabulary 394**
*Prereading Activity:* Identifying Context Clues 394
**"The Language Detectives: How They Found the Tribe That Gave Us Words" 395**
*Comprehension Check* 398

**Chapter 2: Practice in Previewing 399**
*Prereading Activity:* Previewing 399
**"The Pace of Life" 400**
*Comprehension Check* 406

**Chapter 3: Practice in Finding the Main Idea 407**
*Prereading Activity:* Finding the Main Idea 407
**"The Unwritten American Bargain" 408**
*Comprehension Check* 410

**Chapter 4: Practice in Metacognitive Skills 412**
*Prereading Activity:* Developing Questions 412
**"You Must Remember This" 412**
*Comprehension Check* 417

**Chapter 5: Practice in Note Taking 419**
*Prereading Activity:* Preparing to Take Notes 419
**"Hate Speech on Campus" 419**
*Comprehension Check* 421

**Chapter 6: Practice in Problem and Solution 423**
*Prereading Activity:* Examining the Problem 423
**"Old Habits" 423**
*Comprehension Check* 424

**Chapter 7: Practice in Underlining/Annotating, Outlining, and Summarizing 426**
*Prereading Activity:* Previewing to Create Questions 426
**"Interpersonal Influence" 426**
*Comprehension Check* 430
*Comprehension Exercise 1:* Outlining 432
*Comprehension Exercise 2:* Summarizing 434

**Chapter 8: Practice in Reading Chronological Order   434**

*Prereading Activity:* Organizing a Time Line   434

**"Drug Abuse"   435**

*Comprehension Check*   436

**Chapter 9: Practice in Reading Cause and Effect   439**

*Prereading Activity:* Mapping Cause-and-Effect Relationships   439

**"Hard Facts About Nuclear Winter"   440**

*Comprehension Check*   442

**Chapter 10: Practice in Reading Comparison and Contrast   443**

*Prereading Activity:* Previewing   443

**"The Economic Escalator"   443**

*Comprehension Check*   446

*Comprehension Exercise:* Comparing Economic Conditions   447

**Chapter 11: Practice in Reading Issue and Debate   448**

*Prereading Activity:* Stating the Issue   448

**"Back to the Chain Gang?"   448**

*Comprehension Check*   452

*Comprehension Exercise:* Mapping and Essay Writing   453

**Chapter 12: Practice in Reading Research and Statistical Data   454**

*Prereading Activity:* Previewing the Research   454

**"Growing Up Free: Raising Your Child in the 80's"   455**

*Comprehension Check*   460

*Comprehension Exercise:* Designing a Research Study   462

**APPENDIX A   Glossary of Reading Vocabulary   463**

**APPENDIX B   Sample Lecture/Reading Source Materials for Chapter 5 Exercises   473**

**APPENDIX C   Periodical Indexes   483**

*Credits   486*

# List of Readings by Chapter

**PART I**  *The Foundations*

**CHAPTER 1**  **Understanding Context and Learning Vocabulary**

1   *How to Improve Your Vocabulary*
    by Tony Randall    15

2   *Symbols of Humankind*
    by Don Lago    22

Going Beyond: *Don't Talk Dirty to Me*
    by Russell Baker    27


**CHAPTER 2**  **Activating Knowledge to Create Context**

1   *Hypnosis: Altered Consciousness or Role Playing?*
    by Wayne Weiten    35

2   *Chronobiology: Finding Your Peak Time of Day*
    by William John Watkins    45

3   *Sleep as a Biological Rhythm*
    by Wayne Weiten    53

Going Beyond: *All Work and Not Enough Play*
    by Madeline Drexler    63


**CHAPTER 3**  **Understanding the Main Idea**

1   *Get Smart*
    by Madeline Drexler    83

2   *Better Late Than Never*
    by Jack Levin   89

Going Beyond: *What Is Intelligence, Anyway?*
    by Isaac Asimov   94


**CHAPTER 4**   **Understanding Yourself as a Reader and a Learner**

1   *Development of Metamemory*
    by David Shaffer   118

2   *How to Improve Your . . . Oh, Yeah, Memory*
    by Beth Levine   126

Going Beyond: From *Black Boy*
    by Richard Wright   135


**CHAPTER 5**   **Listening and Lecture Notes**

Going Beyond: *Can We Talk?*
    by Diane White   158


**PART II**   *Structures and Strategies*

**CHAPTER 6**   **Problems and Solutions**

1   *Stress and Its Management*
    by M. R. Levy, M. Dignan, and J. Shirreffs   174

2   *Reappraisal: Ellis's Rational Thinking*
    by Wayne Weiten   181

3   *How Much Stress Can You Survive?*
    by Suzanne Ouellette Kobasa   188

Going Beyond: *Problems and Pain*
    by M. Scott Peck   192

# CHAPTER 7    Definitions, Examples, and Lists

1   *Types of Groups*
    by Judson R. Landis   205

2   *Collective Behavior*
    by Judson R. Landis   208

3   *Going "Wilding" in the City*
    by David Gelman with Peter McKillop   214

Going Beyond: *The Male Response to Rape*
    by Roger Rosenblatt   219


# CHAPTER 8    Chronological Order and Narration

1   *Using Alcohol and Drugs*
    by Linda Brannon and Jess Feist   232

2   *Smoking Tobacco*
    by Linda Brannon and Jess Feist   240

Going Beyond: *The Endless Binge*
    by Jerry Adler with Debra Rosenberg   246


# CHAPTER 9    Cause and Effect

1   *Earthly Belches Perturb the Weather*
    from *U.S. News & World Report*   262

2   *The Villain in the Atmosphere*
    by Isaac Asimov   270

3   *Where Have All the Dinos Gone?*
    from *U.S. News & World Report*   276

Going Beyond: *Running Cars on Plain $H_2O$*
    by Sharon Begley with Mary Hager   286


# CHAPTER 10   Comparison and Contrast

1   *Private Versus Public Goods*
    by Philip C. Starr   296

2   *The Isms: Socialism, Communism, Capitalism*
    by Philip C. Starr   301

3   *What Is a Less Developed Country?*
      by Philip C. Starr   307

Going Beyond: *Minds of States*
      by Joshua Fischman   312

**PART III**   *Critical Thinking and Research*

**CHAPTER 11   Issue and Debate**

*Death by the Highway*
by George F. Cole   326

1   *Death*
      by Todd R. Clear and George F. Cole   330

2   *For the Death Penalty*
      by E. Van den Haag   336

3   *Two Editorials on Vigilantism*
      from the *Miami Herald*   343
      from the Manchester, New Hampshire, *Union Leader*   344

Going Beyond: *Getting Away with Murder*
      by Jack Levin   349

**CHAPTER 12   Research Studies and Statistical Data**

1   *Sexual Differentiation*
      by Metta Spencer and Alex Inkeles   365

2   *Biology Influences Sex Roles*
      by Tim Hackler   375

3   *When Siblings Are Unlike Peas in a Pod*
      by Alison Bass   382

Going Beyond: *Where Have All the Smart Girls Gone?*
      by Mary Conroy   389

## PART IV  *Additional Readings for Review*

1  *The Language Detectives: How They Found the Tribe That Gave Us Words*
   from *Strange Stories, Amazing Facts*  495

2  *The Pace of Life*
   by Robert Levine  400

3  *The Unwritten American Bargain*
   by Gen. Colin L. Powell  408

4  *You Must Remember This*
   by Bill Bryson  412

5  *Hate Speech on Campus*
   by Joseph S. Truman  419

6  *Old Habits*
   by Danielle Lewis  423

7  *Interpersonal Influence*
   by James W. Kalat  426

8  *Drug Abuse*
   by Richard Warga  435

9  *Hard Facts About Nuclear Winter*
   by Andrew C. Revkin  440

10  *The Economic Escalator*
    by Jack Levin  443

11  *Back to the Chain Gang?*
    by Larry Reibstein with Ginny Carroll and Carroll Bogert  448

12  *Growing Up Free: Raising Your Child in the 80's*
    by Letty Cottin Pogrebin  455

# To the Instructor

*Reading and Learning Across the Disciplines*, Second Edition, is part of a series of books that brings a whole-language approach to the teaching of reading, writing, and thinking skills, as well as a developmental approach to the instruction of students. Central to the writing of these textbooks is our belief that meaning is constructed by the reader or listener, and that literacy skills should be learned within a meaningful context. The emphasis is on developing reading ability and metacognitive skills within a knowledge domain. Robert Kegan's theory of constructive developmentalism (outlined in his 1982 book, *The Evolving Self*) complements such an integrated theory of comprehension. His theory assumes that at different stages people have different ways of constructing meaning in their lives, and that this qualitatively affects how they view themselves, others, school, and instruction. His ideas are useful in interpreting student responses to reading tasks.

The books in the *Academic Connections* series have three major objectives: (1) to teach reading and study skills within an integrated language framework; (2) to encourage more active and democratic interaction between instructors and learners; and (3) to underscore for students the connections among their personal, social, and academic lives. The books can be used in sequence or independently.

The emphasis in *Reading and Learning Across the Disciplines* is on developing academic reading and study skills within a knowledge domain. The purpose of the text is to acquaint students with text materials similar to those they will encounter in their courses, provide them with a number of strategic options for dealing with these materials, develop necessary background knowledge, and encourage them to develop individual, unique approaches to study tasks.

## How is the text organized?

Because we view reading and studying as personal processes to which students bring individual experiences and learning preferences, this text offers a flexible approach to both. Unlike most study skills texts, *Reading and Learning Across the Disciplines* is organized around rhetorical structures rather than study skills. It emphasizes the intimate relationship among the author's content, purpose, and style, and offers the student a variety of ways to approach the reading selections. Because each rhetorical structure organizes knowledge in a particular way, the structure influences how that knowledge should be analyzed. Consequently, rather than offer one comprehensive reading and study approach, this text encourages students to vary their learning strategies as the readings dictate. The uniqueness of this text lies in the fact that it is content- or subject-driven rather than skills-driven. The skills emanate from the readings rather than being superimposed upon them. Students are encouraged to apply these skills and strategies to their own academic materials, and to adapt them as necessary to their learning preferences.

The book is divided into four parts, and each of the chapters within the four parts are unified around a specific knowledge domain.

Part I contains five chapters that present the basic skills necessary for monitoring reading and study activities. In addition, the chapters attempt to empower students with an increased awareness of their own individual strengths and weaknesses.

Each of the five chapters in Part II focuses on a particular rhetorical structure. Strategies for using these structures to improve reading comprehension and to facilitate the organization and retention of information are presented within a particular academic discipline. Readings include selections from both textbooks and current periodicals.

Part III consists of two lengthy chapters involving critical thinking skills. Its goal is to challenge students to examine the nature of truth in order to form rational, logical opinions.

Part IV is designed as a chapter-by-chapter review of all the skills presented in the text. It offers additional reading and study skills activities and worksheets on which to practice the reading and study skills.

## How is each chapter organized?

Although content and skills vary from chapter to chapter, organization within each chapter is consistent. Each chapter begins with a brief statement of objectives and a chapter outline and checklist. These sections enable instructors to plan and schedule the readings and activities within each chapter. These are previewing and prereading devices as well as time-management aids.

The key concepts and definitions of the chapter are then presented, followed by a warm-up activity and in many cases by brief readings and exercises as well.

The major portion of each chapter consists of a series of two or three readings. Each reading selection is preceded by a prereading activity and followed by a comprehension check that draws on the concepts and skills of the chapter and the content of the reading. Additional comprehension exercises are often included as well.

Each chapter concludes with one or two applications in which students are required to apply the skills to another academic course. In addition, a journal writing activity requires students to synthesize the concepts presented in the readings throughout the chapter and to organize them in the form of an essay.

## What's new in the second edition?

In each chapter you will find:

- additional exercises for practice and reinforcement of skills
- new readings to allow for variation in student ability
- additional questions for journal writing and discussion

Chapter 3 on the main idea has been extensively revised and includes exercises on:

- finding topic sentences
- finding the implied main idea
- locating supporting details
- finding the main idea of longer passages

A new Part IV now includes:

- an additional thematic reading for each chapter
- additional skills exercises for review and application

# Instructor's manual

The organization of *Reading and Learning Across the Disciplines* is somewhat organic; that is, it is an outgrowth of a particular model developed by the authors. However, because we believe that the instructor, not the text, should dictate the content of the course, we have included a comprehensive Instructor's Manual that will enable you to customize your use of the text to suit your course needs and teaching style.

The manual includes:

- a suggested syllabus for planning coverage of topics
- chapter-by-chapter suggestions for in-class and outside activities and assignments
- additional skills exercises, which may be photocopied
- overhead transparency masters for particular exercises
- additional writing assignments and projects

In developing this and the other texts in the *Academic Connections Series*, we have tried to bridge the gap between the integrated and separate skills approaches. We hope that you will respond favorably to our endeavor. We welcome your comments and suggestions and hope that you will respond with your own experiences, so that together we may develop a model that will most effectively enhance student learning.

# Acknowledgments

We would like to thank our colleagues for reviewing and commenting on our manuscript. They are: first edition reviewers: Jane P. Asamani, Tennessee State University; Doralee E. Brooks, Community College of Allegheny County; Beverly Burch, Vincennes University; JoAnn Carter-Wells, California State University, Fullerton; Martha E. Casazza, National College of Education; Lauren Warshal Cohen, Seattle Central Community College; Muriel Davis, San Diego Mesa College; Juliet Emanuel, City University of New York, Borough of Manhattan Community College; Kathryn S. Hawes, Memphis State University; Roberta Hayden, New Hampshire Technical College at Nashua; Constance M. Jones, Grand Valley State University;

Michelle Kalina, Sierra College; Cathy Leist, University of Louisville; Frances McMurtray, San Antonio College; Clyde A. Moneyhun, University of Texas at Arlington; M. Eileen Morelli, Community College of Allegheny County; Thomas E. Nealon, Nassau Community College; Becky Patterson, University of Alaska, Anchorage; Marianne C. Reynolds, Mercer County Community College; Mary Rubin, Cameron University; Coralie Scherer, University of California, Berkeley; Shirley A. Sloan, Evergreen Valley College; Peter E. Sotiriou, Los Angeles City College; Dee Tadlock, Yakima Valley Community College; James E. Walker, Clarion University; Nancy S. Walker, Aims Community College. Second edition reviewers: Margaret Fieler, De Anza College; Pat Gent, Rogers State College; Patricia A. Janson, Suffolk County (NY) Community College; Teresa Kozek, Housatonic Community Technical College; Cathy J. Marsh, Pitt Community College; and Victoria Sarkisian, Marist College.

Mary-Jane McCarthy would also like to thank Michele Copolla McCarthy for reading and commenting on the manuscript, and would like to express special gratitude to Brian, Kimberly, and Marisa for their patience and understanding.

# To the Student

If you have ever tried to put together the pieces of a picture puzzle, you know that your task is much easier if you have an idea of how the puzzle will look when it is finished. For this reason most people start to work on a puzzle by looking at the picture on the box. Next, they locate the straight-edged pieces and fit them together to form the outside frame of the picture. Once they have created the frame of the puzzle, they begin to work on the inside, referring to the picture from time to time to help them figure out where the pieces belong.

Likewise, when you try to read a written selection that requires you to organize and analyze facts, you find it much easier if you have a clear idea of how the author arranged those facts. Once you grasp the overall structure, you have a framework similar to the picture on the puzzle box, which helps you make meaning out of the words on the page.

You can develop a framework for reading:

■ by creating a context that activates prior knowledge

■ by becoming aware of how you function as a reader and learning to monitor your comprehension as you read

■ by learning to identify and utilize the structures by which authors commonly organize their writing

How will *Reading and Learning Across the Disciplines*, Second Edition, help you develop a framework for reading and studying?

Part I, "The Foundations," will teach you to activate knowledge before reading in order to create context, enhance comprehension, and use context to unlock meaning as you read. It will also help you to understand your own learning style and adjust your reading and study strategies accordingly. Furthermore, it will sharpen your listening skills and supply you with a strategy for structuring lecture notes.

Part II, "Structures and Strategies," will teach you to identify and use the common structures by which writers organize their material. You will learn to use these structures to enhance comprehension, to take notes as you read, to become a better test-taker, and to improve your writing skills.

Part III, "Critical Thinking and Research," challenges you to move beyond the literal level of comprehension to a level wherein you are able to analyze and evaluate what you read with a critical eye.

Part IV, "Additional Readings for Review," gives you an opportunity to test your mastery of the skills learned in Parts I, II, and III.

Each chapter of the text includes a warm-up activity, skills exercises, a number of reading selections, reading comprehension checks, skills applications, and a section entitled "Going Beyond" in which you will have an opportunity to verbalize in writing what you have learned in the chapter. By "going beyond" you will be challenged to clarify and synthesize what you have learned in order to truly "make it your own."

CHAPTER 1
**Understanding Context
and Learning
Vocabulary**

CHAPTER 2
**Activating Knowledge to
Create Context**

CHAPTER 3
**Understanding Yourself
as a Learner**

CHAPTER 4
**Understanding Yourself
as a Reader**

CHAPTER 5
**Listening and Lecture**

# The Foundations

I f you were a carpenter's apprentice just beginning to learn the building trade, you would need to start by acquainting yourself with the various implements and materials used in construction. You would then need to learn a number of elementary carpentry skills such as measuring, leveling, sawing, and hammering. And then you would have to practice until you could perform those skills with reasonable proficiency.

As you begin your college studies, consider yourself an apprentice to learning. To become a successful student you must learn a number of important skills. You must be able to read and study effectively; take well-organized, clear lecture notes; organize your time efficiently; and discipline yourself in the midst of a busy and stressful environment.

Part I of *Reading and Learning Across the Disciplines* builds the foundation for your academic success by giving you practice in these very basic and essential academic and personal skills.

**EXERCISE 1**    *Where does comprehension come from?*

When you read you must use context in order to create meaning. Read the passage "Every Saturday Night" and answer the questions or circle the correct answer in the items that follow.

### Every Saturday Night

Every Saturday night four good friends get together. When Jerry, Mike, and Pat arrived, Karen was sitting in her living room writing some notes. She quickly gathered the cards and stood up to greet her friends at the door. They followed her into the living room, but as usual they couldn't agree on exactly what to play. Jerry eventually took a stand and set things up. Finally, they began to play. Karen's recorder filled the room with soft and pleasant music. Early in the evening, Mike noticed Pat's hand and the many diamonds. As the night progressed, the tempo of play increased. Finally, a lull in the activities occurred. Taking advantage of this, Jerry pondered the arrangement in front of him. Mike interrupted Jerry's reverie and said, "Let's hear the score." They listened carefully and commented on their performance. When the comments were all heard, exhausted but happy, Karen's friends went home.

1.  What are the four people doing?  *Playing a game.*

2.  There are two men and two women described in this scene.
    a. true
    b. false
    c. can't tell

3.  How sure are you of your answers to items 1 and 2?
    a. very sure
    b. somewhat sure
    c. unsure

4.  Reread the passage. As you read make a list of the words and phrases that help you create context and make meaning in the passage.

_____ tempo _____          _____

_____ music _____          _____

_____          _____

_____          _____

Discuss your answers with your classmates.

**EXERCISE 2**    *Variations in meaning*

Using the grid on page 11, make a chart comparing the class's answers to the items in Exercise 1. Specifically, do the following:

1.  At the top of the second, third, and fourth columns, write the three most common answers to question 1.

2.  In the left-hand column under the word "Clues," list the words and phrases that helped create meaning in the passage.

3.  Under each of the answers, write a definition for each clue word or phrase. You will need to write more than one definition for each word.

4.  Discuss the variations in meaning. For example, the word *notes* could have a number of meanings depending on what you thought the people were doing. The phrase *took a stand* might mean literally a piece of equipment, or it might be an expression meaning to make a decision.

**EXERCISE 3**  *Identifying context clues*

Each of the sentences below includes some type of context clue. Read each sentence and indicate (a) the meaning of the boldfaced word and (b) the type of clue used.

1. The **manacles** had been on John's wrists for thirty years. Only one person had a key — his wife.

    a.  meaning _____

    b.  clue _____

2. The root is the basic part of the word — its **heritage**, or its origin.

    a.  meaning _____

    b.  clue _____

3. The rattlesnake is poisonous, but the garden snake is completely **innocuous**.

    a.  meaning _____

    b.  clue _____

4. If you are going to be my witness, your story must **corroborate** my story.

    a.  meaning _____

    b.  clue _____

5. A **prefix** is the part that's sometimes attached to the front of a word. Like *prefix*!

    a.  meaning _____

    b.  clue _____

### *Prereading Activity*: **Using context to supply meaning**

This activity will further illustrate how you use context to create meaning as you read. Below is the introduction to Reading Selection One, "How to Improve Your Vocabulary." Fill in the blanks by writing a word that makes sense within the context of each sentence. (Answers will vary.)

Words can make us laugh, cry, _____ to war, fall in love.

Rudyard Kipling _____ words the most powerful drug of _____ . If they are, I'm a hopeless _____ — and I hope to get you _____ , too!

Whether you're still in school _____ you head up a corporation, the _____ command you have of words, the _____ chance you have of saying exactly _____ you mean, of understanding what others _____ — and of getting what you want _____ the world.

English is the richest _____ — with the largest vocabulary on earth. _____ 1,000,000 words!

*You* can express shades of _____ that aren't even possible in _____ languages. (For example, you can differentiate _____ "sky" and "heaven." The _____ , Italians and Spanish cannot.)

Yet, the _____ adult has a vocabulary of only 30,000 _____ 60,000 words. Imagine what we're missing!

_____ are five pointers that help me _____ — and remember — whole *families* of words _____ a time.

They may not look _____ — and won't be at first. But _____ you stick with them you'll find _____ work!

What's the first thing to _____ when you see a word you _____ know?

3.  Some societies developed **syllabic** systems of writing in which several hundred signs corresponded to several hundred spoken sounds.

    type of clue _____

4.  But as technologies evolved, humans **embodied** their thoughts in new ways: through the printing press, in Morse code, in electromagnetic waves bouncing through the atmosphere and in the binary language computers.

    type of clue _____

5.  Today, when the Earth is covered with a swarming interchange of ideas, we are even trying to send our thoughts beyond our planet to other minds in the Universe. . . . Most **exobiologists** believe that when other civilizations attempt to communicate with us they too will use pictures.

    type of clue _____

6.  In **interstellar** communication, we are at the same stage our ancestors were when they used sticks to trace a few simple images in the sand.

    type of clue _____

## *Prereading Activity 2*: **Finding the meaning of new words**

1.  Now take a guess at the meaning of each of the words. Write your guess on the line provided in the second column. Use your knowledge of both context and structure.

2.  As you read the following article, watch for the sentences in which these words are used. (You will be asked to fill in the rest of this chart after you have read the selection.)

| Words | Guess | Modified guess | Dictionary |
|---|---|---|---|
| pictographs | —————— | —————— | —————— |
| ideograms | —————— | —————— | —————— |
| syllabic | —————— | —————— | —————— |
| embodied | —————— | —————— | —————— |
| exobiologists | —————— | —————— | —————— |
| interstellar | —————— | —————— | —————— |

Since humans first learned to capture thought in written symbols, language has served to bring people closer together. As you read Don Lago's article, consider why true communication often eludes us.

## Symbols of Humankind

**BY DON LAGO**

Many thousands of years ago, a man quietly resting on a log reached     1
down and picked up a stick and with it began scratching upon the sand
at his feet. He moved the stick slowly back and forth and up and down,
carefully guiding it through curves and straight lines. He gazed upon what
he had made, and a gentle satisfaction lighted his face.

Other people noticed this man drawing on the sand. They gazed upon     2
the figures he had made, and though they at once recognized the shapes
of familiar things such as fish or birds or humans, they took a bit longer
to realize what the man had meant to say by arranging these familiar
shapes in this particular way. Understanding what he had done, they
nodded or smiled in recognition.

This small band of humans didn't realize what they were beginning.     3
The images these people left in the sand would soon be swept away by
the wind, but their new idea would slowly grow until it had remade the
human species. These people had discovered writing.

Writing, early people would learn, could contain much more infor-    4
mation than human memory could and contain it more accurately. It
could carry thoughts much farther than mere sounds could — farther in
distance and in time. Profound thoughts born in a single mind could
spread and endure.

The first written messages were simply pictures relating familiar ob-    5
jects in some meaningful way — **pictographs**. Yet there were no images
for much that was important in human life. What, for instance, was the
image for sorrow or bravery? So from pictographs humans developed
**ideograms** to represent more abstract ideas. An eye flowing with tears
could represent sorrow, and a man with the head of a lion might be
bravery.

The next leap occurred when the figures became independent of    6
things or ideas and came to stand for spoken sounds. Written figures were
free to lose all resemblance to actual objects. Some societies developed
**syllabic** systems of writing in which several hundred signs corresponded
to several hundred spoken sounds. Others discovered the much simpler
alphabetic system, in which a handful of signs represented the basic
sounds the human voice can make.

At first, ideas flowed only slightly faster when written than they had    7
through speech. But as technologies evolved, humans **embodied** their
thoughts in new ways: through the printing press, in Morse code, in
electromagnetic waves bouncing through the atmosphere and in the binary language of computers.

Today, when the Earth is covered with a swarming interchange of    8
ideas, we are even trying to send our thoughts beyond our planet to other
minds in the Universe. Our first efforts at sending our thoughts beyond
Earth have taken a very ancient form: pictographs. The first messages, on
plaques aboard Pioneer spacecraft launched in 1972 and 1973, featured a
simple line drawing of two humans, one male and one female, the male
holding up his hand in greeting. Behind them was an outline of the
Pioneer spacecraft, from which the size of the humans could be judged.
The plaque also included the "address" of the two human figures: a
picture of the solar system, with a spacecraft emerging from the third
planet. Most **exobiologists** believe that when other civilizations attempt
to communicate with us they too will use pictures.

All the accomplishments since humans first scribbled in the sand have     9
led us back to where we began. Written language only works when two
individuals know what the symbols mean. We can only return to the
simplest form of symbol available and work from there. In **interstellar**
communication, we are at the same stage our ancestors were when they
used sticks to trace a few simple images in the sand.

We still hold their sticks in our hands and draw pictures with them.     10
But the stick is no longer made of wood; over the ages that piece of wood
has been transformed into a massive radio telescope. And we no longer
scratch on sand; now we write our thoughts onto the emptiness of space
itself.

## COMPREHENSION CHECK

Answer the items below by filling in the correct answer or circling the best
answer.

1.  The main idea of this selection is:
    a. Very early in history humans realized the importance of writing.
    b. The tools by which humans communicate have changed over the
       centuries, but the process remains the same.
    c. All the accomplishments in communication are meaningless unless
       individuals know what the symbols mean.

2.  The main limitation of the pictographs was:
    a. They used too many symbols.
    b. They took too long to compose.
    c. They were too limited in what they could express.

3.  People from other planets will probably use pictures to communicate
    with us.
    a. true
    b. false

4. From this selection we can conclude:
   a. Writing will always be the most important method of communication.
   b. Humans are still progressing in their quest to communicate.
   c. There are people on other planets.

5. In the history of communication, which event do you think may have been the most important? Why?

_____

_____


**COMPREHENSION EXERCISE**  *Using context to define new words*

1. Go back to the list of words in the Prereading Activity. In the column provided write a modified guess of the meaning of each word based on your reading. How does your modified guess compare with the guess you made before you read the selection?

2. Now look up each word in a dictionary and write the dictionary definition in the space provided in the list. How close were your guesses to the correct meanings?


**CHAPTER APPLICATION**

Choose a chapter from one of your textbooks (preferably a chapter you are now working on). Select five words you did not know before reading the chapter. Follow the directions for the Comprehension Exercise for Reading Selection One on page 20, looking up the words as directed and writing them in sentences.

When you speak or write, you have to choose which words to use. How do you make these choices?

People use profane language for many reasons. Some use it to get attention, others to create a particular image. But many people use it simply because their limited vocabulary impairs their ability to give an otherwise creative response. As you read "Don't Talk Dirty to Me," think about why you do or do not use dirty language.

### *Prereading Activity*: **Identifying context clues and finding the meaning of new words**

Below are a number of sentences from the selection you are about to read. For each sentence: (1) underline the parts of the sentences that provide clues to the meaning of the boldfaced word, (2) indicate the type of context clue used, and (3) attempt to define each word without using a dictionary.

1.  Still, the passion of the smoke haters is **phenomenal**. You don't see comparable fury applied to curbing any other social habit, like, say, getting drunk or talking dirty.

    a. type of clue _____

    b. definition _____

2.  For two years in the military I lived **immersed** in dirty talk. If Eddie Murphy had come into our outfit and started talking, we would have washed out his mouth with mud for talking clean.

    a. type of clue _____

    b. definition _____

3. Jonathan Yardley of *The Washington Post* recently noted the spread of **vile** language into almost every movie made for adolescents. . . . This suggests that American youth is now as firmly hooked on dirty talk as its parents once were on nicotine.

   a. type of clue _____

   b. definition _____

4. Few of the children will find it easy to free themselves from their **enslavement** to vile and foul-mouthed speech.

   a. type of clue _____

   b. definition _____

5. A ban on dirty talk in movies and television? Absolutely not! No **censorship**! Never!

   a. type of clue _____

   b. definition _____

## Don't Talk Dirty to Me

**BY RUSSELL BAKER**

*So says renowned columnist Russell Baker, who's smoking over what's* really *fouling the air*

There was another one of those smoke fights on an airplane the other day. It's always the same: a smoker so desperate for a cigarette he's ready to start screaming in pain. Somebody willing to die rather than be subjected to cigarette smoke. Pandemonium in the sky, police meeting the plane at the gate. Much assertion of human rights vis à vis tobacco smoke.     1

   Having tried both ways of life, tobacco-stained and nicotine-free, I sympathize with both sides, but pray I never end up on one of those planes where they fight it out. I use the words "end up" by design. It's bad enough up there when you're wondering whether the pilot is using something to revise his brain. We don't need passenger riots to put the thrill back into air travel.     2

Still, the passion of the smoke haters is **phenomenal**. You don't see    3
comparable fury applied to curbing any other social habit, like, say, getting drunk or talking dirty.

This last is a particular grievance of mine. Sidestream smoke, as the    4
Surgeon General reports, may rot lungs, heart and other innards, but dirty talk rots the mind, and I'd like to see a vigorous, aggressive campaign waged against the people who do it. When you try to get a clean talk movement started, though, people think you're joking.

At the airport, for instance: "Smoking or nonsmoking?" they ask.    5
What do I care? I have smoked and I have nonsmoked, and can put up with either condition.

What I'd rather be asked is, "Dirty talking or nondirty talking?" I    6
have dirty talked and I have nondirty talked, and I never want to dirty talk again or associate with the kind of people who do.

For two years in the military I lived **immersed** in dirty talk. If Eddie    7
Murphy had come into our outfit and started talking, we would have washed out his mouth with mud for talking clean.

Near the end of my tour, a trusted companion asked, "Hey, you (dirty    8
talk)ing (dirty talk)er. What the (dirty talk) you gonna do when those (dirty talk)ing (dirty talk)s hand you the (dirty talk), (dirty talk), (dirty talk) pen and ask you to (dirty talk)ing sign up for another two (dirty talk)ing years?"

"I'm (dirty talk)ing gonna tell the (dirty talk)ing, (dirty talk)s to take    9
that (dirty talk)ing pen and shove it . . ."

At this point I broke down and told my friend, "I'm getting out, pal."    10

"You're (dirty talk)ing kidding!" he expostulated.    11

"I mean it," I said. "I want to go once again to a place where a man    12
can ask, 'What in the world do you think you're doing?' and 'Isn't this a devil of a mess?' and 'By George, he's got it; I think he's got it!' without being exiled for talking weird."

I'm not an **absolutist** on this. Live and let live is my philosophy.    13
Jonathan Yardley of *The Washington Post* recently noted the spread of **vile** language into almost every movie made for adolescents, which is almost every movie made nowadays. This suggests that American youth is now as firmly hooked on dirty talk as its parents once were on nicotine.

Just as millions of those parents have broken their cigarette addiction,    14
so millions of American youngsters can probably break their dependence
on dirty talk. It would be cruel, however, to expect them to break the
habit cold turkey. Few of their parents were able to give up cigarettes
without a struggle; few of the children will find it easy to free themselves
from their **enslavement** to vile and foul-mouthed speech.

For humane reasons, then, an all-out attack on dirty talk would be    15
excessively cruel. We must proceed gradually, subtly. Just inside door-
ways, windows or attic dormers . . . let us place small signs that say,
"Thank you for not talking dirty."

Let taxicab drivers plaster the interiors of their cabs with stickers that    16
say, "No vile language. Driver allergic to dirty talk."

Let restaurants establish dirty talking sections for diners too weak to    17
break the chains that bind them.

A ban on dirty talk in movies and television? Absolutely not! No    18
**censorship**! Never!

With sufficient bullying by an aroused public, however, theater mar-    19
quees and printed television schedules might carry the message: "Warning: This entertainment contains dirty talk which may . . . create the
depressing **illusion** that you are trapped in a military barracks with
people who think you are weird."

Crusaders against smoke want everybody to live longer, but if it    20
means everybody will have more years to spend talking dirty, what's the
point?

## JOURNAL WRITING

1.  How you express yourself orally and in writing tells the world a great
    deal about you. Using what you have learned from the readings in this
    chapter, write about how *you* use the English language to accomplish
    your goals.

2.  What is your opinion on the use of profane, or "dirty," language today?
    Has it gone too far? Should we reevaluate the use of language on televi-
    sion and movies? Give at least three reasons to support your opinion.

3.  The words you choose, even the tone with which you speak, varies depending on your relationship with your audience, as well as on the circumstances or setting of the conversation. For example, you might address your girlfriend or boyfriend as "honey" when no one else is present, but would most likely refer to him or her by name in the presence of fellow workers. Describe three or four situations in which you would use different language, and give examples of the words you might use.

4.  Sometimes we use concrete objects to represent ideas or emotions. For example, the color green is sometimes used to symbolize money or greed and other times to symbolize newness, freshness, or youth. Choose a word that can be used symbolically. How do you think this word came to symbolize what it does? Explain what the word symbolizes to you, and why. Give examples of when and where the word might be used.

5.  Describe an experience in which you had difficulty explaining what you wanted to convey, either orally or in writing. What were the major factors that prevented you from expressing yourself? What was the outcome of the experience?

## CHAPTER 2

# Activating Knowledge
# to Create Context

After studying Chapter 2 you should be able to:

■ understand the importance of background knowledge in comprehension

■ preview reading materials to activate background knowledge and experience

■ organize your time more efficiently

## CHAPTER CHECKLIST

Use the following checklist to help you plan for the text, readings, and activities in this chapter.

| Date Assigned | Date Completed | |
|---|---|---|
| _____ | _____ | Activating prior knowledge |
| _____ | _____ | WARM-UP: Measuring background knowledge |

### READING SELECTION ONE

| | | |
|---|---|---|
| _____ | _____ | *Prereading Activity*: What do you know about hypnosis? |
| _____ | _____ | **"Hypnosis: Altered Consciousness or Role Playing?"** |
| _____ | _____ | COMPREHENSION CHECK |
| _____ | _____ | Previewing by scanning and skimming |
| _____ | _____ | EXERCISE 1: Skimming for main ideas |

### READING SELECTION TWO

| | | |
|---|---|---|
| _____ | _____ | *Prereading Activity*: Previewing an article |
| _____ | _____ | **"Chronobiology: Finding Your Peak Time of Day"** |
| _____ | _____ | COMPREHENSION CHECK |

### READING SELECTION THREE

| | | |
|---|---|---|
| _____ | _____ | *Prereading Activity*: Previewing an article |
| _____ | _____ | **"Sleep as a Biological Rhythm"** |
| _____ | _____ | COMPREHENSION CHECK |

| Date Assigned | Date Completed | |
|---|---|---|
| —— | —— | **CHAPTER APPLICATION 1** |
| —— | —— | **CHAPTER APPLICATION 2** |
| —— | —— | **GOING BEYOND:** "All Work and Not Enough Play" |
| —— | —— | **JOURNAL WRITING** |

# Activating Prior Knowledge

The passage "Every Saturday Night" in Chapter 1 was intentionally written to be ambiguous. Fortunately, authors usually include more specific details that serve as clues to the context. Nonetheless, they write with the expectation that their readers will be able to bring a certain amount of knowledge to the subject at hand.

In Chapter 2 you will learn how to activate knowledge to improve both your comprehension and your level of retention.

**WARM-UP** *Measuring background knowledge*

What you bring to a reading selection depends upon your prior knowledge of the subject matter. Let's imagine that the range of potential knowledge about any subject runs along a continuous line and that your knowledge of a given subject can be represented by placing an X at the appropriate place on that line. For example:

| *none* | *a little* | *some* | *a lot* | *a great deal* |
|---|---|---|---|---|

ecology ——————————X—————————————————————

Indicate what your level of knowledge might be for the following topics by placing an X at the appropriate place on the line.

| | *none* | *a little* | *some* | *a lot* | *a great deal* |
|---|---|---|---|---|---|

rock music _____

group interactions _____

nuclear fission _____

coping with stress _____

hypnosis _____

Let's take hypnosis, for example. If you have never read anything about hypnosis, initially you might place the X under "a little." However, if you examine your experiences more closely, you may recall having seen a professional hypnotist on TV or in a nightclub. You may have seen a movie in which someone was hypnotized or have heard about someone using hypnotism to give up smoking or lose weight. If so, you know something about what hypnotism is, how it is performed, and what it can do. You may actually have "a lot" of information about hypnotism. Activating that information will increase your comprehension and facilitate retention of facts as you read.

**READING SELECTION ONE**

### *Prereading Activity*: **What do you know about hypnosis?**

Before reading the following excerpt, let's see how much you know about hypnosis. Read the following statements and mark each one as either true or false.

_____ 1. Hypnotism is sometimes used as an anesthetic.

_____ 2. Anyone can be hypnotized.

_____ 3. Hypnotism was first developed in Austria by a man named Franz Mesmer.

_____ 4. It is primarily the voice of the hypnotist that induces the trance.

_____ 5. One explanation for what occurs under hypnosis is that the subject is merely playing a role.

Now read the following excerpt from a college psychology text to determine how much background knowledge you have on the topic of hypnosis. When you finish, check your answers against those in the Prereading Activity by completing the summary that follows.

## Hypnosis: Altered Consciousness or Role Playing?

### BY WAYNE WEITEN

Have you ever seen a show put on by a stage hypnotist? If so, you probably saw some unusual demonstrations that you may have found perplexing. For instance, I once saw a stage hypnotist tell a hypnotized subject that he had just returned from Mars and that he should tell the audience what it was like — in his native Martian tongue. The young man started speaking energetically, but in absolute gibberish (at least to earthling ears). Another subject frantically dropped a pencil when informed that it was a red-hot piece of iron, and a third began to crawl about the stage as if she were a mountain lion.      1

What's going on here? The power of theatrical hypnotists to produce foolish behavior in members of the audience symbolizes for many what hypnosis is all about. In the classic explanation of hypnosis, its effects are achieved by putting subjects into a special state of consciousness, commonly called a *hypnotic trance*. As you will soon see, this explanation has been hotly debated.      2

Hypnosis has a long and checkered history. It all began with a flamboyant 18th-century Austrian physician named Franz Anton Mesmer. Working in Paris, Mesmer claimed to cure people of paralysis and other illnesses through an elaborate routine involving a "laying on of hands." Although Mesmer had some complicated theories about how he had harnessed "animal magnetism," he had simply stumbled onto the power of suggestion. It was rumored that the French government offered him a princely sum to disclose how he effected his cures. He refused, probably because he didn't really know. Eventually he was dismissed as a **charlatan** and run out of town by the local authorities.      3

Although officially discredited, Mesmer inspired followers — practitioners of "mesmerism" — who continued to ply their trade, putting interested people into apparent trance states. To this day, our language      4 preserves the memory of Franz Mesmer: when we are "under the spell" of an event or a story, we are *mesmerized*.

Eventually, a Scottish physician, James Braid, became interested in   5 the trancelike state that could be induced by the mesmerists. He thought that perhaps the trance could be used to produce anesthesia for surgeries. It was Braid who popularized the term *hypnotism* in 1843, borrowing it from the Greek word for sleep. With a new name and a modest bit of scientific credibility, hypnotism gained some acceptance within the medical profession. However, just as it was catching on as a technique for producing general anesthesia, more powerful and reliable drug anesthetics were discovered, and interest in hypnotism dwindled.

Since then hypnosis has led a curious dual existence. On the one   6 hand, it has been the subject of numerous scientific studies. Furthermore, it has enjoyed considerable use as a clinical tool by physicians, dentists, and psychologists for over a century. Meanwhile, an assortment of entertainers and quacks have continued in the less respectable tradition of mesmerism, using hypnotism for parlor tricks and **chicanery**. It is not surprising, then, that most people don't know what to make of the whole subject. In this section, we'll work on clearing up some of the confusion surrounding hypnosis.

## Hypnotic induction and susceptibility

*Hypnosis* is a systematic procedure that typically produces a height-   7 ened state of suggestibility. Hypnosis may also lead to passive relaxation, narrowed attention, and enhanced fantasy.

If only in popular films, virtually everyone has seen a *hypnotic induc-*   8 *tion* enacted with a swinging pendulum. But this is only one of a variety of hypnotic induction techniques — Kroger (1977) lists over 20. Generally, it is the hypnotist's verbal behavior that plays the crucial role in the induction. Usually, the hypnotist suggests to the subject that he or she is relaxing. Repetitively, softly, subjects are told that they are getting tired, drowsy, or sleepy. Often, the hypnotist vividly describes bodily sensations that should be occurring. Subjects are told that their arms are going limp, their feet are getting warm, their eyelids are getting heavy. Gradually, most subjects succumb and become hypnotized.

People differ in how well they respond to hypnotic induction. Ernest   9 and Josephine Hilgard have done extensive research on this variability in *hypnotic susceptibility.* Not everyone can be hypnotized. About 10% of the population doesn't respond well at all. At the other end of the continuum, about 10% of people are exceptionally good hypnotic subjects (Hilgard, 1965). . . .

Although a number of theories have been developed to explain hyp-  10
nosis, it is still not well understood. The most crucial theoretical issue is whether hypnosis involves a unique altered state of consciousness or a normal state of consciousness characterized by dramatic role playing.

**Hypnosis as role playing**    Theodore Barber (1969, 1979) has been a  11
leading advocate of the view that hypnosis produces a normal mental state in which suggestible people act out the role of a hypnotic subject. According to this notion, good hypnotic subjects get caught up in their role and try to behave as they think hypnotized people are supposed to. Barber argues that it is subjects' role expectations that produce hypnotic effects rather than a special trancelike state of consciousness. . . .

**Hypnosis as an altered state of consciousness**    In spite of the doubts  12
raised by Barber, many prominent theorists maintain that hypnotic effects *are* attributable to a special, altered state of consciousness (Beahrs, 1983; Fromm, 1979; Hilgard, 1986). These theorists argue that role playing probably cannot explain all hypnotic phenomena. For instance, they assert that even the most cooperative subjects are unlikely to endure surgery without an anesthetic drug just to please their physician and live up to their expected role.

Of late, the most influential explanation of hypnosis as an altered  13
state is Ernest Hilgard's (1986) theory, which holds that hypnosis creates a dissociation in consciousness. *Dissociation* involves a splitting off of mental processes into two separate, simultaneous streams of awareness. In other words, Hilgard theorizes that hypnosis splits consciousness into two streams. One of these is in communication with the hypnotist and the external world, while the other is a difficult-to-detect "hidden observer." Hilgard believes that many hypnotic effects are a product of this divided consciousness. For instance, he suggests that a hypnotized subject might appear unresponsive to pain because the pain isn't registered in the portion of consciousness that communicates with other people.

## COMPREHENSION CHECK

Read the following summary of Reading Selection One and fill in the blanks.

Hypnotism was first developed by an Austrian physician named

_____ _____ , who claimed to cure illnesses by a technique

involving _____ _____ _____ _____ . Although he was

eventually discredited, his followers continued to practice "_____ ,"

which involved putting people into a trancelike state. Later, a Scottish

physician began to use the technique as an anesthetic and renamed it

_____ , based on the Greek word for sleep.

Hypnosis is defined as "a systematic procedure that typically produces

a heightened state of _____ . It is enacted in a variety of ways, but it is

the hypnotist's _____ that is crucial. Hypnotic susceptibility varies,

with about 10 percent of the population responding poorly and another

_____ percent responding exceptionally well.

Two conflicting theories have been developed to explain hypnosis. One,

the role-playing theory advocated by _____ _____ , states that

susceptible subjects are merely acting out a role. The other theory purports

that hypnotism is actually an elevated state of mind. One advocate of this

theory, Ernest Hilgard, believes that the hypnotic state involves a

dissociation of _____ in which the consciousness splits into two

streams.

Until further scientific research validates one of these theories,

hypnotism will remain a mysterious and fascinating phenomenon.

# Previewing by Scanning and Skimming

One technique for activating knowledge and preparing yourself to read is **previewing**. The word *preview* is derived from the Latin prefix *pre-*, which means "before," and the French verb *voir*, "to see." A preview is a glimpse of what is to come.

For example, when you watch the preview of a movie, you see brief scenes from the whole movie — usually the best parts. The purpose of the preview is to whet your appetite so that you will want to see the whole thing. Likewise, when you preview something you are about to read, you get a glimpse of the whole selection. You set the scene or context and create a picture of what is to come. In short, you build a framework much like the outside edge of the picture puzzle mentioned in the introductory section "To the Student." This framework helps you fit the facts of the reading selection together.

The process of previewing involves scanning and skimming a selection to activate knowledge before reading.

Scanning and skimming are two very simple techniques you perform all the time. **Scanning** really isn't reading. It involves running the eyes quickly over material to locate a specific item, then reading only that particular item. You scan when you look up a number in a telephone book.

**Skimming** is a little more complicated. It involves scanning to locate specific material and then reading the specific material more carefully. You probably skim a menu when you go out to dinner. For example, if you prefer fish you might first scan to locate the fish section and then quickly read, or skim, the selections on that part of the menu, perhaps looking for certain ingredients or forms of preparation or the least expensive items. Finally, you read more carefully to see exactly what those selections offer.

By scanning and skimming you get an idea of what is available on the menu and can make your choice quickly and wisely. In the same way, skimming a reading selection gives you a general idea of what the selection is about. It helps you decide whether the article is appropriate for your needs and how to approach the article as you begin to read.

Skimming a reading selection usually involves reading the first and last paragraphs, the first sentence of each paragraph, and words in bold print or italics, as well as reviewing any graphic material such as pictures or charts.

### How to Use Scanning and Skimming to Preview a Reading Selection

1. Skim (read quickly) the title and author's name. Consider what the title might mean. Note the author's credentials and their relevance to the topic.

2. Skim the introduction (first paragraph) and conclusion (last paragraph). State the main idea of these paragraphs in your own words.

3. Scan to locate and read all headings, subheadings, and other prominent type.

4. Skim illustrations, charts, graphs, and the like, being sure to read all information including titles and captions. Think about how these add to your understanding of the selection.

5. Scan for italicized and boldfaced words, terms, quotes, numbers, names, dates, and so on. Skim the sentences surrounding these words to learn more about their importance.

6. Acquaint yourself with the meanings of words that are essential to your understanding of the selection.

7. Using all the information you have gleaned by scanning and skimming, write a few sentences stating what you think the selection is about.

**EXERCISE 1**    *Skimming for main ideas*

Skim the following selections by reading *only* the boldfaced sentences and words. Then attempt to state the main ideas by filling in the blanks in the sentences that follow.

## *Geologic time*

**Humanity is a new experiment on planet Earth.** For most of its history, life on Earth was restricted to the sea. Living things began to populate the land slightly over **400 million years ago**, and humans have existed for no more than **3 million years**.

**One way to represent the evolution of life is to compress the 4.6-billion-year history of Earth into a 1-year-long film.** In such a film, Earth forms as the film begins on **January 1**, and through all of January and February it cools and is cratered and the first oceans form. But those oceans remain lifeless until sometime in **March** or early **April**, when the first living things develop. The **4-billion-year history of Precambrian** evolution lasts until the film reaches mid-November, when primitive ocean life begins to evolve into complex organisms such as trilobites.

**If we examine the land instead of the oceans, we find a lifeless waste.** But once our film shows planet and animal life on the land, about **November 28**, evolution proceeds rapidly. **Dinosaurs**, for example, appear about **December 12** and vanish by **Christmas** evening, as **mammals** and birds flourish.

**Throughout the 1-year-run of our film there are no humans, and even during the last days of the year as the mammals rise and dominate the landscape, there are no people.** In the early evening of **December 31**, vaguely human forms move through the grasslands, and by late evening they begin making stone tools. The **Stone Age** lasts until about **11:45 p.m.**, and the first signs of civilization, towns and cities, do not appear until 11:54 p.m. **The Christian era begins only 14 seconds before the New Year, and the Declaration of Independence is signed with 1 second to spare.**

In relation to the geological age of the _____ , human beings have existed for only a few _____ .

## *Ants: The oldest farm in the world*

**Anthropologists think ancient humans began farming 10,000 years ago.** *Puh-leeze*: **by then, leaf-cutter ants had been raising tidy little gardens of fungus for 23 million years**. But that's not all: according to a paper in the current issue of the journal *Science*, they had been **tending the** *same* **fungal lineage** for all that time, too. "It's as if your family passed along the same starter culture for yogurt or sourdough for millions of generations," says coauthor Ted Schultz of Cornell University.

**The 190 species of leaf-cutter ants live mostly in Latin America.** In Belize, they've been known to spirit away entire vegetable gardens in a night, carrying the leaves down the holes of the nest and chewing them to soft pulp. The ants then pluck a tuft of fungus from another part of their farm and plant it on the new leaf. They eat the fungal shoots. The first leaf cutters probably got their starter fungi from the wild. But today, when queens leave the nest to found a new colony, they take along starter pellets.

**Fungi in the nests of highly evolved leaf cutters in Brazil, Trinidad, Costa Rica, Nicaragua and three states in the United States, the scientists find, are clones of each other**; that is, they are apparently genetically identical. Using DNA analysis, the scientists calculate that the clone has been around for 23 million years, says Cornell's Ulrich Mueller. Which raises a question: if ants have had so long to farm, why do they always show up at our picnics?

For over _____ years, the _____ ant has been farming _____ generated from the same fungal source.

## *Prereading Activity*: **Previewing an article**

Try previewing the article "Chronobiology: Finding Your Peak Time of Day" by following the directions in this activity and writing your responses on the worksheet on page 44.

1. *Read the title. Write it down and think about your level of knowledge on this topic.* If the word "chronobiology" is foreign to you, try to relate its parts to other, more familiar words such as "biology" or "chronic." Think about the meaning of the word "peak." What might "peak time of day" mean? Set a purpose for reading by writing down something you want to learn about the topic.

   Now *read the name of the author.* Notice there is no indication that he is an authority on this topic.

2. As there is no formal introduction or summary, *read the first and last paragraphs of the article. Summarize the main idea of the paragraphs in your own words.*

3. *If there were headings in this article to separate paragraphs, you would read them and write them down.* Headings indicate the role of the paragraphs they precede and make it easier for the reader to understand the framework. Since there are no headings, *skim the quotes and paraphrase them using your own words.*

4. *Scan for quotes, italics, bold face, proper names, and the like. Write down those you feel might be important, and skim the surrounding sentences for clues to their meaning or importance.* For example, in paragraphs 3 and 4:

   "about a day" refers to circadian cycles. These occur in most animals and people.

   "24-hour period" — What happens over a "24-hour period"?

   Dennis LaSalle — What contribution has he made to the study of chronobiology?

   It is not necessary to write down every quote, italic, name, and so on. *Decide how much you need in order to grasp the basic facts of the article.*

5. *Write definitions for the key words in the selection.* At this point it is essential that you know the meaning of "chronobiology."

6. *Read over your notes. Write one paragraph summarizing what you have learned.*

## "Chronology" Preview Worksheet

1.  Title and purpose _____
    _____
    _____

2.  Main idea of introduction and conclusion _____
    _____
    _____

3.  Important headings and quotes

    a. _____

    b. _____

    c. _____

4.  Important terms and names

    _____     _____

    _____     _____

    _____     _____

5.  Unfamiliar vocabulary words and definitions

    a. _____

    b. _____

    c. _____

    d. _____

6.  Main idea of the selection _____
    _____
    _____

Because you have previewed this difficult selection, you should be able to comprehend and retain the facts easily. When you finish reading it, try to answer as many of the Comprehension Check questions as you can without referring back to the article.

## Chronobiology: Finding Your Peak Time of Day

BY WILLIAM JOHN WATKINS

**"I'd have done a lot better on those college boards,"** my son said, 1 **"if I didn't have to take them in the middle of the night."** For him, 8 a.m. on Saturday literally *is* the middle of the night. And he is not the only person who finds early morning the wrong time of day to do any heavy thinking. An architect friend told me recently, "I get more work done between five and seven than I do all day long, and it's not just because the interruptions stop at five. I just feel better. I think better, and I feel more like working."

**Both my friend and my son are touching on an old truth that** 2 **has gotten a lot of support recently from an emerging field of science called chronobiology.** Chronobiology holds the promise of improving our work, our play, our learning and our health by allowing us to understand the daily cycle of energy and rest our bodies go through. It may even hold the key to increasing productivity, which so many experts claim is the real key to stopping inflation. The field of chronobiology has been in existence for about ten years, although it has been resisted strongly by some scientists because its acceptance could mean that billions of dollars worth of research would be open to question and might have to be redone.

**Chronobiology deals with the cycles that go on within our** 3 **bodies every day, from week to week, and even from moment to moment.** The most important and most easily recognized of these cycles are the *circadian* **("about a day") cycles** that occur in most people and animals. Body temperature, blood sugar, heart rate, blood pressure, respiration, brain waves and over a dozen chemical levels in the blood rise and fall over a roughly 24-hour period. The result of these circadian rhythms is a peak and a valley of attention and energy once each day.

**The cycles, however, vary from person to person, a fact that**    4
**has important ramifications in the field of education. Dennis**
**LaSalle, a Connecticut chronobiologist,** discovered in working with
children that their addition skills and memory varied with the time of day
the testing was done. While every individual has a slightly different cycle,
people can be broken down roughly into two groups: **"day people,"**
whose circadian peaks occur in early morning, and **"night people,"**
whose peaks occur later in the day or at night. Science seems finally to
have discovered what common experience has shown all along, that
different people function best at different times of the day.

**Eventually home computers may allow students to learn at**    5
**the precise time of the day when they are mentally and physi-**
**cally at their best, but in the meantime, Dr. LaSalle suggests two**
**immediate scheduling changes that could have far-reaching ef-**
**fects.** Since a sizable percentage of any group of students are at a physiological low point during the morning, Dr. LaSalle suggests rotating class
schedules so that the same class is not given at the same time every day.
In this way, both groups would be at their most alert during some part of
the teaching and thus would not fall behind by always being at their low
point. Any "night" person who has had to take geometry at eight o'clock
in the morning might wonder why it has taken scientists so long to come
to that conclusion and why it has taken educators even longer to do
something about it.

**The idea of doing things when the mind and body are at peak**    6
**efficiency could have an important effect on how we work as**
**well.** We work best when we feel like working, and we feel most like
working when we are alert and energetic. As we have seen, this varies
from person to person, but if each person were scheduled to work during
a stretch of time that included his or her point of peak efficiency, production would inevitably rise.

**The increased introduction of "flex-time," in which employ-**    7
**ees set their own hours outside the rigid nine-to-five work day**
**of most businesses, is a step in the right direction.** This is especially
true in terms of shift work. Few industries assign shifts according to their
employees' circadian cycles, with the result that **"day"** people assigned
to night shift are not as alert as they would be if their shift coincided with
their personal and mental peak times. The result, of course, is lower

efficiency, reduced productivity and an increase in accidents that tend to occur when employees get tired and let their attention slip.

**There is a second health effect of shift work**. Physiologically, 8 the "slow rotation" practiced by many factories is the worst possible schedule employees could be put on, although the rotation is often done to accommodate the workers, who universally dislike certain shifts and do not want to be on them for very long. In slow rotation, a worker is assigned to one of three shifts for a period of one week. At the end of that time, they are rotated into the next shift and a week later into a third shift.

---

*Since a sizable percentage of any group of students is at a physiological low point during the morning, Dr. LaSalle suggests rotating class schedules so that the same class is not given at the same time every day.*

---

**Unfortunately, it takes four to nine days for many of the** 9 **most important cycles within the body to readjust to the new schedule**, with the result that the person has barely become adjusted to the new shift when he or she is forced to change again. In some people, body temperature, which has a great deal to do with when and how easily people get to sleep, never fully adjusts, leaving workers perpetually tired and out of sorts. The long-term health effects of slow rotation have not been adequately studied, but the economic results should be obvious.

**The effect of circadian rhythms on health is one of the most** 10 **important and most controversial areas of chronobiology**. According to studies by **Dr. Franz Halberg** of the University of Minnesota, we are less resistant to certain drugs at different times of the day. The effectiveness of drugs varies with a person's individual cycle. This is especially true for medication given to lower blood pressure, which may vary by as much as twenty points during one circadian cycle. Since less medication is needed at the time of day when blood pressure is normally low, a precise scheduling of medication can keep a patient from getting too much medicine at some times and too little at others. The same thing may be true of cancer treatments, since cell division has also been shown to have a circadian cycle. Even the cancer cells themselves may have daily cycles of strength and weakness that could increase the efficiency of treatment that is timed to take advantage of these low points in the cells' daily cycle.

**According to Dr. Frederick Bartter, a University of Texas en-**   11
**docrinologist, the rhythmic susceptibility to drugs occurs in all**
**drugs known to have been tested for that effect.** It is, in fact, the
matter of drug effectiveness that is the most controversial part of chronobiology. Some recent studies have shown that animals, particularly ones
who are normally active at night, have a much lower resistance to drugs
in the daytime. This is important because the maximum safe dosage of a
drug is determined by giving larger and larger doses of the drug to a group
of animals until more than half of them die. At the point in their daily
cycle when they are least resistant to the drug, more mice will die of
overdoses. As a result, some drugs that may be safe and more effective in
higher doses are labeled as being dangerous or **lethal**.

---

*The effect of circadian rhythms on health is one of the most controver-*
*sial areas of chronobiology. According to studies by Dr. Franz Halberg*
*of the University of Minnesota, we are less resistant to certain drugs at*
*different times of the day.*

---

**The opposite may also be true. Drugs given when the mice**   12
**are at their peak have far less effect on them, with the result**
**that the same dose may kill most of the mice or very few of them**
**depending on the time of day it is administered.** This finding has
stirred a great deal of opposition from both drug companies and scientists
because it means that many, if not all, drugs will have to be retested with
experiments that take the time of day and the experimental animal's daily
cycle into consideration.

**Many experiments in all branches of science are conducted**   13
**with mice and other *nocturnal* animals with little or no regard**
**for the effect of daily cycles, and, because scientists are normally**
**active in the day while mice are normally active at night, a great**
**deal of scientific research that has already been accepted may**
**have to be redone.** The cost of redoing even a small percentage of this
research would be in the billions of dollars, so the debate over chronobiology is likely to go on for a long time.

**In the meantime, there is a way you can establish for yourself**   14
**what your own daily cycles are and schedule your life accord-**
**ingly**. There are three very simple ways to determine your circadian
cycles. The first is to keep every day for a week an hourly diary, in which
you rate your alertness, mood and sensitivity on a scale of one to ten. A
second way is to record your hourly temperature, and the third is to
record your pulse rate.

**Body temperature varies between one and a half and two**   15
**degrees over a 24-hour period, while pulse rate may vary by as**
**much as 30 beats a minute from the high point of the cycle to**
**the low point**. The easiest way to take your pulse is to place your middle
finger just under the corner of your jaw where your pulse is strongest.
Count the number of beats for fifteen seconds and multiply by four. Even
after a few days, you should be able to see where your daily peaks and
valleys tend to be. You will probably find that the physical variations
match up pretty well with your feelings about how energetic and alert
you are.

**Once you have established what your circadian cycles are,**   16
**you can use them to get the most out of whatever you are doing**.
The low points in your cycle — when your pulse is down and your temperature low — are good for **sedentary** activity, like watching television,
just resting, or listening to music. The low point in your temperature cycle
is a good time to go to sleep for the night or even to take a short nap so
you can do some effective work later when your temperature rises.

**Times of high temperature and alertness should be used for**   17
**study**, reading and physical activity. In fact, if you're a competitive person whose peaks are in late afternoon, you might find it to your advantage
to schedule that next tennis match well after lunch instead of in the
morning. **While pressures of daily routine may prevent large-**
**scale changes in your lifestyle, you may find that rearranging**
**your schedule in little ways to take advantage of your daily**
**highs and lows can add pleasure to your living and perhaps, if**
**researchers are right, years to your life.**

## COMPREHENSION CHECK

Complete the following items by filling in the blanks or circling the correct answer.

1. Summarize the main idea of paragraph 3 by filling in the blanks of the following sentence:

   Chronobiologists claim there is a natural rhythm called the _____

   cycle that causes _____ and valleys of attention and _____

   within the body each day.

2. Paragraph 2 contains the main idea of the entire selection. Try to state it in your own words.

   _____

   _____

3. What specific alterations does the author suggest schools might make to accommodate students' circadian rhythms?

   _____

   _____

   *(You may look back at the passage to answer questions 4–6 on vocabulary.)*

4. What does the word *lethal* in paragraph 11 mean? _____

   What type of context clue is used (see Chapter 1)? _____

5. What does the word *nocturnal* in paragraph 13 mean? _____

   What type of context clue is used? _____

6. What does the word *sedentary* in paragraph 16 mean? _____

   What type of context clue is used? _____

7. Why are some scientists reluctant to accept chronobiology as a valid science?

   _____

   _____

8. The author of this article probably uses the theory of chronobiology to plan his own schedule.
   a. true
   b. false

9. Explain the steps involved in taking your pulse. (You may need to refer back to the article to answer this question.)

   a. _____

   b. _____

   c. _____

10. Describe two ways you think you could use chronobiology to help you in your daily work or school activities.

    a. _____

    b. _____

## READING SELECTION THREE

### *Prereading Activity*: **Previewing an article**

Using the worksheet on page 52, preview the selection "Sleep as a Biological Rhythm" following the italicized portions of the six steps on page 43.

## "Sleep as a Biological Rhythm" Preview Worksheet

1. Title and purpose _____

   _____

   _____

2. Main idea of introduction and conclusion _____

   _____

   _____

3. Important headings or quotes

   a. _____

   b. _____

   c. _____

4. Important terms and names

   _____     _____

   _____     _____

   _____     _____

5. Unfamiliar vocabulary words and definitions

   a. _____

   b. _____

   c. _____

   d. _____

6. Main idea of the selection _____

   _____

   _____

Read the selection carefully, keeping in mind the arguments advanced by the previous selection as you proceed. When you finish, again, try to answer as many of the Comprehension Check questions as you can without referring back to the reading.

## Sleep as a Biological Rhythm

BY WAYNE WEITEN

A rhythmic quality pervades the world around us. The daily alternation    1
of light and darkness, the annual pattern of the seasons, and the phases
of the moon all reflect this rhythmic quality of repeating cycles. Humans
and many other animals display biological rhythms that are tied to these
planetary rhythms (Luce, 1971). *Biological rhythms* **are periodic fluctuations in physiological functioning**. Birds beginning a winter mi-
gration or raccoons going into hibernation are showing the influence of
a yearly cycle, just as a student trying to fight off sleep while studying late
at night is showing the influence of a daily cycle of activity and rest. The
existence of these rhythms means that organisms have biological clocks
that somehow monitor the passage of time.

### Biological rhythms in humans

Four time cycles appear to be related to behavior in humans. Our    2
biological rhythms include cycles corresponding roughly to periods of
1 year, 28 days, 24 hours, and 90 minutes (Aschoff, 1981). The yearly, or
seasonal, cycle has been related to patterns of sexual activity and the
onset of mood disorders such as depression (Smolensky et al., 1981; Wehr
et al., 1986). Women's menstrual cycles are tied to the 28-day **lunar**
month: This cycle has been related to fluctuations in mood, although the
data are complex and controversial. Men may experience similar but less
obvious 28-day cycles that affect their hormonal secretions (Parlee, 1973,
1982). The 90-minute cycle appears related to fluctuations in alertness
and daydreaming (Lavie, 1982). Our yearly, monthly, and 90-minute
time cycles appear to exert only a modest influence over our mental states
and behavior. In contrast, our daily rhythms appear to exert considerably
more influence.

### Circadian rhythms

Our most obvious biological rhythms are our daily cycles, or circa-   3
dian rhythms. The term *circadian* is derived from two Latin roots: *circa*
(about) and *dies* (a day). Thus, **circadian rhythms are the 24-hour
biological cycles found in humans and many other species**. In
humans, circadian rhythms are particularly influential in regulating sleep
(Webb, 1982), but they also produce variations in body temperature,
blood pressure, urine production, and hormone secretion, as well as
other physical functions . . . (Aschoff & Wever, 1981). For instance, your
body temperature varies by about 3 degrees Fahrenheit over the period of
a day, usually peaking in the afternoon and descending to a low in the
depths of the night.

A study by Charles Czeisler and his colleagues indicates that we gen-   4
erally fall asleep as our body temperature begins to drop and awaken as
it begins to ascend once again (Czeisler et al., 1980). Researchers have
concluded that our circadian rhythm can leave us physiologically primed
to fall asleep most easily at a particular time of day. This optimal time
varies from one person to another, depending on unique personal schedules, but it's interesting to learn that each of us may have an "ideal" time
for going to bed.

Our circadian clocks are apparently regulated internally, because they   5
continue to run even when we're cut off from exposure to the cycle of
day and night. For instance, when people stay in a cave or a closed-off
room without windows or clocks, their circadian rhythms generally persist even though information about the light-dark cycle is eliminated.
Interestingly, however, when people are isolated in this way, *they tend to
drift toward a 25-hour cycle* (Aschoff & Wever, 1981). This peculiar trend is
charted for one experimental subject in Figure 5.4. . . .

Although our biological clocks continue to function when we're cut   6
off from the daily cycle of light and darkness, our biological rhythms tend
to become more **erratic** or less rhythmic. This observation led many
theorists to conclude that exposure to daylight *readjusts* our biological
clocks. The readjustments may be necessary to correct for our tendency
to drift toward a 25-hour cycle.

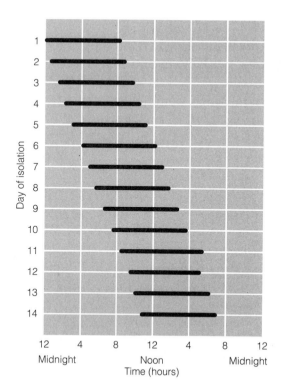

**Figure 5.4**  Changes in sleep periods of a subject isolated from the day-night cycle. The drift of the sleep periods to the right is characteristic of studies in which subjects are deprived of information about day and night. Subjects typically drift toward a 25-hour "day," retiring later and later with each day spent in isolation. When subjects are reexposed to light-cycle cues, they quickly return to a 24-hour rhythm.

Scientists aren't sure how our basic timekeeping mechanism works. One theory is that the body's ability to track time is tied to the synthesis of proteins (Jacklet, 1978). However, researchers do have a pretty good idea of how the day-night cycle resets our biological clocks. There is evidence that exposure to sunlight affects the activity of the *pineal gland* (Binkley, 1979). The pineal gland's secretion of a neurotransmitter (serotonin) and a hormone (melatonin) is closely related to the cycle of light and darkness. The connection between the day-night cycle and activity in the pineal gland probably accounts for how our biological clocks are readjusted.

### Ignoring our circadian rhythms

What happens when you ignore your biological clock and go to sleep    8
at a time that is unusual for you? Typically, the quality of your sleep
suffers. This is the reason for what we call *jet lag*. When you fly across
several time zones, your biological clock keeps time as usual, even though
official clock time changes. You then go to sleep at the "wrong" time and
are likely to experience agitated, poor-quality sleep (Tepas, 1982). This
inferior sleep, which can continue to occur for several days, can make
people sluggish and irritable.

People differ in how quickly they can readjust their biological clocks    9
to compensate for jet lag (Colquhoun, 1984). In addition, the speed of
readjustment depends on several factors, including the distance and direction traveled. Generally, it's easier to fly westward and lengthen your
day than it is to fly eastward and shorten it (Klein et al., 1977). It takes
longer to **resynchronize** after flying east. Why? Perhaps because of our
curious tendency to drift toward a 25-hour cycle. Apparently, there is a
natural drift toward lengthening the daily cycle, which is exactly what
you do when you fly westward. Flying eastward goes against this drift,
much like swimming against a river current. Researchers are currently
investigating whether certain drugs can be used to help people reset their
biological clocks and so reduce the effects of jet lag. Thus far, the results
are promising but inconclusive (Rosenfeld, 1986).

The findings on jet lag have led researchers to distinguish between    10
two types of alterations in circadian rhythm. When your schedule is
altered so that you lengthen your day, you are said to experience a *phase-
delay* shift. If you shorten your day, you go through a *phase-advance* shift.
The evidence on jet lag suggests that we can accommodate phase-delay
changes more easily than phase-advance changes (see Figure 5.5).

Of course, you don't have to hop a jet to get out of sync with your    11
biological clock. Just going to bed a couple of hours later than usual can
affect how you sleep. For instance, Charles Czeisler and his colleagues
found that people who were at home but out of phase with their usual
sleep schedule tended to sleep much longer than those who were in phase
(Czeisler et al., 1980).

Rotating time shifts that force people to keep changing their sleep    12
schedule also play havoc with biological rhythms. Rotating shifts are

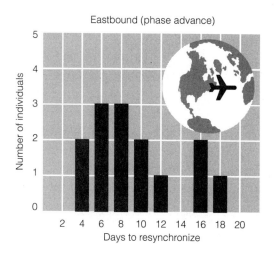

Eastbound (phase advance)

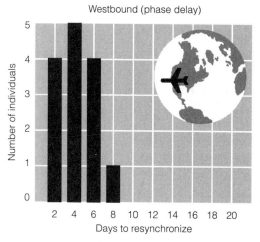

Westbound (phase delay)

**Figure 5.5** Circadian rhythms and jet lag. Air travelers generally adjust to local time more slowly after flying east (which shortens their day) than after flying west (which lengthens it). The explanation for this phenomenon may be our natural drift toward a longer daily cycle; it is easier to extend our biological cycle than to shorten it.

common among nurses, pilots, police officers, and many kinds of industrial workers. People who rotate shifts often complain bitterly about their sleep problems, and scientific research indicates that their complaints are well founded. Studies show that shift rotation can have a negative impact on the quality of employees' sleep, not to mention their productivity at work and their physical and mental health (Bell & Telman, 1980; Webb, 1975).

## COMPREHENSION CHECK

Answer the following items by circling or filling in the correct answer.

1. This selection is mainly about:
   a. sleep
   b. time shifts
   c. biological rhythms
   d. circadian rhythms

2. Which selection appears to be more scientific: "Chronobiology" or "Sleep as a Biological Rhythm"? Why?

   _____

   _____

   _____

3. In your own words explain the four "time cycles" related to human behavior.

   _____

   _____

   _____

   _____

4. What happens to natural body cycles when people are cut off from the daily cycle of light and darkness?

   _____

   _____

5. In your own words state the physiological explanation for how the body readjusts its biological clock.

   _____

   _____

6. Why is it harder to readjust the body system when flying east? _____

   _____

7. What is a "phase-advance" shift? _____

   _____

8. Using the context of the sentence define the word *erratic* in paragraph 6.

   _____

   What type of context clue is used? _____

9. Using the context of the sentence define the word *resynchronize* in paragraph 9.

   _____

   What type of context clue is used? _____

10. Can you see a relationship between the belief in astrology and the scientific study of biological rhythms? If so, what is it? If not, why not?

    _____

    _____

    _____

**CHAPTER APPLICATION 1**

Using the Time Organizer chart on page 60, keep track of your daily activities for one week. In filling in your chart, you should focus on the following activities:

| | | |
|---|---|---|
| sleeping | talking on the phone | studying |
| grooming (bathing, dressing, etc.) | watching TV | work |
| eating | socializing | exercise/sports |
| | attending classes | |

# Time Organizer

| | Monday | Tuesday | Wednesday | Thursday | Friday | Saturday | Sunday |
|---|---|---|---|---|---|---|---|
| 6:00 A.M. | | | | | | | |
| 7:00 | | | | | | | |
| 8:00 | | | | | | | |
| 9:00 | | | | | | | |
| 10:00 | | | | | | | |
| 11:00 | | | | | | | |
| 12:00 | | | | | | | |
| 1:00 P.M. | | | | | | | |
| 2:00 | | | | | | | |
| 3:00 | | | | | | | |
| 4:00 | | | | | | | |
| 5:00 | | | | | | | |
| 6:00 | | | | | | | |
| 7:00 | | | | | | | |
| 8:00 | | | | | | | |
| 9:00 | | | | | | | |
| 10:00 | | | | | | | |
| 11:00 | | | | | | | |
| 12:00 | | | | | | | |
| 1:00 A.M. | | | | | | | |
| 2:00 | | | | | | | |
| 3:00 | | | | | | | |
| 4:00 | | | | | | | |
| 5:00 | | | | | | | |

At the end of the week analyze your time schedule by answering the following questions (round off to the nearest hour):

1. How many hours did you spend sleeping each day? _____

2. How many hours did you spend grooming (bathing, dressing, etc.)?

   _____

3. How many hours did you spend eating? _____

4. How many hours did you spend on the phone? _____

5. How many hours did you spend watching television? _____

6. How many hours did you spend socializing? _____

7. Did you spend three hours studying for each hour spent in class?

   _____

8. How many hours did you spend at your job? _____

9. How many hours did you spend exercising or playing sports? _____

10. What other activities consumed more than one hour of your time during the week? How much time?

   _____

   _____

Now answer these questions:

1. Which three activities took up the most time in your week, and how much time did you spend on them?

   a. _____

   b. _____

   c. _____

2. Which three activities took up the least time, and how much did they take?

   a. _____

   b. _____

   c. _____

3. Which activities would you like to spend less time on?

   a. _____

   b. _____

4. Which activities would you like to spend more time on?

   a. _____

   b. _____

5. On a separate piece of paper, summarize how you might adjust your time schedule in the weeks to come.

## CHAPTER APPLICATION 2

Looking at your Time Organizer chart, try to recall your feelings while performing certain activities. Using the Circadian Rhythm chart, plot your daily highs and lows for each day of the week by doing the following:

1. Place a P for peak at the time of day (morning, afternoon, evening, or night) when you felt the most energetic each day.

2. Place a V for valley at the low point in your energy level each day.

3. Using a red pen, connect the Ps to establish your high-energy pattern.

4. Using a different-color pen, connect the Vs to establish your low-energy pattern.

Using the information you have acquired by filling in your Time Organizer and your Circadian Rhythm charts, create a daily schedule that will make optimum use of your body rhythms.

| Circadian Rhythm | | | | | | | |
|---|---|---|---|---|---|---|---|
| | *Monday* | *Tuesday* | *Wednesday* | *Thursday* | *Friday* | *Saturday* | *Sunday* |
| Morning | | | | | | | |
| Afternoon | | | | | | | |
| Evening | | | | | | | |
| Night | | | | | | | |

## GOING BEYOND

It is important to organize and make the best use of your time if you are to succeed in college, but "all work and not enough play" tends to make for frayed nerves and an unbalanced life. According to Madeline Drexler, Americans are worn down by the work ethic.

What are your ideas on spending leisure time? How do the findings in this article fit with your ideas?

## All Work and Not Enough Play

### BY MADELINE DREXLER

In a world where no one worked more than four hours a day, wrote    1
philosopher Bertrand Russell, there would be "happiness and joy of life, instead of frayed nerves, weariness, and dyspepsia." His 1932 essay titled "In Praise of Idleness" made an eloquent case for expanded leisure time. Nearly 60 years later, time-starved Americans, craving open, unscheduled hours, couldn't agree more.

Though the work week has remained steady at about 40 hours for   2
the last 50 years, an increasing proportion of Americans are toiling for
longer stretches. In 1990, according to the US Bureau of Labor Statistics,
23 percent of Americans worked 49 hours or more a week. "Ours is a
culture of work," says Benjamin Kline Hunnicutt, professor of leisure
studies at the University of Iowa, "and the idea that leisure should increase is ideologically foreign to us."

Not all observers agree, however, that we have become work addicts.   3
Sociologist John Robinson, director of the Americans' Use of Time Project, at the University of Maryland, has found that, contrary to conven-
tional wisdom, Americans actually have more free time than they used
to. Men have an average of 41 leisure hours a week, up from 34 in 1965,
and women have an average of 40, up from 34. Robinson defines free
time as what's left over after subtracting the hours people spend working
and commuting to work, caring for their families, doing housework,
shopping, sleeping, eating, and grooming. He suggests that free time has
grown because fewer households have children, more Americans are
spending more of their lives unmarried, people take time off during the
work day for personal chores, and because—for women—housework
consumes less time.

Whether or not we are in fact working less, Americans clearly hanker   4
for more free time. Nearly a third of the participants, ages 18 to 64, in
Robinson's 1985 study reported that they "always" feel rushed to do the
things they have to do.

One reason may be that our lives are fragmented. There is a sharp   5
boundary between work and play. And in most cases, play is consigned
to weary weeknights or hyperactive weekends.

Robert Grudin, who teaches English at the University of Oregon,   6
believes each of us needs a "nest of time": an inviolable period for leisure
pursuits. In his book *Time and the Art of Living* he writes: "Such periods
unify us, concentrating our energy, judgment and emotion upon a single
point. Conversely, they relieve us from all other considerations and so
give us profound refreshment. They give us, if temporarily, ourselves."

Others note that our free time is seldom free, but instead consists of   7
tightly scheduled exercises in consumerism and self-improvement. "This
is a 'doing' culture," Robinson says. "There is not a lot of time given to
contemplation. It just doesn't fit."

Yet this drive toward activity takes a psychic toll. "If you start to view    8
your leisure time as something demanded of you, you could easily feel
you've lost your ability to sit and loaf," says Tom Juster, an economist at
the University of Michigan Survey Research Center.

Some suggest that, worn down by the work ethic, we have lost our    9
ability to find fulfillment in leisure. "Work is 'this for that.' It's less intrin-
sic and more extrinsic," Hunnicutt says. "But what is the activity of
freedom? What is worth doing for itself?" One of the more alarming of
Robinson's findings is that much of our free time — 38 percent — is spent
watching television. By contrast, reading a book, newspaper, or magazine
accounts for less than 10 percent, or fewer than three hours a week.
Relaxing and thinking fill up all of an hour.

One notion researchers agree on is that many Americans now value    10
free time as much as money. Some white-collar employee groups are
pressing for guaranteed four- or six-week vacations and the option of
shorter work weeks. But Hunnicutt suspects the trend isn't limited to the
affluent. He believes that people on the bottom rungs of employment —
those who can find only transient or dead-end jobs in a shrinking economy — will by virtue of their alienation see more meaning in nonwork
activities. "Work is increasingly one of those gods that failed," he says.

Yet Robinson counters that there is inherent satisfaction in work and    11
that many Americans would not welcome enforced repose. A survey he
conducted in Jackson, Michigan, asked people where they found more
enjoyment: in their free time, in work, or in both equally. Twenty-five
percent said they enjoyed their free time more, 15 percent preferred their
work time, and 60 percent enjoyed them the same amount. "I think that
work is getting a bad rap," Robinson says, although he concedes that
these results could spring from the fact that the leisure we fashion "isn't
that great."

In the diary reports, people who rated themselves happiest were those    12
who were "sometimes rushed." As Robinson sees it, "There's a sense that
being busy is important. It confers status." But the temporal ideal, he
says, is a happy medium: "neither too busy nor having too much time on
your hands."

## JOURNAL WRITING

1. How much leisure time do you allow yourself each week? What do you do with that time? Is there a particular leisure activity you would pursue if you had more time? If you had unlimited amounts of money and did not have to work, what would you do with yourself?

2. Describe your attitude toward time and how it affects your behavior. For example, do you always, sometimes, or seldom feel rushed? Are you always, sometimes, or never on time?

3. Characterize the findings and opinions of each of the following researchers and writers as found in Drexler's article:

   a. Bertrand Russell

   b. Benjamin Kline Hunnicutt

   c. John Robinson

   d. Tom Juster

4. If you could plan a two-week fantasy vacation with anyone in the world, whom would you take, where would you go, and what would you do? Discuss what this vacation might reveal about your attitudes toward work and leisure.

5. According to this article the happiest people are those who are "sometimes rushed." "There's a sense that being busy is important, it confers status," notes one of the researchers. What does this statement mean and how does it reflect American attitudes towards work and leisure?

## CHAPTER 3

# Understanding the Main Idea

After studying Chapter 3 you should be able to:

- locate the topic sentence of a paragraph
- state the main idea of a paragraph
- state the main idea of a longer reading selection
- understand your potential as a learner

Use the following checklist to help you plan for the text, readings, and activities in this chapter.

| Date<br>Assigned | Date<br>Completed | |
| --- | --- | --- |
| _____ | _____ | The main idea and the building block approach to writing |
| _____ | _____ | WARM-UP 1: Finding the stated main idea of a paragraph |
| _____ | _____ | EXERCISE 1: Finding the topic sentence |
| _____ | _____ | WARM-UP 2: Finding the implied main idea of a paragraph |
| _____ | _____ | EXERCISE 2: Inferring the main idea when there is no topic sentence |

### READING SELECTION ONE

| | | |
| --- | --- | --- |
| _____ | _____ | *Prereading Activity*: Finding the topic sentence |
| _____ | _____ | **"Get Smart"** |
| _____ | _____ | COMPREHENSION CHECK |

### READING SELECTION TWO

| | | |
| --- | --- | --- |
| _____ | _____ | *Prereading Activity*: Rating yourself |
| _____ | _____ | **"Better Late Than Never"** |
| _____ | _____ | COMPREHENSION CHECK |
| _____ | _____ | CHAPTER APPLICATION |

# The Main Idea and the Building Block Approach to Writing

Understanding your learning preferences is a fundamental ingredient in becoming a successful student, but even more essential is the ability to comprehend what you read. Chapters 1 and 2 introduced two keys to comprehension: utilizing context and activating prior knowledge. This chapter focuses on perhaps the most important skill of all — your ability to understand the main idea of a reading selection. In order to become proficient in this skill, it is helpful to know something about how writers express ideas.

Writers, particularly textbook authors, often take a building block approach to writing. That is, they break the writing task down into distinct components or blocks — subject and predicate, sentences of various types, paragraphs of various types — and then fit the blocks together to form the finished product — the essay. Let's look at each of the "blocks" in a little more detail.

## The sentence

Writers begin building concepts by writing down single thoughts or ideas to create **sentences**. In English the subject often appears at the beginning of the sentence, followed by the predicate. For example:

> Intelligence as measured on I.Q. tests appears to be related to success in school but seems to have little to do with achievement in careers.

> *Subject* (what is being discussed)
> Intelligence as measured on I.Q. tests

> *Predicate* (what is being said about the subject)
> appears to be related to success in school but seems to have little to do with achievement in careers.

## The paragraph

Next, writers combine sentences to develop their thoughts and ideas into **paragraphs**. Sometimes they include one sentence that states the main idea. This is the sentence that the rest of the paragraph supports or explains. It is called the **topic sentence**.

The topic sentence might be thought of as the "subject" of a paragraph because it states what the paragraph is about. Similarly, the remaining sentences might be construed as the "predicate" of a paragraph because they constitute the particular things being said about the subject. These sentences are the supporting details of the paragraph.

The topic sentence (or subject) usually appears in the first few sentences of the paragraph, but sometimes it is found at the end or even in the middle of the paragraph. Many paragraphs do not have a topic sentence, in which case the reader must infer the main idea from the related sentences.

Finding the main idea of a paragraph involves three steps:

1. Find the subject or topic by asking, "Who or what is the paragraph about?"

2. Locate the specific details by asking, "What is being said about the subject?"

3. Look for a topic sentence that answers the question, "What do the details tell me about the subject?"

## The essay

When writers wish to express a number of ideas in order to prove or support a concept, they combine several paragraphs to construct **articles** or **essays**.

In order to prepare readers for what is to come in an article or essay, writers often begin with an **introduction** — a few paragraphs that outline the topic and/or state the main idea. The introduction is to the essay what the subject is to the sentence or what the topic sentence is to the paragraph.

The group of paragraphs that supports or elaborates on the main point is sometimes called the **body** of the selection. The body is similar to the predicate of a sentence or to the supporting details of the paragraph, because it elaborates on or supports the topic. It follows the introduction and usually constitutes the largest part of the essay.

Most reading selections also contain a **conclusion,** which either relates to or summarizes the main ideas of the selection.

Finding the main idea of an article or essay is similar to finding the main idea of a paragraph. As you read the selection, do the following:

1. Look for the topic or subject in the introduction. Often the main idea is stated in the first paragraph. Sometimes, however, the first paragraph merely sets the scene or provides background, in which case the main idea may be in a later paragraph.

2. Figure out the main idea of each paragraph, noting how each one supports or relates to the topic.

3. Look for a summary of the details in the last paragraph. This summary or conclusion may be a clue to the main idea.

The figure on page 72 summarizes the key components of the building block approach to writing.

### Rule of Thumb for Finding the Main Idea of a Paragraph or Essay

1. Determine the topic of the passage.

2. Locate the details that support or explain the topic.

3. Summarize the details that support or explain the topic.

**WARM-UP 1**  *Finding the stated main idea of a paragraph*

Let's look at a paragraph where the main idea is stated in a topic sentence:

Memories fade away rapidly when not reviewed or used. The curve of forgetting is like a slide; facts slip away almost immediately after we learn them. In fact, unless we put them to use most learning leaves us within 24 hours. Motor learning seems to be better retained than verbal learning because actions accompany the motor learning. The acts have to be completely done to be done at all, and so require a higher degree of organization and competency.

**Article or Essay**

Introduction (what is being discussed — main idea introduced)

Body (what is being said about the topic — support or elaboration)

Conclusion (summarizes or relates ideas from the body of the selection)

**Paragraph**

Topic sentence (what is being discussed or the topic)

Supporting sentences (what is being said about the topic)

Concluding sentence (summarizes or link to the next paragraph)

**Sentence**

Subject (what is being discussed)

Predicate (what is being said about the subject)

The Building Blocks of Writing

First, find the subject by asking yourself, "Who or what is the paragraph about?" (Which words, or synonyms, are repeated?) The subject of the paragraph is memory, or learning. Notice how many times the word *learning* is used in the paragraph. Memorizing is one type of learning.

Next, locate the details by asking yourself, "What specifically is being said about learning?" There are basically three supporting details: (1) facts slip away almost immediately after being learned, (2) if we don't use them, memories are gone within twenty-four hours, and (3) motor learning lasts longer because it involves action.

Finally, find the sentence that sums up the details. "Memories fade away rapidly when not renewed or used" is the topic sentence because the details explain (a) how quickly memory fades and (b) why one type of learning is retained (memorized) better than another.

**EXERCISE 1**    *Finding the topic sentence*

Read the following paragraphs and then complete the items that follow. Remember that although the most common placement of the topic sentence is at the beginning, it may appear at the end or even in the middle of the paragraph.

1.  Researchers believe that, from birth to adolescence, we are laying down the basic circuitry of the brain. As we grow up, the world subsequently makes its mark physically. Exposure to new tasks and new stimuli generates the development of new circuits and synapses for handling them. From then on, continued stimulation throughout life further strengthens these pathways and enhances their interconnections.

State the topic or subject of the paragraph in a few words.

_____

List the details, or what is being said about the topic.

_____

_____

_____

Write the sentence that best explains or sums up all the details.

_____

2.  For years, experts had believed that an individual's ability to learn was
    a fixed capacity. During the last two decades, however, leading psy-
    chologists and educators have come to think otherwise. "We have in-
    creasing proof that human intelligence is expandable," says Jack
    Lochhead, director of the Cognitive Development Project at the Uni-
    versity of Massachusetts at Amherst. "We know that with proper
    skills people can actually improve their learning ability."

State the topic or subject of the paragraph in a few words.

_____

List the details, or what is being said about the topic.

_____

_____

_____

Write the sentence that best explains or sums up all the details.

_____

3.  A poor showing on tests was once a signal to all concerned — child,
    teacher, parents — that greater effort was needed to learn, or to teach,
    what was required. It didn't mean that a child couldn't learn. But the
    damaging assumption behind testing as it is now employed in many
    schools is that only those who test well are capable of learning what is
    needed to escape an adult life restricted to menial dead-end jobs. This
    new message imparted by our schools is that test-measured ability, not
    effort, is what counts, and what many students are learning is that they

are not equal to everybody else. What's tragic about this change is not just that it's unjust — but that it's untrue.

State the topic or subject of the paragraph in a few words.

_____

List the details, or what is being said about the topic.

_____

_____

_____

Write the sentence that best explains or sums up all the details.

_____

4.  Looking back on my childhood, I am convinced that naturalists are born and not made. My father was a keen naturalist, but although we all shared the same upbringing, my siblings were not hooked on plants and insects in the way I was. They soon abandoned their pressed flowers and butterfly nets. Unlike them, I had no ear for music and languages, I was not an early reader and I could not do mental arithmetic. But I had a retentive memory and was deeply, passionately fond of animals and keenly interested in everything connected with them.

State the topic or subject of the paragraph in a few words.

_____

List the details, or what is being said about the topic.

_____

_____

_____

Write the sentence that best explains or sums up all the details.

_____

5. When we talk about intelligence, we do not mean the ability to get a good score on a certain kind of test, or even the ability to do well in school. These are at best only indicators of something larger, deeper, and far more important. By intelligence we mean a style of life, a way of behaving in various situations, and particularly in new, strange, and perplexing situations. The true test of intelligence is not how much we know how to do, but how we behave when we don't know what to do.

State the topic or subject of the paragraph in a few words.

_____

List the details, or what is being said about the topic.

_____

_____

_____

Write the sentence that best explains or sums up all the details.

_____

6. Curiosity is the key to doing well in a learning environment. In high school you could wait passively for a teacher to tell you what to learn. In college, however, your most valuable learning comes from asking questions and searching for answers. An essential skill developed by successful college students is that of asking and answering questions. They actively seek and find useful information. They do not sit back and wait for someone to tell them what they need to know.

State the topic or subject of the paragraph in a few words.

_____

List the details, or what is being said about the topic.

_____

_____

_____

List the details, or what is being said about the topic.

_____

_____

_____

Write a sentence that sums up the details.

4.  One of Albert Einstein's biographers tells a story about an encounter
    between the physicist and a neighborhood girl that took place as he
    was walking through slush and snowdrifts on his way to teach a class at
    Princeton. After they had chatted for a while, the girl looked down at
    Einstein's moccasins, which were soaking wet. "Mr. Einstein, you've
    come out without your boots again," she said. Einstein laughed and
    pulled up his trousers to show his ankles. "And I forgot my socks," he
    confessed.

State the topic or subject of the paragraph in a few words.

_____

List the details, or what is being said about the topic.

_____

_____

_____

Write a sentence that sums up the details.

_____

5.  For Asian Americans, a college campus remains an excellent place
    to learn the skills to prepare for a rewarding career. For recent immi-
    grants, it is ideal for acquiring language skills and for broadening their
    understanding of their adopted culture. A college education, then,
    should prepare the students to participate fully in all aspects of Amer-
    ican life. This will assure all of the benefits that come from the rich
    blend of two distinct cultures, Asian and American.

State the topic or subject of the paragraph in a few words.

_____

List the details, or what is being said about the topic.

_____

_____

_____

Write a sentence that sums up the details.

_____

## READING SELECTION ONE

### *Prereading Activity*: **Finding the topic sentence**

Read the following paragraph (excerpted from Reading Selection One) and then answer the questions or complete the items.

> There isn't any single, immutable entity called "intelligence." Rather, there are many kinds of intelligence, all of which play critical roles in how we adapt to the world. These range from the ability to adjust to novel situations and learn from experience to sorting out knowledge and carrying on abstract thinking. Other facets of intelligence include the way we behave with others, make choices, and persevere despite setbacks. To underscore the distinction between these pragmatic skills and the traditional notion of a single, quantifiable intellect, researchers have labeled our real-world survival mechanisms "practical intelligence."

1. Find the subject or topic by asking yourself, "Who or what is the paragraph about?"

_____

5. The main idea of paragraph 8 is found in:
   a. sentence 1
   b. sentence 2
   c. sentence 4
   d. sentence 5

6. The topic or subject matter of the entire article is:
   a. intelligence tests
   b. the theory of multiple intelligences
   c. the theory of practical intelligence

7. State the main idea of the entire selection by writing a few sentences that summarize how the details support or explain the topic.

   _____

   _____

8. The purpose of paragraph 1 is to:
   a. provide background information
   b. state the main idea
   c. create interest in the topic

9. The word *pragmatic* in the last sentence of paragraph 2 can be deciphered by using clues from the previous sentence as well as words within the sentence itself. Write a synonym for *pragmatic*.

   _____

10. The phrase *immutable entity* is used in paragraph 2 to describe the traditional notion of intelligence. Explain what the phrase means by drawing on your understanding of the entire article.

    _____

    _____

    _____

## READING SELECTION TWO

### *Prereading Activity*: **Rating yourself**

Before reading the selection "Better Late Than Never," answer the following questions:

1. How would you rate yourself as a student in high school?
   a. excellent
   b. good
   c. average
   d. fair
   e. poor

2. How involved with extracurricular activities were you in high school?
   a. very
   b. somewhat
   c. a little
   d. not at all

3. At what age did you decide that you wanted to go to college? —————

4. Was there another person who was influential in your decision? If so, what was the relationship of this person to you?

   _____

5. How would you rate yourself as a student in college?
   a. excellent
   b. good
   c. average
   d. fair
   e. poor

In the selection "Better Late Than Never" the author describes the factors that contribute to educational "late blooming" — a phenomenon in which mediocre students later become serious-minded and dedicated to learning. As you read the selection, consider the factors that have influenced your own educational career.

## Better Late Than Never

BY JACK LEVIN

*Individual success doesn't always follow a strict schedule*

Dr. William Levin is professor of sociology at Bridgewater State College, an award-winning teacher and the **prolific** author of a number of re-spected books in his field. He also flunked the eighth grade.    1

I met Bill Levin almost 20 years ago as his master's thesis advisor in what was then the School of Public Communication at Boston University. We hit it off almost immediately. Not only did we share the same last name (though not the same parents), but we also discovered we were both educational late bloomers — **mediocre** high-school students who later developed into serious-minded, dedicated college students (I can't say that I flunked the eighth grade, but I can still "brag" about being on academic probation during my first year of college).    2

Bill Levin's escape from educational mediocrity is far from unique. In fact, there are thousands of educational late bloomers who go on to become brilliant college or graduate students. Thousands more interrupt their collegiate pursuits, only to return years later. In fact, we live in a society where second chances are fast becoming a way of life, especially in the educational field. We tolerate late blooming, but do we know why? Trying to answer just that question, Bill and I recently talked with college students in the Boston area. And in interviews with both late and early bloomers, we were able to identify four important factors: capacity, opportunity, a triggering event and a period of readiness to accept change.    3

Intellectual capacity is a **prerequisite** for almost any success, when-     4
ever it occurs in the life cycle. But for late bloomers, capacity has an
important emotional component. Those who lack intellectual capacity
more than make up for it with commitment and involvement. Many of
the late bloomers we interviewed were, as high-school students, almost
fanatically devoted to a cause, a hobby, a job, a sport or an idea. For
example, while in high school, one late bloomer became committed to
physical exercise. Hard-pressed to find the time to study, he still managed
to jog, run, lift weights, bike and swim on a regular basis. Another student
was heavily into illicit drugs. He spent hours in the library, but not doing
his homework. Instead, he read and researched articles related to his
addiction. Then there was the mechanical engineering major who now
has a 3.6 grade-point average, but had only a 2.5 average in high school.
He, however, was a member of his school's debating team and chorus in
addition to working more than 20 hours a week.

In a sense, the presence of emotional commitment in high school     5
may indicate later academic potential. The question is how do we transfer
that commitment from an extracurricular activity, athletics or a cause to
the college classroom?

Part of the answer involves the second factor in late blooming: the     6
presence of opportunity. Almost everywhere outside the United States,
the timing of academic success is inflexible. Students must achieve high
grades and achievement test scores early in their academic careers; they
must also enter college by a specified age. . . .

In sharp contrast, the American educational system gives students a     7
second, third, even a fourth chance for a college education. If they or
their parents are able to pay the bills, even students who have low grades
in high school are granted an opportunity to enroll in higher education.
One-third of all colleges have open admission policies.

But capacity and opportunity are not always enough for late bloom-     8
ing to occur. Bill Levin, for example, had the opportunity to attend college
because his parents saved the money to send him. And like millions of
other middle-class students, he went to college primarily because that's
what was expected of him. But for Levin and others like him, the commitment to education only materialized because of a triggering event — a
reward, a punishment or both that provided a rationale for making a
profound change in their lifestyle.

For some of the late bloomers we studied, that triggering event was a    9
work experience during college. Some suggested that a job showed them,
perhaps for the first time, the strong connection between grades and the
kind of work they were likely to do after they graduated. Even an unpleas-
ant job during college was motivating; it forced them to deal with the
likelihood that, unless things changed drastically, this was the kind of
boring, monotonous work they might expect to be doing for the rest of
their lives.

Other late bloomers pointed to more positive events as triggering their    10
commitment to academics. Some, such as Bill Levin, gave credit to a great
teacher who had inspired them to study or to a course that was new and
exciting to them. Others were a few years older than their classmates,
having dropped out to work for a year or two; transferred from another
college; or spent a few years in the military. Peers also made a difference.
For example, one late-blooming college senior reported that it was a
bright, achievement-oriented girlfriend who motivated him by threatening to end their relationship if he didn't "buckle down."

If the series of triggering events is effective, a student enters a period    11
of readiness to change. During this stage, the academic community gradually becomes an important reference point, a source of norms and values. The student frequently changes his or her major based on personal
interest rather than practicality or parental guidance. For the first time,
grades are used as markers of personal worth and school takes on primary
importance. The individual is ready to bloom. He talks informally with
instructors during their office hours and after classes; she discusses a
lecture with her friends. He spends more time in the library; she writes
for the campus newspaper and runs for student government.

Given our present state of knowledge, we are not able to predict who    12
will and will not turn out to be a late bloomer. Until our theories and
methods permit such accurate predictions, we must treat every student
as a potential late bloomer. This means that we must never give up on
anyone. Bill Levin is living proof and he has plenty of company.

## COMPREHENSION CHECK

For each of the following items either circle the correct answer or fill in the blank.

1. The purpose of the first paragraph is to:
   a. create interest
   b. introduce the subject
   c. state the main idea

2. The main idea of paragraph 3 is stated in:
   a. sentence 1
   b. sentence 2
   c. sentence 4

3. The last sentence of paragraph 3 is:
   a. a concluding sentence — it ties up the thoughts
   b. a supporting detail sentence — it supports the main idea
   c. a transitional sentence — it serves to link ideas between paragraphs

4. The topic sentence in paragraph 6 is:
   a. sentence 1
   b. sentence 2
   c. sentence 3

5. What characteristic does the author feel is as important for academic success as intellectual capacity?

   _____

6. In two words what is the topic of the entire selection?

   _____

7. State the main idea of the entire selection by explaining what the supporting details tell you about the topic.

   _____

   _____

8. The last paragraph:
   a. summarizes the ideas of the article
   b. draws a conclusion from the ideas in the article
   c. states the main idea of the article

9. The word *mediocre* in paragraph 2 means "weak" or "average." What type of context clue is used in that paragraph?
   a. synonym
   b. example
   c. inference
   d. contrast

10. The author feels that anyone can be a late bloomer.
    a. true
    b. false

## CHAPTER APPLICATION

Write an essay about a significant educational experience, one that changed the way you felt about school—for better or for worse. Select a key idea to focus on in your introduction, and then develop or explain this idea in a series of paragraphs. Be sure your essay includes the following:

- an introduction that creates interest, introduces the subject matter, and/or states the main idea

- a body of paragraphs that develop or support the main idea

- an ending that summarizes the main points or draws a conclusion

## GOING BEYOND

As you read this selection written by a man considered to be a genius, think about what the word *smart* really means.

# What Is Intelligence, Anyway?

### BY ISAAC ASIMOV

What is intelligence, anyway? When I was in the army I received a kind 1 of aptitude test that all the soldiers took and, against a normal of 100, scored 160. No one at the base had ever seen a figure like that, and for two hours they made a big fuss over me. (It didn't mean anything. The next day I was still a buck private with KP as my highest duty.)

All my life I've been registering scores like that, so that I have the 2 complacent feeling that I'm highly intelligent, and I expect other people to think so, too. Actually, though, don't such scores simply mean that I am very good at answering the type of academic questions that are considered worthy of answers by the people who make up the intelligence tests — people with intellectual **bents** similar to mine?

For instance, I had an auto repairman once, who, on these intelli- 3 gence tests, could not possibly have scored more than 80, by my estimate. I always took it for granted that I was far more intelligent than he was. Yet, when anything went wrong with my car, I hastened to him with it, watched him anxiously as he explored its **vitals**, and listened to his pronouncements as though they were divine **oracles** — and he always fixed my car.

Well then, suppose my auto repairman devised questions for an intel- 4 ligence test. Or suppose a carpenter did, or a farmer, or, indeed, almost anyone but an **academician**. By every one of those tests, I'd prove myself a moron. And I'd *be* a moron, too. In a world where I could not use my academic training and my verbal talents but had to do something **intricate** or hard, working with my hands, I would do poorly. My intelligence, then, is not **absolute** but is a function of the society I live in and of the fact that a small subsection of that society has managed to foist itself on the rest as an **arbiter** of such matters.

Consider my auto repairman, again. He had a habit of telling me jokes 5 whenever he saw me. One time he raised his head from under the automobile hood to say, "Doc, a deaf-and-dumb guy went into a hardware store to ask for some nails. He put two fingers together on the counter and made hammering motions with the other hand. The clerk brought him a hammer. He shook his head and pointed to the two fingers he was hammering. The clerk brought him nails. He picked out the sizes he wanted, and left. Well, doc, the next guy who came in was a blind man. He wanted scissors. How do you suppose he asked for them?''

**Indulgently**, I lifted my right hand and made scissoring motions    6
with my two fingers. Whereupon my auto repairman laughed raucously and said, ''Why, you dumb jerk, he used his *voice* and asked for them.'' Then he said, **smugly**, ''I've been trying that on all my customers today.'' ''Did you catch many?'' I asked. ''Quite a few,'' he said, ''but I knew for sure I'd catch *you*.'' ''Why is that?'' I asked. ''Because you're so god-damned educated, doc, I *knew* you couldn't be very smart.''

And I have an uneasy feeling he had something there.    7

## JOURNAL WRITING

1.  The articles in this chapter should have increased your understanding of what it means to be intelligent. Using this new information, describe a person you consider to be "smart." Include specific examples to support why you consider this person to be "smart."

2.  Isaac Asimov explains that one kind of intelligence is rated by the ability to answer academic questions. Identify other kinds of "smarts" you associate with the following occupations:

    a. a professional soccer player
    b. a drummer
    c. a trail guide
    d. a marriage counselor
    e. an interior decorator

3.  What kinds of intelligence were valued by you and your friends in elementary school? In high school? Discuss whether these values have changed or been influenced by other factors since you became a college student.

4. What are your present career objectives? What are the essential skills or kinds of intelligences necessary for success in that profession? Discuss the particular abilities you possess that will qualify you for your chosen career. Which aspects of the career do you think will be easiest for you? Which will be the most difficult?

5. Are you a "late bloomer" — someone whose desire for education surfaced later than usual? If so, does your educational history resemble the typical late bloomer, as described by sociologist Jack Levin? Was there a triggering event that sparked your desire to learn? Did you have a passion for some hobby or pursuit other than learning in your early years? Describe your educational experiences and explain how and why your attitudes have changed over the years.

## CHAPTER 4

# Understanding Yourself
# as a Reader
# and a Learner

After studying Chapter 4 you should be able to:

- identify your own learning style
- adjust your learning style as necessary
- identify your strengths and weaknesses as a reader
- set goals and adjust your rate as you read
- paraphrase as you read
- monitor your comprehension as you read
- summarize a selection after reading it

## CHAPTER CHECKLIST

Use the following checklist to help you plan for the text, readings, and activities in this chapter.

| Date Assigned | Date Completed | |
|---|---|---|
| _____ | _____ | Learning styles |
| _____ | _____ | WARM-UP 1: Learning style inventory |
| _____ | _____ | Coordinating your learning style with your instructor's |
| _____ | _____ | EXERCISE 1: Adapting your learning style for tests |
| _____ | _____ | Coordinating your learning style with the task |
| _____ | _____ | EXERCISE 2: Creating a study group |
| _____ | _____ | Metacognition and reading comprehension |
| _____ | _____ | WARM-UP 2: Reading profile |
| _____ | _____ | Improving your reading through metacognitive monitoring |

### READING SELECTION ONE

| | | |
|---|---|---|
| _____ | _____ | *Prereading Activity 1*: Paraphrasing |
| _____ | _____ | *Prereading Activity 2*: Creating questions |

| Date Assigned | Date Completed | |
| --- | --- | --- |
| ⸺ | ⸺ | **"Development of Metamemory"** |
| ⸺ | ⸺ | COMPREHENSION CHECK |
| | | **READING SELECTION TWO** |
| ⸺ | ⸺ | *Prereading Activity*: Remembering |
| ⸺ | ⸺ | **"How to Improve Your . . . Oh, Yeah, Memory"** |
| ⸺ | ⸺ | COMPREHENSION CHECK |
| ⸺ | ⸺ | CHAPTER APPLICATION |
| ⸺ | ⸺ | GOING BEYOND: From *Black Boy* |
| ⸺ | ⸺ | JOURNAL WRITING |

# Learning Styles

> Charley was a pretty fair college high jumper until the day his coach decided to improve him. The coach taught him a new way to get over the rail, but Charley couldn't jump grass with it. Finally, the coach gave up and told Charley to return to his old form, but Charley was never the same after that.
>
> — Paul Chance, *Psychology Today*

Learning is a very mysterious phenomenon that often takes place even when we are not aware of it. You may remember the moment when you began to read, but do you remember the steps that brought you to that point?

The learning experience differs for each individual. Although most people learn best when they utilize as many senses as possible, we all have preferences for the way we receive and process information. For example, watching an exercise workout on videotape is usually easier than simply listening to an audiotape of the same workout because with the video you have both sight and sound to help you. And if you physically follow the directions as you listen and watch, the experience is further enhanced. Suppose you could choose only one modality — sight or sound — would you choose a soundless videotape or an audiotape? Your choice has something to do with what we call your *learning style*.

Just as some of us prefer reading to watching television, and some prefer a museum visit to a concert, all of us have our own learning style. For example, some of you might prefer a class where you actively participate, and others a class where you listen. But sight and sound are not the only learning preferences we have. For a given task some of us plan out precisely what we are going to do while others create as we go along. In the same vein, those of us who like to make plans probably prefer the deductive teaching method in which the instructor presents the concepts first and then gives the examples, while those of us who follow a more creative path may prefer the inductive teaching method in which we are shown examples and are asked to arrive at a conclusion. Do you prefer a professor to outline the main ideas and then lecture to fill in the details? If so, you prefer deduction. If you would rather discuss concepts and synthesize ideas to draw conclusions, then you prefer induction. Do you like to work alone or with others? Do you proceed with caution or with haste? All of these tendencies make up your individual learning style.

Becoming aware of your learning style will help you to (1) understand why you have difficulty with certain learning experiences, (2) adjust to the various teaching styles you encounter during your schooling, and (3) plan your course of study and perhaps your career.

In Chapter 4 you will examine yourself as a student — what you like and don't like, what you do well and what you do poorly. Then, throughout the rest of the book, you will be presented with a number of strategies designed to improve your chances for success as a student. If, like Charley, the college high jumper, you already have a successful strategy for a particular skill, by all means keep it. Studies show that some students have more success with techniques they develop on their own than with those they are taught. However, studies also show that many students benefit a great deal from learning new strategies. Once you have a grasp of your strengths and weaknesses, you will be able to select and adapt strategies in this text to your specific learning style.

**WARM-UP**  *Learning style inventory*

Following are several series of statements adapted from a number of formal learning style inventories designed to pinpoint a person's learning style. Rate the items from 1 to 5, with 1 being your highest rating (that is, 1 denoting an item you strongly agree with or prefer) and so on down to 5 as your lowest rating.

*Receiving Information*

_____    1. I prefer reading directions.

_____    2. I prefer having directions explained to me orally.

_____    3. I enjoy lectures.

_____    4. I enjoy large-group discussion.

_____    5. I enjoy small-group discussion.

_____    6. I enjoy hands-on group activities.

_____    7. I enjoy self-directed computer work.

_____    8. I enjoy self-directed work using an audiotape.

_____    9. I memorize things by writing them out.

_____    10. I memorize things by repeating them orally.

*Processing Information*

_____    1. I get more done when I work alone.

_____    2. I like to work with others.

_____    3. I like to make a plan and follow it as I work.

_____    4. I like to begin working and follow my instincts.

_____    5. I like to know why things happen.

_____    6. I like to know all the details.

_____    7. I prefer objective tests to essay tests.

_____    8. I work quickly and am willing to make mistakes.

_____    9. I like to relate information to myself and things I know.

_____   10. I like to use information to solve problems.

*Instructor Characteristics*

_____    1. I prefer an instructor who is mainly interested in transmitting knowledge.

_____    2. I prefer an instructor who helps me to gain personal insights.

_____    3. I prefer an instructor who helps me apply my knowledge.

_____    4. I want an instructor who is primarily interested in challenging me intellectually.

_____    5. I like an instructor who lectures, allowing occasional discussion.

_____    6. I like an instructor who holds many large-group discussions.

_____    7. I prefer an instructor who uses a variety of group activities.

_____    8. I prefer an instructor who holds mainly small-group discussions.

_____    9. I want an instructor who explains exactly what to do and how to do it.

_____   10. I prefer an instructor who allows the students to organize and take charge of their own learning.

Place the statements you ranked 1 or 2 from the first two lists under the heading "Student" on the chart below. Place the statements you ranked 1 or 2 from the third list under "Instructor."

*Student*                                    *Instructor*

_____         _____

_____         _____

_____         _____

_____         _____

_____         _____

_____         _____

Now read over the chart you have just created to get an idea of your learning preferences. Then write a few paragraphs on a separate sheet of paper describing your learning style (what you like and don't like about learning and instructional methods). Finally, describe a course from which you learned a great deal (and perhaps in which you also received a good grade). Think about the instructional style of the teacher, and explain why you think it may have meshed with your individual learning preferences.

## Coordinating Your Learning Style with Your Instructor's

Because the way we process information is reflected in how we ultimately express that information, your instructors' teaching styles will reflect their own personal learning preferences. Therefore, if you understand your instructors' preferences, you should be able to predict the test questions they will create.

For example, I recall an instructor in an eighteenth-century literature course I took as an undergraduate. Although literally hundreds of poets and poems were represented in the five-inch-thick anthology, he discussed only a few poets from each period. He was meticulous about details, even including footnotes in his discussion.

There was so much information to study for the midsemester exam that I hardly knew where to begin. Understanding his penchant for detail, however, I began with an intense review of the history and characteristics of each period. I studied footnotes, sidenotes, even glossary notes. Then I chose two poems from each period: one that had been discussed in class and one that hadn't. I carefully analyzed every line of each poem. I figured that if I understood a few representative poems, I would be able to transfer this knowledge to others.

As I expected, the first half of the exam included fifty obscure identifications, some of which had been taken from the footnotes. The second half of the exam involved one poem to be analyzed in depth. It was not a poem that had been discussed in class, but it *was* one I had chosen to study. I thought about why I had chosen that particular poem and realized that it was representative of one of the instructor's favorite poets.

---

**EXERCISE 1**    *Adapting your learning style for tests*

Consider a course in which you did not perform as well as you wished on the exams. Describe the instructor's teaching method by listing two or three classroom strategies the instructor used. Compare these with the types of test questions the instructor asked. Were the instructor's teaching methods reflected in the types of exam questions? How did you study for those exams? Would another study technique have been more appropriate?

*Instructor Behaviors*                    *Types of Test Questions*

_____          _____

_____          _____

_____          _____

Write a few sentences describing the method you used in studying for the exams. Then write a few sentences describing what you might have done differently.

_____

_____

_____

_____

# Coordinating Your Learning Style with the Task

A learning strategy that is successful in one course or with one instructor may not necessarily be successful in another. And because most instructors do not individualize their courses to suit the learning styles of their students, there are times when you must adjust your strategies to suit the tasks of the course. Imagine the following scenario:

Your psychology instructor has informed you that the midterm exam will be an essay test covering class lectures and the first six chapters of the textbook. You are more comfortable with objective tests because generating and memorizing facts has always been easier for you than organizing ideas. John, who sits next to you in class, suggests that you study with him and a few other students. You reject his offer because you feel you study better alone.

That evening you go to the library and begin to study by reading over your class notes. You then read over the pertinent chapters in your texts hoping to get a grip on the concepts and developing a list of important terms as you go along. You soon realize this is too time-consuming so you concentrate on the review questions at the end of each chapter. After studying in this manner for four or five hours, you feel you know most of the important information.

John, on the other hand, is good at organizing ideas and prefers essay to objective tests. He enjoys working in groups and sharing ideas with other people, so that evening he meets with two other students in the cafeteria, and they pool their ideas about possible exam questions. They begin by skimming the chapter titles and introductions to determine the major concepts covered in the text. They then compare the concepts in the text to those covered by the instructor in class. Past experience has taught them that instructors tend to test them on the concepts that have been emphasized in class.

After deciding on a list of twelve possible questions, each person chooses four and, using the text and class notes, develops an outline for each answer. Next, they discuss the outlines, modifying them as needed. When they have agreed on the answers, they make copies of all twelve outlines so that each person will have study guides to review later that evening.

The next day you are nervous as the exam begins. You read the exam questions carefully and then choose the four you feel most confident about. However, as you begin you are confused and unsure. So many facts and ideas are bubbling around in your head that you are unable to focus or organize them in a coherent manner. In a panic you begin to furiously write down *everything* you know about each question. When class ends you are still writing, but you notice that John has already finished and is reading over his test.

When you receive the results of your test you are very disappointed. In addition to giving you a C, the instructor has included these comments:

> Essays poorly focused. For example, in question 1 you define the basic methods of conflict avoidance and offer examples of each, but the question asked you to evaluate the effectiveness of the methods in particular situations. . . .

Understanding *how* to study for a particular test is just as important as knowing *what* to study. Simply knowing a lot of information will not guarantee success, but once you know how to use and relate that information, you will be able to master both essay and objective tests. In later chapters we will discuss the best way to approach each type of test.

## EXERCISE 2    *Creating a study group*

Working in groups of four or five, compare your learning styles with those of your classmates. Locate at least one person in the group whose style is different from your own. Work with that person to draw up a list of behaviors that will complement one another. Which of your strengths will compensate for your partner's weaknesses and vice versa?

*Your Strengths*                              *Partner's Weaknesses*

_____            _____

_____            _____

_____            _____

_____            _____

*Your Weaknesses*                          *Partner's Strengths*

_____          _____

_____          _____

_____          _____

_____          _____

Before the next major exam in this course, meet with your partner and determine the following:

1.  Your instructor's teaching style _____

    _____

2.  Predicted types of questions _____

    _____

3.  Strategies you might use to study _____

    _____

4.  Ways you might help one another _____

    _____

# Metacognition and Reading Comprehension

There is a long-standing debate among English instructors regarding the nature and extent of corrections on student essays. Some instructors argue that if they do not correct the obvious grammatical errors, students will assume there are none. Others claim that an abundance of red marks on a composition is not only demoralizing but also useless, because students don't learn simply by correcting what they didn't know in the first place.

Students, too, are divided. Some ask, "How can we revise if we don't know what we don't know?" Others verify their professors' fears that red marks simply frustrate and discourage them.

One thing both schools of thought agree on is that writing does improve through constant revision. Becoming aware that something needs to be changed is the first step toward changing it.

The same is true for improving reading comprehension. To be a skilled reader you must first be aware of when you do and do not fully comprehend what you have read. Then you must learn to reread and to reevaluate your initial perceptions. In other words, you must practice *metacognition*, or what Arthur Costa has defined in his article "Mediating the Metacognitive" (*Educational Leadership*, 1984) as the ability to know what you know and what you don't know. More specifically, according to David Cooper in *Improving Reading Comprehension* (Boston: Houghton Mifflin, 1986),

> metacognition refers to the knowledge and control which students have over their own thinking and learning activities. It appears to involve two basic components:
>
> 1. awareness of the process and skills needed to complete a task successfully,
>
> 2. the ability to tell whether one is performing a task correctly and to make corrections during the task if needed; this process is termed cognitive monitoring.

A number of factors distinguish skilled readers from weak ones: (1) skilled readers are *aware* of their strengths and weaknesses, (2) they establish goals for reading and adjust their rate of speed and level of concentration according to the difficulty level of the material and their reasons for reading, and (3) they consciously summarize information as they read, rereading passages that are confusing or of special importance. In short, skilled readers utilize **metacognitive monitoring**.

Learning to monitor your reading comprehension will enhance your confidence in your reading skills.

## Paraphrasing and rereading for clarification

Unless you can explain what you have read in your own words, you can't be sure that you comprehend it. That is why skilled readers paraphrase as they read. If they have difficulty paraphrasing, they reread until they are able to state the information in their own words.

Paraphrasing is one of the most useful skills you can apply to college reading. In addition to clarifying your reading comprehension, it will also enhance your ability to (1) take more meaningful notes, (2) recall what you have read for studying, and (3) avoid plagiarism.

Paraphrasing is a difficult process that involves a number of steps. To illustrate the process let's examine how we might paraphrase the first sentence of Reading Selection One, "Development of Metamemory."

> **Metacognition** is a term cognitive psychologists use to refer to what we know of the human mind and its capabilities, including our awareness of our own mental strengths and liabilities and the ways in which we monitor and control our cognitive processes.

1. If the sentence contains a technical term, begin by looking up the term in the dictionary or glossary. For example:

   *metacognition* — an understanding of how one acquires knowledge

   *cognitive* — related to the process of acquiring knowledge

2. Break the sentence into clauses (groups of words with subjects and predicates) and phrases. Commas, semicolons, dashes, and conjunctions (*and, but, because,* etc.) sometimes separate clauses and phrases. For example:

   Metacognition is a term [*clause*]

   cognitive psychologists use to refer to [*clause*]

   what we know of the human mind and its capabilities [*clause*]

   including our awareness of our own mental strengths and liabilities and the ways in which [*phrase*]

   we monitor and control our cognitive processes [*clause*]

**3.** Pick out the core words — the nouns and verbs that convey meaning — in each clause or phrase. For example:

Metacognition   term

psychologists   refer

know   mind   capabilities

awareness   mental strengths   liabilities

ways   monitor   control   cognitive process

**4.** Substitute synonyms for some of the words. For example:

Metacognition   word

psychologists   relate

knowledge   mind   can do

be aware   mind's strong points   weaknesses

ways   manage and direct   process of gaining knowledge

**5.** Put the sentence "back together" in paraphrase form by using your substitute words. For example, in this case, reread the original sentence, and try to paraphrase it by filling in the blanks:

Metacognition is a term which relates to our _____ of what the mind can do, including our _____ of our mental strengths and weaknesses, and the ways we _____ and _____ the process of gaining _____.

---

**READING SELECTION ONE**

## *Prereading Activity 1*: **Paraphrasing**

Using the five-step process outlined on pages 113–114, paraphrase the following sentences from "Development of Metamemory." Use two separate sentences, invert the order of phrases and clauses, or even list the main points if you wish. Keep in mind that no two people will paraphrase the same sentence in quite the same way. Be creative!

1.  Your own store of metacognitive knowledge might include an under-standing that you are better at math than at word problems; that you must selectively attend to the most relevant information if you hope to solve difficult problems; or that it is wise to double-check a proposed solution to a problem before concluding that it is correct.

*Step 1 (definitions)* _____

_____

*Step 2 (phrases/clauses)* _____

_____

_____

_____

*Step 3 (core words)* _____

_____

_____

_____

*Step 4 (synonyms)* _____

_____

_____

_____

*Step 5 (paraphrase)* _____

_____

_____

_____

_____

2. Although a 4-year-old may know that very short lists are easier to remember than long ones and that it will take more effort to remember the
   longer list, children younger than age 7 usually overestimate how well
   they will perform on memory tasks while underestimating the amount of
   study that is necessary to learn the materials.

*Step 1 (definitions)* _____

_____

*Step 2 (phrases/clauses)* _____

_____

_____

_____

*Step 3 (core words)* _____

_____

_____

_____

*Step 4 (synonyms)* _____

_____

**GOING BEYOND**

Most of us take for granted the right to read and withdraw books from a library. But this has not always been the case for many Americans. In this thought-provoking narrative, Richard Wright describes his experiences as a young African American who had to lie in order to check books out of the library. As you read the following selection, compare your own attitudes toward reading with those of the author.

## From *Black Boy*

*BY RICHARD WRIGHT*

I entered the library as I had always done when on errands for whites, but I felt that I would somehow slip up and betray myself. I doffed my hat, stood a respectful distance from the desk, looked as unbookish as possible, and waited for the white patrons to be taken care of. When the desk was clear of people, I still waited. The white librarian looked at me.  1

"What do you want, boy?"  2

As though I did not possess the power of speech, I stepped forward and simply handed her the forged note, not parting my lips.  3

"What books by Mencken does he want?" she asked.  4

"I don't know, ma'am," I said, avoiding her eyes.  5

"Who gave you this card?"  6

"Mr. Falk," I said.  7

"Where is he?"  8

"He's at work, at the M——— Optical Company," I said. "I've been in here for him before."  9

"I remember," the woman said. "But he never wrote notes like this."  10

Oh, God, she's suspicious. Perhaps she would not let me have the books? If she had turned her back at that moment, I would have ducked out the door and never gone back. Then I thought of a bold idea.  11

"You can call him up, ma'am," I said, my heart pounding.  12

"You're not using these books, are you?" she asked pointedly.  13

"Oh, no, ma'am. I can't read."  14

"I don't know what he wants by Mencken," she said under her    15
breath.

I knew now that I had won; she was thinking of other things and the    16
race question had gone out of her mind. She went to the shelves. Once or
twice she looked over her shoulder at me, as though she was still doubt-
ful. Finally she came forward with two books in her hand.

"I'm sending him two books," she said. "But tell Mr. Falk to come in    17
next time, or send me the names of the books he wants. I don't know
what he wants to read."

I said nothing. She stamped the card and handed me the books. Not    18
daring to glance at them, I went out of the library, fearing that the woman
would call me back for further questioning. A block away from the library
I opened one of the books and read a title: *A Book of Prefaces*. I was nearing
my nineteenth birthday and I did not know how to pronounce the word
"preface." I thumbed the pages and saw strange words and strange
names. I shook my head, disappointed. I looked at the other book; it was
called *Prejudices*. I knew what that word meant; I had heard it all my life.
And right off I was on guard against Mencken's books. Why would a man
want to call a book *Prejudices*? The word was so stained with all my
memories of racial hate that I could not conceive of anybody using it for
a title. Perhaps I had made a mistake about Mencken? A man who had
prejudices must be wrong.

When I showed the books to Mr. Falk, he looked at me and frowned.    19

"That librarian might telephone you," I warned him.    20

"That's all right," he said. "But when you're through reading those    21
books, I want you to tell me what you get out of them."

That night in my rented room, while letting the hot water run over    22
my can of pork and beans in the sink, I opened *A Book of Prefaces* and
began to read. I was jarred and shocked by the style, the clear, clean,
sweeping sentences. Why did he write like that? And how did one write
like that? I pictured the man as a raging demon, slashing with his pen,
consumed with hate, denouncing everything American, extolling everything European or German, laughing at the weaknesses of people, mock-
ing God, authority. What was this? I stood up, trying to realize what
reality lay behind the meaning of the words . . . Yes, this man was fighting, fighting with words. He was using words as a weapon, using them

as one would use a club. Could words be weapons? Well, yes, for here they were. Then, maybe, perhaps, I could use them as a weapon? No. It frightened me. I read on and what amazed me was not what he said, but how on earth anybody had the courage to say it.

Occasionally I glanced up to reassure myself that I was alone in the room. Who were these men about whom Mencken was talking so passionately? Who was Anatole France? Joseph Conrad? Sinclair Lewis, Sherwood Anderson, Dostoevski, George Moore, Gustave Flaubert, Maupassant, Tolstoy, Frank Harris, Mark Twain, Thomas Hardy, Arnold Bennett, Stephen Crane, Zola, Norris, Gorky, Bergson, Ibsen, Balzac, Bernard Shaw, Dumas, Poe, Thomas Mann, O. Henry, Dreiser, H. G. Wells, Gogol, T. S. Eliot, Gide, Baudelaire, Edgar Lee Masters, Stendahl, Turgenev, Huneker, Nietzsche, and scores of others? Were these men real? Did they exist or had they existed? And how did one pronounce their names? 23

I ran across many words whose meanings I did not know, and I either looked them up in a dictionary or, before I had a chance to do that, encountered the word in a context that made its meaning clear. But what strange world was this? I concluded the book with the conviction that I had somehow overlooked something terribly important in life. I had once tried to write, had once reveled in feeling, had let my crude imagination roam, but the impulse to dream had been slowly beaten out of me by experience. Now it surged up again and I hungered for books, new ways of looking and seeing. It was not a matter of believing or disbelieving what I read, but of feeling something new, of being affected by something that made the look of the world different. 24

As dawn broke I ate my pork and beans, feeling dopey, sleepy. I went to work, but the mood of the book would not die; it lingered, coloring everything I saw, heard, did. I now felt that I knew what the white men were feeling. Merely because I had read a book that had spoken of how they lived and thought, I identified myself with that book. I felt vaguely guilty. Would I, filled with bookish notions, act in a manner that would make the whites dislike me? 25

I forged more notes and my trips to the library became frequent.    26
Reading grew into a passion. My first serious novel was Sinclair Lewis's
*Main Street*. It made me see my boss, Mr. Gerald, and identify him as an
American type. I would smile when I saw him lugging his golf bags into
the office. I had always felt a vast distance separating me from the boss,
and now I felt closer to him, that I could feel the very limits of his narrow
life. And this had happened because I had read a novel about a mythical
man called George F. Babbitt.

The plots and stories in the novels did not interest me so much as the    27
point of view revealed. I gave myself over to each novel without reserve,
without trying to criticize it; it was enough for me to see and feel something different. And for me, everything was something different. Reading
was like a drug, a dope. The novels created moods in which I lived for
days. But I could not conquer my sense of guilt, my feeling that the white
men around me knew that I was changing, that I had begun to regard
them differently.

Whenever I brought a book to the job, I wrapped it in newspaper—a    28
habit that was to persist for years in other cities and under other circumstances. But some of the white men pried into my packages when I was
absent and they questioned me.

"Boy, what are you reading those books for?"    29
"Oh, I don't know, sir."    30
"That's deep stuff you're reading, boy."    31
"I'm just killing time, sir."    32
"You'll addle your brains if you don't watch out."    33

I read Dreiser's *Jennie Gerhardt* and *Sister Carrie* and they revived in    34
me a vivid sense of my mother's suffering; I was overwhelmed. I grew
silent, wondering about the life around me. It would have been impossible for me to have told anyone what I derived from these novels, for it
was nothing less than a sense of life itself. All my life had shaped me for
the realism, the naturalism of the modern novel, and I could not read
enough of them.

Steeped in new moods and ideas, I bought a ream of paper and tried    35
to write; but nothing would come, or what did come was flat beyond
telling. I discovered that more than desire and feeling were necessary to
write and I dropped the idea. Yet I still wondered how it was possible to
know people sufficiently to write about them? Could I ever learn about

life and people? To me, with my vast ignorance, my Jim Crow station in life, it seemed a task impossible of achievement. I now knew what being a Negro meant. I could endure the hunger. I had learned to live with hate. But to feel that there were feelings denied me, that the very breath of life itself was beyond my reach, that more than anything else, hurt, wounded me. I had a new hunger.

In buoying me up, reading also cast me down, made me see what was possible, what I had missed. My tension returned, new, terrible, bitter, surging, almost too great to be contained. I no longer *felt* that the world about me was hostile, killing; I *knew* it. A million times I asked myself what I could do to save myself, and there were no answers. I seemed forever condemned, ringed by walls. 36

I did not discuss my reading with Mr. Falk, who had lent me his library card; it would have meant talking about myself and that would have been too painful. I smiled each day, fighting desperately to maintain my old behavior, to keep my disposition seemingly sunny. But some of the white men discerned that I had begun to brood. 37

"Wake up there, boy!" Mr. Olin said one day. 38

"Sir!" I answered for the lack of a better word. 39

"You act like you've stolen something," he said. 40

I laughed in the way I knew he expected me to laugh, but I resolved to be more conscious of myself, to watch my every act, to guard and hide the new knowledge that was dawning within me. 41

If I went north, would it be possible for me to build a new life then? But how could a man build a life upon vague, unformed yearnings? I wanted to write and I did not even know the English language. I bought English grammars and found them dull. I felt that I was getting a better sense of the language from novels than from grammars. I read hard, discarding a writer as soon as I felt that I had grasped his point of view. At night the printed page stood before my eyes in sleep. 42

Mrs. Moss, my landlady, asked me one Sunday morning: 43

"Son, what is this you keep on reading?" 44

"Oh, nothing. Just novels." 45

"What you get out of 'em?" 46

"I'm just killing time," I said. 47

"I hope you know your own mind," she said in a tone which implied that she doubted if I had a mind. 48

I knew of no Negroes who read the books I liked and I wondered if   49
any Negroes ever thought of them. I knew that there were Negro doctors,
lawyers, newspapermen, but I never saw any of them. When I read a
Negro newspaper I never caught the faintest echo of my preoccupation in
its pages. I felt trapped and occasionally, for a few days, I would stop
reading. But a vague hunger would come over me for books, books that
opened up new avenues of feeling and seeing, and again I would forge
another note to the white librarian. Again I would read and wonder as
only the naïve and unlettered can read and wonder, feeling that I carried
a secret, criminal burden about with me each day.

## JOURNAL WRITING

1.  When Richard Wright read Mencken for the first time, he discovered
    that words are powerful weapons. How did reading empower him? How
    did it change his life? How might reading empower you?

2.  Have you ever read something that influenced your thinking? Explain
    what it was and how it affected you.

3.  Compare Wright's situation as an "unlettered" and "naïve" young Afri-
    can American in the early years of the twentieth century with your
    own. Do you consider reading and writing paths to knowledge and
    freedom as he did? How has the value of reading and writing changed
    since Wright's day?

4.  Although television provides us with much of the same information that
    newspapers and magazines do, why do you think newspapers and mag-
    azines are still so popular? What are some of the advantages of the
    printed word over electronic media?

5.  Have you ever seen a movie version of a book you read? Which did you
    prefer? Why? Explain the advantages and disadvantages of each form.

## CHAPTER 5

# Listening and
# Lecture Notes

After studying Chapter 5 you should be able to:

- listen more actively
- organize your lecture notes
- listen and watch for important organizational cues
- monitor your note taking

Use the following checklist to help you plan for the text, readings, and activities in this chapter.

| Date Assigned | Date Completed | |
| --- | --- | --- |
| _____ | _____ | Being an active listener |
| _____ | _____ | WARM-UP: Improving your note taking |
| _____ | _____ | EXERCISE 1: How actively do you listen to a lecture? |
| _____ | _____ | EXERCISE 2: The importance of active listening |
| _____ | _____ | Why take notes? |
| _____ | _____ | The three stages of note taking |
| _____ | _____ | EXERCISE 3: Preparing to take lecture notes |
| _____ | _____ | EXERCISE 4: Condensing and abbreviating |
| _____ | _____ | EXERCISE 5: Practicing note taking |
| _____ | _____ | EXERCISE 6: Monitoring by summarizing |
| _____ | _____ | CHAPTER APPLICATION |
| _____ | _____ | GOING BEYOND: "Can We Talk?" |
| _____ | _____ | JOURNAL WRITING |

# Being an Active Listener

Although today's professors utilize a wide variety of instructional methods, the traditional lecture approach still seems to be the most common. And the instructors who favor the lecture method often develop their exam questions primarily from their lectures. Consequently, the ability to take good lecture notes is a skill you must master if you are to become a successful student. In order to take good lecture notes, you must, above all else, become an active listener.

In Chapter 5 you will learn some of the basic dos and don'ts of note taking, evaluate your present note-taking habits, and practice note-taking strategies in a lecture setting. Keep in mind that, like most of the reading and studying strategies presented in this text, note taking is unique to the individual note taker. Therefore, you should adapt and modify the suggested strategies to fit your individual learning style.

**WARM-UP**   *Improving your note taking*

Consider the following scenario:

You are having difficulty following your psychology professor's lectures. You always seem to be a few words behind and to lose the focus of the material trying to catch up. Your notes are disorganized, and when you read them over for a quiz or test, they make no sense at all. What should you do?

   **a.**   Ask the professor to slow down.

   **b.**   Tape record the class so that you can listen to it again.

   **c.**   Copy someone else's notes each day.

   **d.**   None of the above.

The answer, surprisingly, is "**d.** None of the above." While all of these suggestions have some surface appeal, each has, as we say, a brief "shelf life." Let's examine the reasons each of these strategies has only limited effectiveness.

**a.**  Asking a professor to slow down might help for the remainder of a lecture, but the tempo of the lecture may not be the real issue. It could be that the topic is complex and your background knowledge inadequate. In that case you may need to spend more time before class acquainting yourself with the subject matter.

**b.**  Tape recording the class is a bad idea because when you know the recorder is getting the information you tend to relax and tune out. As a result there is little interaction between you and the professor and no means of clarifying or monitoring your understanding of the material.

For example, suppose your mass communications professor is talking about "interaction process analysis." You recall a recent discussion group where one person monopolized the conversation, and you think it may be an example of this concept. By asking the professor for feedback, you can clarify the concept for yourself, and probably for others in the class as well.

Also, when you listen to a tape, you do not have the advantage of what we call "visual cues." Physical actions such as hand gestures, facial expressions, and body movements may alter the meaning of the instructor's words. Suppose the professor states in a serious tone, "Communism is still a far better system than capitalism." At the same time he shrugs his shoulders, raises his eyebrows, and gestures toward the class as if soliciting a response. Without the advantage of the visual cues, you might not detect that the statement was made to generate discussion rather than as a statement of fact.

Lastly, tape recording lecture notes is bad time management. Listening to the notes is one more thing you have to do each night, and if you procrastinate you may end up with hours of extra work. You may even fail to review the lectures.

**c.**  Copying someone else's notes also has its drawbacks. First, you have no guarantees that the other person's notes are accurate and/or complete. Second, you may have difficulty understanding the other person's handwriting and abbreviations. Most people have their own systems for organizing and highlighting important concepts, and sometimes these systems make sense only to them.

Most importantly, each of these strategies encourages you to remain a passive listener. To get the most out of the classroom experience, you must become more active in your listening habits.

Remember, there are as many different teaching styles as there are learning styles, and there is rarely a perfect fit between student and instructor. Some lecturers are very organized, use lots of signal words, and explain clearly and precisely what they want you to know. Others spend more time digressing and explaining applications, in which case you may have to rely more heavily on your text for the facts and use the lectures for reinforcement. The important thing to do is "size up" the teaching style and adjust your note-taking methods accordingly.

**EXERCISE 1**  *How actively do you listen to a lecture?*

The following list contains some of the characteristics of a good note taker. Place a check mark in front of those that best describe your note-taking style.

_____ 1. I acquaint myself with the material before class by reading the assignment and preparing questions.

_____ 2. I listen attentively from the very beginning of the lecture until the very end.

_____ 3. I listen for clue words that indicate main ideas, such as "the three types of group leadership" or "the basic characteristics of groups."

_____ 4. I listen for signal words that indicate a change of topic or a pattern of organization such as comparison-and-contrast or cause-and-effect.

_____ 5. I paraphrase the instructor's words.

_____ 6. I abbreviate as much as possible.

_____ 7. I am aware of how audio and visual signals such as voice, tone, and gesture affect lecture delivery.

_____    8.   I interact in class by asking questions when I do not understand or by adding information that I think is relevant to the discussion.

_____    9.   I listen to what other students have to say.

Now list the note-taking strategies you think you need to work on:

1. _____

2. _____

3. _____

4. _____

5. _____

**EXERCISE 2**   *The importance of active listening*

This activity demonstrates how feedback gained by actively listening enhances the accuracy of note taking. To complete this exercise students should form groups of four. One student will serve as the sender while the other three will act as receivers. Then do the following:

1. One at a time, the sender will describe, using only words, the first group of figures on page 473 in Appendix B. The receivers will reproduce each of the figures on paper according to the sender's directions. Receivers cannot ask questions or look at one another's papers.

2. The sender will then give directions for the second group of drawings on page 473. This time, however, receivers may ask questions to make sure they are following directions accurately. The sender can orally answer their questions.

Once the two sets of drawings are complete, you may turn to page 473 to check your drawings for accuracy in terms of size, shape, and so on. Then discuss the following questions:

1.  How many drawings were accurately drawn?

2.  Were the results better with two-way communication?

3.  Was one-way communication more frustrating for the sender? For the receivers?

Based on your answers to these questions, discuss why asking questions in the classroom might help both the student and the instructor.

# Why Take Notes?

At this point you still may question whether you need to take good lecture notes. Perhaps you view yourself as an active listener. Maybe you like to participate in class. Or perhaps the instructor just rehashes the book. Therefore, you don't think you need to take notes. Right?

Wrong! There are many reasons you should take notes. First, the semester is usually four or five months long, and studies show that students forget 80 percent of what they learn in just two weeks. Thus, you need to have an accurate written record of the material covered. Second, because knowledge is acquired through the six senses, you facilitate learning when you use more than one sense at a time. Therefore, attempting to *write* what you hear enhances your ability to understand and remember the material. Third, taking notes during a class lecture is like monitoring and paraphrasing as you read. It helps you determine whether you understand what the instructor has said. Remember: Unless you can restate what you hear, you cannot be sure you understand it. Finally, class lectures, unlike texts, give you insight into what the *professor* thinks. Instructors have their own perspectives and agendas. Understanding those perspectives and agendas will enable you to predict questions at exam time.

# The Three Stages of Note Taking

Good note taking begins before you enter the classroom and ends after you leave it. Why? Consider this scenario:

Two people who know nothing about guitar playing decided to take guitar lessons. The first person attends the initial lesson, listens carefully, attempts to imitate the instructor during the lesson, but neglects to practice until the next lesson. The second person, on the other hand, reads a self-help book on how to play guitar before attending the first lesson. Because the book has provided him with a mental image of how to execute the exercises, he understands the instructor's directions quite well. In addition, the next day he practices while the instructions are still fresh in his mind. Which student do you think will have more success not only with the first guitar lesson but with guitar playing in general?

As with guitar playing, the key to successful and meaningful note taking is not simply writing down (or "imitating") everything the instructor says (or does). Rather, it is a three-stage process: (1) preparation, (2) actual note taking, and (3) review. Let's examine each of these stages in detail.

## Stage 1: Prelecture preparation

It might seem strange to speak about preparing for a lecture, but you can do specific things to enhance your readiness to listen actively and take good notes.

*First, always read and complete assignments before going to class.* This will acquaint you with new and/or difficult concepts and increase your understanding of the lecture. Being aware of unfamiliar names, terms, or definitions will facilitate your ability to visualize them in print. This is especially important when your instructor does not use the board very often. We have all had the experience during a lecture of being unable to write a name because we had no idea how to spell it! In addition, doing your reading directs your thinking and makes you a more active listener. The questions you generate as goals during the reading process will also become your goals for listening in the classroom.

*Second, if you have time before the lecture begins, look over any notes you may have taken while reading to refresh your memory and activate knowledge.*

*Finally, always write the date on the top line to the left of the margin.* The date is useful for organizational and reference purposes. If you miss a class you will be able to identify which notes are missing at a later date, and if your classmates date their notes as well it will facilitate the process of group study.

**EXERCISE 3**    *Preparing to take lecture notes*

This exercise demonstrates the importance of reading assignments before class. To complete the exercise do the following:

*(As homework)*

1.  Read the text excerpt "Communication on the Group Level" on page 474 of Appendix B, monitoring yourself carefully as you read.

*(In class)*

2.  Before the class lecture begins, quickly scan the selection you read for homework.

3.  Listen and take notes as your instructor reads the selection "Communication on the Group Level."

4.  Listen and take notes as your instructor reads the selection "A Group's Life Cycle" on page 477 of Appendix B.

Once you have completed taking and comparing notes, discuss the following questions:

1.  Are your notes for the first excerpt more thorough than those for the second?

2.  Did the prelecture reading enable you to take more complete notes?

3.  Were you better able to write down technical terms having seen them before?

4. Was your spelling of the various terms more accurate in the first excerpt?

5. What did you learn by completing this exercise?

## Stage 2: During the lecture

After a few classes you should have an idea of the instructor's lecturing style. For example, are the lectures merely an explanation of the assigned readings, or are they extended explanations and applications of a few specific topics? Once you understand the kind of lectures the instructor gives, you can adjust your note-taking style accordingly.

*Page Set-up*   There are a number of ways to organize your notes on the page, and you should search for a method with which you are comfortable. You may also wish to vary your page set-up to adjust to the instructor's style or to a particular lecture objective. The following system offers a great deal of flexibility to the note taker:

1. Set the left- and right-hand margins about one-quarter of the way in from the edges of the paper.

2. Use the left-hand margin to write the date, main topics, and key words such as example (EX), definition (DEF), and important (IMP). (This system will be explained in more detail in the section on the note-taking process.)

3. Use the space between the margins to write the subject of the lecture (at the top) and the important supporting details that pertain to the main ideas, indenting and numbering subordinate details and examples.

4. Use the right-hand margin for monitoring yourself during and after the lecture by writing assignment and exam information, questions about the material, and personal observations or applications. This margin may also be used to write periodic summaries during and after the lecture.

The figure on page 151 shows how this set-up should look.

| **Date:** 3/21 | **Topic:** Note-taking strategies | **Monitoring Column** |
|---|---|---|
| **Main Topics** | | Assignment: 3/25 |
| Active Listening | Aids comprehension and retention | Read Ch. 4 |
| Three Stages of Note Taking | A. Prelecture | |
| |    1. Read assignments before class | |
| |    2. Look at notes before class | |
| |    3. Write the date on the top line | |
| | B. During Lecture | |
| |    1. Page set-up (3 sections) | |
| |      a. left margin: main topics | |
| |      b. middle margin: important details | |
| |      c. right margin: monitor during + after?? | Clarification (summarizing as you listen) |
| |    2. Process | |
| |      a. be alert | |
| |      b. skim outlines | |
| EX |      c. listen for signal words (ex. *characteristics*) | |
| EX |      d. use graphics (ex. 1, 2, a, b) | |
| |      e. abbreviate | |
| |      f. note audio + visual clues | |
| DEF |    3. Monitoring — summarizing as you listen to lecture | Summary: Must be active before, during, + after lecture |
| | C. Postlecture | |
| |    1. Discuss after class | |
| |    2. Reread + modify notes | Important to review notes immediately |
| |    3. Highlight important ideas | |
| |    4. Summarize in right margin | |

Sample Note-Taking Page Set-up

*The Note-Taking Process*  Once you've established how you will set up the page, you need to develop an effective system for taking actual notes. The following suggestions should help you in this process.

1. **Be alert**. Listen critically from the very beginning to the very end of the class. At the beginning of class many instructors state their objectives and/or topics for the lecture. In this case write the topic on the top line in the middle column and use this cue to activate your memory. Other instructors will begin class by summarizing what was covered in the last class and/or giving assignments and exam dates. Be sure to record this information in the right-hand margin.

2. **Read or skim outlines**. Sometimes an instructor will give you a preview of the lecture by putting an outline on the board or on an overhead projector. If so, jot it down if you have time, but not at the expense of hearing what the instructor is saying. It may be better simply to read it quickly to activate knowledge and write down the information as the lecture progresses.

3. **Listen for signal words**. There are many words that signal organizational framework. If you listen carefully for these words, you will understand how the important ideas and details of the lecture fit together. For example, an instructor may begin by saying "First we will discuss the characteristics of group communication." You would write (or abbreviate) the words "characteristics of group communication" in the left-hand margin. As the lecture proceeds listen for words that signal enumeration (first, second, third, etc.). These would indicate the "characteristics" and would probably be followed by explanations of pertinent details. Because the "characteristics" would be main topics, you would write them in the left-hand margin. You would then place the supporting ideas and specific details in the middle of the page.

4. **Use graphic variations**. To visually differentiate subordinate ideas, you might use capital letters for the main ideas and lowercase letters for the details. When writing details you might indent those that explain or define others. This is similar to the way many outlines are structured.

5. **Condense and abbreviate**. It is not possible — or necessary — to take down every word the instructor says. Instead, listen before you write, and think about what is being said. Then write down only key words, not complete sentences, using abbreviations and condensed versions whenever possible. Condensing and abbreviating, like paraphrasing, are somewhat subjective — no two people will take identical notes. There are, however, some common rules. These are summarized in the table below.

| Rules for Condensing and Abbreviating | | |
|---|---|---|
| *Rule* | *Long Version* | *Condensed Version* |
| Use standard symbols | and | & or + |
| | money | $ |
| | therefore | ∴ |
| | equals | = |
| | at | @ |
| | number | # |
| Shorten dates | September 20, 1992 | 9/20/92 |
| Use first syllable and/or the first few letters of the second | history | hist |
| | approximately | approx |
| | information | info |
| | example | ex |
| | experiment | exp |
| Omit vowels | develop | dvlp |
| | complex | cmplx |
| | individuals | indvls |
| Omit prepositions and articles | a, of, the, on (etc.) | — |
| After first use abbreviate proper nouns | National Liberation Front | NLF |
| | International Students Association | ISA |

6. **Pay attention to auditory and visual cues.** Sometimes instructors will indicate progression from one topic to another by pausing or by shuffling their notes. Listen and watch for a change of direction. Instructors will also signal levels of importance by vocally stressing or repeating particular words. For example, if you hear "This is important" or "Remember . . ." place a star next to these topics and write the letters "Imp" in the left-hand margin. Finally, the information an instructor writes on the board is usually important and therefore should be included in your notes.

**EXERCISE 4**    *Condensing and abbreviating*

For each of the following sentences, practice condensing and abbreviating the key information. The first one has been done for you to serve as a model. Be creative!

1. The life cycles of groups often become a bit more complex when individuals who do not know one another come together to form a group, particularly a task group of some type.

   *Life cycl grps grow cmplx when unacquainted indiv form grp for partic task.*

2. We often make a distinction between small-group communication, which involves approximately three to twenty-five people, and large-group communication, which involves more than twenty-five people.

   _____

   _____

3. Groups are fundamental to human existence. We are, for example, born into what sociologists call a primary group.

   _____

   _____

4. An organizational group is a collection of individuals who represent some formal part of a business, institution, or organization, such as the people in the accounting office, the receptionist, or the "marketing" group.

_____

_____

5. A circumstantial group is a collection of individuals brought together by some course of events, often accidental or coincidental, as with a group of individuals who find themselves waiting in line at the bank or who are traveling together in a section of an airplane.

_____

_____

6. Typically, we consider group communication to be face-to-face, with speech and nonverbal communication as the main media.

_____

_____

***Monitoring Your Note Taking***   Just as you need to monitor your comprehension while reading, you need to monitor your understanding of the lecture during note taking. If you use the right-hand margin for monitoring, you will be able to compare your monitoring notes with the initial ones.

If you miss information, are confused, or do not understand something, ask questions. If the instructor prefers that students hold questions until the end of the lecture, place a question mark (?) or briefly describe the problem in the right-hand margin. Then, when the instructor answers your question, write the explanation in the right-hand margin as well. That way the clarification remains separate from original notes.

When there is a lull in the lecture or the instructor digresses with a lengthy example, take advantage of the break to summarize important concepts. You may want to use a technique such as mapping or charting to visualize the notes. You may simply want to write a sentence or two that paraphrases the ideas. Just as paraphrasing helps to monitor and reinforce information as you read, it serves to clarify your thoughts when taking notes.

**EXERCISE 5**   *Practicing note taking*

On a separate piece of paper take notes following the suggestions below while a friend or your instructor reads you the lecture "Group Leadership" from page 479 of Appendix B.

1.  Draw the margins as described in the section on page set-up.

2.  Listen for and write words that signal main topics and organizational framework in the left-hand margin.

3.  Write key words such as "example" and "definition" in the left-hand margin.

4.  Write main ideas and important supporting details in the middle column, numbered and indented to indicate subordinate ideas.

5.  Condense throughout, and abbreviate as much as possible.

**EXERCISE 6**   *Monitoring by summarizing*

In this exercise your instructor or a friend will again read you the lecture, this time pausing at a number of strategic places in the lecture. When there is a pause in the lecture, quickly paraphrase or diagram the material using the right-hand margin of your note page from Exercise 5. If you are working in class, compare notes with a classmate.

***Note Taking During Discussion Classes***   Many students think there is no need to take notes during a discussion. To the contrary, because discussions often clarify difficult and confusing concepts, it can be extremely helpful to take discussion notes as part of the monitoring process. In addition, if a professor uses discussion as the primary vehicle for instruction, the ideas discussed are obviously the focus of the course and most likely will constitute the material for the exams.

| Date | Topic: Group Dynamics | |
|------|----------------------|--|
| *Questions:* How do you behave during a group discussion? | *Answers:* 1. Shy — don't speak out 2. Like to say what I feel 3. Speak when I feel strongly | *Summaries:* Illustrates factors that affect group dynamics |

Sample Discussion Class Notes

When taking notes on a discussion, divide your paper as you would for a lecture. Use the left-hand margin for the questions or problems posed, the middle column for the answers, and the right-hand column for summarizing ideas. The figure above shows how this process would look.

## Stage 3: Postlecture

Because you tend to forget information almost immediately after you have heard it, it is important to reinforce your classroom experience as soon as possible. To review the lecture and ensure maximum retention of material, you should do the following:

1. Discuss your notes with a classmate immediately after class.

2. Read over your notes that afternoon or evening.

3. As you reread your notes, add or modify main ideas.

4. Number, underline, or otherwise clarify and highlight details.

5. Use the right-hand margin to paraphrase the important ideas.

This process may appear time consuming, but as with previewing and note taking for your textbooks, any reinforcement of material during the term will save many hours at exam time.

**CHAPTER APPLICATION**

The only way to test your note-taking skills is to try taking notes during an actual class. For this activity do the following:

1.  Choose a class where the instructor relies heavily on the lecture method.

2.  Take notes as described in this chapter.

3.  Read and reorganize your notes at home.

4.  Xerox your notes and bring them to class.

5.  Working with a partner, exchange notes and evaluate your partner's notes on the basis of clarity and form.

**GOING BEYOND**

True communication occurs only when the parties involved interact with one another. Therefore, one-way communication not only results in misunderstanding but also inhibits, and often prevents, the development of relationships. In her review of Deborah Tannen's book *You Just Don't Understand: Women and Men in Conversation*, Diane White explains why some men and women have difficulty communicating. As you read, think about your own ability, or inability, to communicate with the opposite sex and whether you agree with her assertions.

## Can We Talk?

**BY DIANE WHITE**

Recently a friend told me he'd finally discovered the secret of making    1
women happy. "I just shut up and listen," he said.

Imagine, he figured this out all by himself, and he's only 45. But at    2
least he figured it out.

If my friend's discovery strikes me as funny, it's because I used to be a    3
girl, a girl who grew up being told over and over again that if she wanted
to be popular with boys she must listen to them, encourage them to talk
about themselves, draw them out.

Few boys are given similar instructions about girls. Boys expect girls    4
to listen to them. They don't expect to have to listen to girls. So it isn't
surprising that women who want men to listen to them are often
disappointed.

In her book "You Just Don't Understand: Women and Men in Con-    5
versation," Deborah Tannen writes that many men don't like to listen to
anyone, female or male, because they believe that the act of listening is a
subordinate role. Men never want to be one-down in conversation. It's
just the way they are.

Her basic thesis is that men and women use language differently, and    6
that those differences begin when they're children.

Girls play in small groups or pairs, they have best friends and spend a    7
lot of time talking. Girls learn to use language to gain intimacy, to make
connections. Boys, on the other hand, tend to play competitive games in
larger, hierarchical groups. Boys grow up learning that other people are
going to push them around, and they use language to assert themselves.

These separate styles of communicating persist into adulthood and,    8
according to Tannen, cause all sorts of confusion and misunderstandings
between the sexes. For example, when women marry what they often
want and expect in a husband is a new and improved version of a best
friend, someone they can tell everything to and who, in turn, will share
all his secrets. "This is not what men expect," Tannen said, perhaps
unnecessarily.

A young man asked [her] why his girlfriend persists in talking about    9
their relationship when he thinks everything is settled. The question,
Tannen said, gave her the opportunity to say one of her favorite things
about the differences in the way men and women communicate. "Many
women feel the relationship is working so long as you keep talking about
it," she said. "And many men feel the relationship isn't working if you
keep having to work it over."

Tannen is not trying to step up hostilities in the war between the    10
sexes, on the contrary. One of the points she tries to get across is that
many of the misunderstandings in communication between men and
women are not the fault of the individual but of cultural conditioning.
We must learn to understand our different ways of communicating, she
says. "The danger is that if we don't realize that these are systematic
differences in conversational style we make interpretations that aren't
valid."

Consider the listening problem. "Sometimes men give [women] the    11
impression they're not listening because they're not looking at them,"
Tannen said. This, too, is part of the different ways men and women
communicate. In videotapes of research she's conducted on the body
language of children talking to a friend of the same sex, at every age, from
5 to 15, the girls sit face to face, and look at each other. And at every age
the boys sit side by side, talking intently, listening, and looking everywhere but at one another. So that man who appears to be ignoring you
may in fact be hanging onto your every word. But don't count on it.

## JOURNAL WRITING

1.  Tannen claims she is not trying to step up hostilities between the
    sexes, but rather is trying to help men and women enhance their rela-
    tionships through better communication. What do *you* think the impact
    of her ideas may be? Why? (If you dare, you might want to exchange
    journals with a friend of the opposite sex and ask him or her to
    respond!)

2.  There are many factors that influence your ability or inability to com-
    municate with someone. Describe an experience in which you had dif-
    ficulty communicating with a particular person. What was the root of
    the difficulty? Were you able to overcome the problem?

3. Today we have many alternatives to face-to-face communication. We can write a letter, use a telephone, even send a message through a computer. What are some of the advantages and disadvantages of each method of communication? Give an example of a situation in which you would prefer to use one particular method rather than another.

4. Describe a course in which you had trouble with the communication process. What were the problems? What did you do, or what could you have done, to alleviate the problems?

5. Cultural factors often influence how we interact during conversation. For example, in some cultures it is considered disrespectful for young children to look directly at adults when being spoken to. Describe any cultural factors that may influence your behavior during conversation. Have these behaviors ever been misinterpreted by persons from other cultures?

CHAPTER 6
**Problems and Solutions**

CHAPTER 7
**Definitions, Examples,
and Lists**

CHAPTER 8
**Chronological Order
and Narration**

CHAPTER 9
**Cause and Effect**

CHAPTER 10
**Comparison and
Contrast**

As you work through Part II of this text, you will learn how to identify and use these structures to understand what you read, take notes from texts, study for and take tests, and organize your writing.

Keep in mind that active engagement of some kind does improve recall and test performance. Active engagement can take the form of underlining, summarizing, mapping, outlining, or simple note taking. Although there is little agreement as to which of these techniques is most effective, methods involving student decision making and application have been found to be the most valuable. In short, if you actively respond to your texts and learn to adapt your methods to the needs of the subject matter, you will achieve the greatest success.

Each chapter of Part II of *Reading and Learning Across the Disciplines* covers:

- a different rhetorical structure
- readings organized around a particular academic theme
- the specific note-taking or study skill strategies most suitable for each structure

Once you understand these structures and strategies, you will be able to make meaningful decisions about your reading and study skills.

# Problems and Solutions

After studying Chapter 6 you should be able to:

- comprehend a reading selection about a problem or a solution
- analyze and solve problems
- evaluate your ability to handle stressful experiences
- cope with stressful situations

## CHAPTER CHECKLIST

Use the following checklist to help you plan for the text, readings, and activities in this chapter.

*Date Assigned*    *Date Completed*

_____   _____   Questions and answers

_____   _____   WARM-UP: Generating solutions

_____   _____   Viewing problems as effects

_____   _____   Solving problems

_____   _____   EXERCISE 1: Solving a personal problem

### READING SELECTION ONE

_____   _____   *Prereading Activity*: Previewing the selection

_____   _____   **"Stress and Its Management"**

_____   _____   COMPREHENSION CHECK

_____   _____   COMPREHENSION EXERCISE: A stress management program

### READING SELECTION TWO

_____   _____   *Prereading Activity*: Previewing the selection

_____   _____   **"Reappraisal: Ellis's Rational Thinking"**

_____   _____   COMPREHENSION CHECK

_____   _____   COMPREHENSION EXERCISE: Reappraising a stress-inducing situation

### READING SELECTION THREE

—— ——  *Prereading Activity*: Previewing the selection

—— ——  **"How Much Stress Can You Survive?"**

—— ——  COMPREHENSION CHECK

—— ——  CHAPTER APPLICATION

—— ——  GOING BEYOND: "Problems and Pain"

—— ——  JOURNAL WRITING

## Questions and Answers

**Q:**  *Help! I'm graduating from college this year and I still bite my nails. No matter what I tell myself, I can't quit. Will I have to go through life this way?*

**A:**  You have lots of company: Between 25% and 36% of college students bite their nails, but by the age of 40 the nail-crunching population drops to about 8%. By this age, social pressures induce many nail-biters to stop. Smoking, drinking or teeth grinding often replace nail chewing.

If you want normal nails by graduation, you might want to try the following technique. At the risk of looking eccentric, carry around an envelope, make a mark on it every time you bite your nails, and put the parings into it. Total your bites-per-day each night and record them on a graph.

Measure your nails weekly to monitor your progress and reward yourself with a manicure if you go a week without biting them. Keep your nails polished for some positive reinforcement and file away those tempting rough edges.

This isn't the only tactic. Some people find it helpful to apply a bitter-tasting coating to their nails. The envelope-and-graph technique was drawn from behavioral therapy, and another option might be to consult a trained behavioral therapist. But try the envelope suggestion first; it might do the trick.

Problems, problems, problems. We encounter them every day. Some are as trivial as nail biting, others as catastrophic as drug addiction. Whatever the extent of the problem, viable solutions can be extremely elusive. Graphing your nail bites per day and rewarding yourself with a manicure sounds like a simple enough solution, but applying that solution requires time, energy, and discipline. In fact, *devising* the solution is only the first step in solving the problem.

Chapter 6 introduces the rhetorical structure of **problem and solution**. It explains how to use this structure to improve your reading comprehension and suggests strategies to help you solve problems and reduce stress in your life.

**WARM-UP**    *Generating solutions*

Three possible solutions are offered to the nail-biter. Working in groups of two or three, do the following:

1.  Generate as many other solutions as you can.

2.  List the strengths and weaknesses of each solution.

3.  Choose the best solution and write a few sentences explaining your choice.

Use the chart on page 171 to record your solutions and their relative merits.

## Viewing Problems as Effects

Problems result when factors act on one another in such a way that they create conflict. In this sense we can think of problems as the effects of cause-and-effect relationships.

Let's consider the following scenario:

It's Thursday and you have not even begun the rough draft for a term paper that is due on Monday. So you're faced with the prospect of spending the entire weekend working on the paper. To complicate matters, Friday afternoon your boss asks you to work for a few hours on Saturday morning.

| Curing Nail Biting | | |
| --- | --- | --- |
| *Solutions* | *Strengths* | *Weaknesses* |
| envelope and graph | | |
| bitter-tasting coating on nails | | |
| therapy | | |
| | | |
| | | |
| | | |

To top it all off, you also learn that some of your friends have planned a party for Saturday evening. We might summarize the scenario in this way:

*Problem*: term paper to write

*Cause*: procrastination

*Effect*: lost weekend

*Conflict*: schoolwork, job, party

Possible solutions include the following:

■ You could stay home the entire weekend, forfeit the funds and the fun, and do the best possible job on your paper.

■ You could go to work, but stay home on Saturday evening and produce a mediocre paper.

■ You could go to work and to the party on Saturday, pass in an inferior paper, and probably receive a poor grade.

■ You could go to work, attend the party, pass in the paper late, and hope the professor will not penalize you too severely.

Your decision will depend on your priorities and the strength of your commitment to each of them.

Of course this problem might never occur if you adhere to a good time-management system. But even if you are a good time manager, unexpected events can alter plans, and creativity in problem solving becomes necessary.

## Solving Problems

Barry Anderson in his book *The Complete Thinker* has outlined five steps for attacking a problem:

1. **State the problem**. Be specific. For example, you would not say, "My friend has a drug problem," but rather, "My friend has been addicted to cocaine for three years."

2. **Get the facts**. Examine the who, what, where, why, when, and how. For example: *Who* supplies him? *Where* does he get the money? *Why* does he use it? *When* does he use it? *How* often does he use it? *How* does he function?

3. **Focus on the important facts**. Identify the factors that influence the facts you have generated in step 2. For example, if someone uses drugs at work, how might this affect fellow workers?

4. **Generate ideas**. Think of solutions that attack one, some, or all of the factors. Be creative. Consider unusual or far-out ideas such as organizing fellow workers to ostracize him.

5. **Choose the best idea**. Evaluate the strengths and weaknesses of each solution. For example, the far-out solution given in step 4 may alienate him and lessen his self-esteem, exacerbating the addiction.

**EXERCISE 1**  *Solving a personal problem*

Think of a minor personal problem you have right now such as how to get to your afternoon job or settle a disagreement with a roommate, relative, or friend. Attack the problem using Anderson's five steps, generating at least three possible solutions in step 4. Carefully consider the effects of each solution and choose the one that best reflects your priorities.

*Step 1 (problem)* _____

*Step 2 (facts)* _____

_____

*Step 3 (factors)* _____

_____

*Step 4 (possible solutions)* _____

_____

_____

*Step 5 (best solution)* _____

_____

**READING SELECTION ONE**

## *Prereading Activity*: **Previewing the selection**

The following selection is excerpted from an introductory college textbook on health issues. Preview the selection by scanning and skimming the first paragraph, the headings and subheadings, italicized and boldfaced words, and any other prominent typographical features. Then complete the following paragraph:

This selection discusses the nature of _____ and how it might affect one's _____ . In particular, it describes problems that might cause stress for the _____ _____ and offers some suggestions on how to _____ it.

Now read the selection carefully. As you read consider the sources of stress in your own life and how the information in this article might help you cope with it.

───────────

## Stress and Its Management

### BY M. R. LEVY, M. DIGNAN, AND J. SHIRREFFS

### The nature of stress

Stress is a term used to describe certain physical and psychological reactions that human beings (and other animals) exhibit in response to any **stimulus**, or marked change in their environment. The Greek physician Hippocrates, writing in the fifth century B.C., may have been the first to suggest a relationship between stress and illness. It was not until 1914, however, that American physiologist Walter Cannon probably coined the term *stress* to describe a powerful psychophysiological process that appeared to influence emotions. Cannon viewed stress as a potential cause of medical problems and suggested that emotional disturbances often trigger physical reactions.

For a long time, scientists have known that some of the ways we respond to a stimulus are *specific* to that stimulus: If we are exposed to extreme heat, we perspire; if we are exposed to extreme cold, we shiver. In the mid-1930s, however, the pioneering stress researcher Hans Selye observed certain similarities in our responses to any stressor — heat, cold, good news, bad news, winning money, losing money. He called them *nonspecific* physical reactions, because any stressor will initiate the same series of responses — pale skin, rapid breathing, quickened heart rate, elevated blood pressure, plus, often, extreme mental alertness, muscle tension, nausea, vomiting, diarrhea. These nonspecific responses are what Selye called stress. . . .

### The stress mechanism's effects on the body

Today, the "fight or flight" response is still useful if a physical reaction (such as dodging a speeding car) is called for, or if we have to meet some short-term psychological challenge (such as giving a speech or taking an

1

2

3

exam). Our bodies are equipped to handle stress without damage — *if* we are able to relax after we have mobilized our physical resources and taken the short-term action that was called for. After the stressful situation has passed, we need a chance to regain our original balanced state — what is known as our bodily **homeostasis**. Just as our bodies need to maintain a normal temperature of about 37° C (98.6° F) most of the time, so do they need to keep other aspects of functioning in balance most of the time. These aspects include blood pressure, the volume of fluids, and the level of hormones in the blood.

Trouble arises when one arousal reaction is piled on top of another and the body does not get a chance to return to normal. Many of our modern stressors are psychological. We can neither fight them nor flee them. Stress tends to build up and disrupt our body's functioning, particularly through the action of hormones released by the **endocrine** glands under stress. Epinephrine, for example, may keep muscles tense and the blood pressure and heart rate high for several days, or even longer. It may also interfere with the immune system, lowering our resistance to disease. . . .

**4**

**Stress and the college student**    Not all adults realize that college students are under a variety of stresses that can make their college experience quite difficult. Some of these are discussed below.

**5**

*Poor time management*    The college experience places large demands on students' time. Students often feel rushed and overextended. Many do not budget their time effectively, do not set priorities for tasks, or put things off until the last minute — and some do all three. Usually, students' problems are due not to the work load, but to poor time management.

**6**

*Lack of balance between work and play*    Fearing failure and under pressure to meet deadlines for assignments, some students turn to a pattern of "all work and no play." Yet without some form of recreation, rest, and relaxation, we set ourselves up for **chronic** stress problems. Work and play are both important parts of a college student's life, though the right balance is hard to achieve.

**7**

*Noisy and crowded living conditions*    A physical environment that is    8
noisy and cramped (as dormitory rooms typically are) can be a significant source of stress. Experiments have shown that continuous
exposure to loud music will induce a stress response in both animals
and humans — as will surroundings that restrict free movement.

*Pressure to conform*    Many college students, especially freshmen, are    9
living away from home for the first time, and this alone can be stressful. The situation is often made worse when wanting to be accepted
by the peer group makes students accept and participate in behaviors
that conflict with their established values and standards.

*Career anxiety*    A common concern for today's college student is find-    10
ing employment after graduation. The high costs of college education
mean that many young people are deeply in debt by the time they
graduate. Even if the student has a marketable skill, his or her future
is less assured in uncertain economic times, as when the unemploy-
ment rate is high.

*Fear of rejection and failure*    Certain learning and testing situations    11
are a source of stress, especially if undue emphasis has been placed
on grades or the attainment of specific skills. Competitive students
often victimize one another with merciless competition, and social
organizations such as fraternities and sororities can put students under physical, emotional, and social pressures. . . .

## Coping with stress

In setting up your personal stress management program, you should    12
begin by deciding which of the stressors in your life are unavoidable, or
at least beyond your control. Then make a mental list of the stressors you
can avoid *totally*. And finally, list the stressors in your life that are ones
you can do something about. Some stressors you can modify: If you can't
stand the noise in your dormitory, for example, you can at least get on a
dorm committee and work to have rules imposed to limit the noise to
certain hours. Other stressors may be subject to even more control: those
you contribute to, or even create for yourself, through poor planning,
putting things off, expecting the worst (though it seldom happens), and
so on.

Make some notes about concrete ways you can reduce some of the    13
stresses you are under — from "Start studying in the library, where it's
quiet" to "Do lab assignments earlier in the week" to "Stop worrying
about what my parents will say about my future."

***Managing your time better***    You will greatly reduce your stress level if    14
you adopt some of the "time management" techniques that stress experts
have been discussing recently. Time management requires you to plan
everything you do carefully, and really get tough with yourself about
putting aside nonessential tasks and doing essential things *now*. Interestingly, time management also requires you to set aside some of your ego-
involvement in your activities. You have to give up the feeling that you
can do *everything*, and all at the same time. You have to stop feeling that
you must be at the center of all activities and that no one can replace you.

For really constructive time management, some experts recommend    15
that you take a long look at your values and goals and try to determine
which of them *really* matter. Decide which ones represent what *you* believe in and want, not what other people think you should want. Then
divide these goals into three categories: self, work, and family. Most of us
have to balance goals from all three of these categories. No single category
can be sacrificed in favor of the others without producing inner psychological conflict or rebellion.

The most important step is to establish priorities among all your goals    16
in each of the three categories. You might label the most urgent goals A
and the least important ones C; all others would be rated B. If you can't
decide whether an item is a B or a C, make it a C for the time being; you
can upgrade it later, if necessary. You should always have your list of
priorities clearly in mind, so that trivial tasks don't distract you from
pursuing important goals.

You should also bear in mind that these priorities are flexible, subject    17
to revision as emergencies, conflicts, and compromises arise. It would be
self-defeating to use time-management techniques to lock yourself into a
pattern that imposes *more* stress on you. There is no point in clinging
rigidly to a set of time priorities that no longer apply to your situation.
The idea is for you to learn to manage time, not to let time manage you.

## COMPREHENSION CHECK

Complete the following items by filling in the blank or circling the correct answer.

1. What is stress? _____

2. In your own words explain how stress affects the body.

   _____

   _____

3. Paraphrase the author's suggestions for coping with stress. _____

   _____

   _____

4. State the main idea of this selection by explaining the problem and the solution being described.

   _____

   _____

5. In your own words explain *homeostasis* as used in paragraph 3.

   _____

   _____

6. Explain the difference between specific and nonspecific reactions.

   _____

   _____

7. Stress of any kind is harmful to the body.
   a. true
   b. false

8. Which of the causes of stress among college students affects you the most, and why? Which the least?

_____    _____

_____

_____

_____

9. How might stress affect your ability to make a thoughtful, sound decision?

_____

_____

_____

_____

10. Which specific details in the section "Coping with Stress" imply that the author is writing for college students?

_____

_____

**COMPREHENSION EXERCISE**    _A stress management program_

## A. Setting up the program

Use some of the suggestions in Reading Selection One to set up a personal stress management program. Using the chart on page 180, do the following:

1. Write down the items listed under "Stress and the College Student" that are sources of stress or conflict for you.

2. Determine whether the source of stress is avoidable, unavoidable, or adjustable.

| Personal Stress Management Program | | |
|---|---|---|
| *Stressor* | *Source of the Stressor* | *Reduction Strategy* |
| 1. | | |
| 2. | | |
| 3. | | |
| 4. | | |
| 5. | | |
| 6. | | |

3.  Create a specific strategy for coping with each situation.

## B. Following up

Choose a partner and do the following:

1.  Discuss your stress reduction strategies. Adjust strategies if necessary.

2.  When you have a firm list of strategies, write them on another piece of paper.

3.  Place the paper in an envelope, writing your name and the date one month from today on the front of the envelope.

4.  Seal and exchange envelopes with your partner.

5.  In one month's time return the envelopes to each other and reread the list of strategies.

6.  Check off the strategies that worked for you and consider new strategies for those that didn't.

### *Prereading Activity*: **Previewing the selection**

Preview Reading Selection Two by skimming and scanning the title, the first paragraph, and the boldface and italic text, and by looking very carefully at the diagram. When you have finished previewing, answer the following question: What do you think Ellis means by "you feel the way you think"?

---

---

Now read the selection carefully. This excerpt is from a "chapter application" section of the college psychology textbook *Psychology: Themes and Variations*. It describes a stress-coping mechanism called reappraisal developed by theorist Albert Ellis. As you read the selection, be thinking about what the concept of reappraisal might entail and how you might apply it to your own life.

## Reappraisal: Ellis's Rational Thinking

**BY WAYNE WEITEN**

Albert Ellis (1977, 1985) is a prominent theorist who believes that we can    1
short-circuit our emotional reactions to stress by altering our **appraisals** of stressful events. Stone and Neale call this strategy *situation redefinition.* . . . Ellis's insights about stress appraisal are the foundation for a widely used system of therapy that he devised. *Rational-emotive therapy* **is an approach to therapy that focuses on altering clients' patterns of irrational thinking to reduce maladaptive emotions and behavior**.

Ellis maintains that *you feel the way you think*. He argues that proble-    2
matic emotional reactions are caused by negative self-talk, which he calls catastrophic thinking. *Catastrophic thinking* **involves unrealistically pessimistic appraisals of stress that exaggerate the magnitude of one's problems**. Ellis uses a simple A-B-C sequence to explain his ideas (see Figure 13.18).

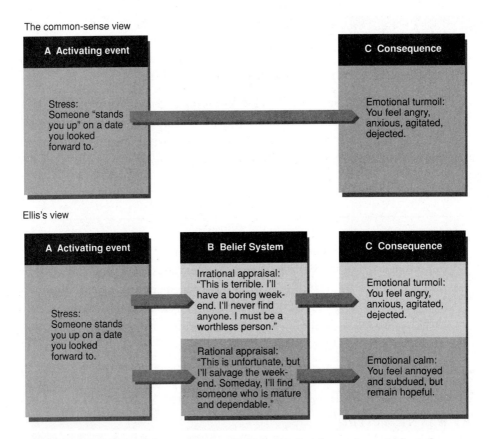

The common-sense view

Ellis's view

**Figure 13.18** Albert Ellis's A-B-C model of emotional reactions. Although most of us are prone to attribute our negative emotional reactions directly to events, Ellis argues that we *feel* the way we *think*.

■ A: *Activating event.* The A in Ellis's system stands for the activating event that produces the stress. The activating event may be any potentially stressful transaction. Examples might include an automobile accident, the cancellation of a date, a delay while waiting in line at the bank, or a failure to get a promotion you were expecting.

- B: *Belief system*. B stands for your belief about the event. This represents your appraisal of the stress. According to Ellis, we often view minor setbacks as disasters. Thus, we engage in catastrophic thinking: "How awful this is. I can't stand it! Things never turn out fair for me. I'll never get promoted."

- C: *Consequence*. C stands for the consequence of your negative thinking. When your appraisals of stressful events are terribly negative, the consequence tends to be emotional distress. Thus, we feel angry, or outraged, or anxious, or panic-stricken, or disgusted, or dejected.

Ellis asserts that most of us don't understand the importance of phase   3
B in this three-stage sequence. We unwittingly believe that the activating event (A) causes the consequent emotional turmoil (C). However, Ellis maintains that A does *not* cause C. It only appears to do so. Instead, Ellis asserts, B causes C. Our emotional distress is actually caused by our catastrophic thinking in appraising stressful events.

According to Ellis, it's commonplace for people to turn inconvenience   4
into disaster and to make "mountains out of molehills." For instance, imagine that someone "stands you up" on a date that you were looking forward to eagerly. You might think as follows: "Oh, this is terrible. I'm going to have another rotten, boring weekend. People always mistreat me. I'll never find anyone to fall in love with. I must be a crummy, worthless person." Ellis would argue that such thoughts are terribly irrational. He would point out that it doesn't follow logically, just because you were stood up, that you (1) must have a lousy weekend, (2) will never fall in love, and (3) are a worthless person.

Ellis theorizes that unrealistic appraisals of stress are derived from   5
**irrational assumptions** that we hold. He maintains that if you scrutinize your catastrophic thinking, you'll find that your reasoning is based on a logically indefensible **premise**, such as "I must have approval from everyone" or "I must perform well in all endeavors." These faulty assumptions, which we often hold unconsciously, generate our catastrophic thinking and our emotional turmoil. . . .

How can you reduce your unrealistic appraisals of stress? To accom-   6
plish this, Ellis asserts that you must learn (1) how to detect catastrophic
thinking and (2) how to dispute the irrational assumptions that cause it.
Detection involves acquiring the ability to spot unrealistic **pessimism**
and wild exaggeration in your thinking. Examine your self-talk closely.
Ask yourself why you're getting upset. Force yourself to verbalize your
concerns, silently or out loud. Look for key words that often show up in
catastrophic thinking, such as *should, ought, never,* and *must.*

Disputing your irrational assumptions requires subjecting your entire   7
reasoning process to **scrutiny.** Try to root out the assumptions from
which you derive your conclusions. We're often unaware of these assumptions. Once they're unearthed, their irrationality may be quite obvious. If your assumptions seem reasonable, ask yourself whether your
conclusions follow logically. Try to replace your catastrophic thinking
with lower-key, more rational analyses. These strategies should help you
to redefine stressful situations in ways that are less threatening. Strangely
enough, another way to make stressful situations less threatening is to
turn to humor.

**COMPREHENSION CHECK**

Complete the following items by filling in or circling the correct answer.

1. Is this selection mainly about a problem or a solution? _____

2. Explain what is meant by "catastrophic thinking."

   _____

   _____

3. In the A-B-C sequence of Ellis's theory, which part of the sequence
   actually causes stress? Explain.

   _____

   _____

_____

_____

4. The main idea of this selection is:
   a. Unrealistic appraisal of stress is derived from irrational assumptions we hold.
   b. Catastrophic thinking results from negative self-talk.
   c. Albert Ellis believes that we can lessen the effects of stressful events by changing our appraisal of the events themselves.
   d. The A-B-C sequence explains how our thinking can create stressful reactions to events.

5. Paraphrase the author's definition of rational-emotive therapy.

_____

_____

6. What common analogy does Ellis use to explain what we do when we use "catastrophic thinking"?

_____

_____

7. The word *assumption* is used a number of times in the second half of the selection. In that context the best meaning for the word is:
   a. knowledge of a situation or idea
   b. an irrational idea
   c. a previously held idea or belief

8. The word *pessimistic* in the definition of "catastrophic thinking" probably means

_____

9. From this selection we can infer that Albert Ellis is probably:
   a. an optimist
   b. a pessimist

10. Describe a situation in which you were guilty of catastrophic thinking. What was the irrational assumption that caused the catastrophic thinking?

_____

_____

_____

**COMPREHENSION EXERCISE**     *Reappraising a stress-inducing situation*

Pretend you are in the following stress-activating situations (A). Now think a "catastrophic thought" (B) and record it in the "belief system" column. Then describe the ensuing emotions or consequences (C).

*(A) Activating Event*     *(B) Belief System*     *(C) Consequences*

You are stuck in
heavy traffic on your    → _____  → _____
way to school
                            _____     _____

                            _____     _____

You fail your first      → _____  → _____
biology test
                            _____     _____

                            _____     _____

You think you are        → _____  → _____
"in love" with two
people                      _____     _____

                            _____     _____

Now reappraise *one* of the situations by answering the following questions.

Situation: _____

1. What assumption was your catastrophic thought based on?

   _____

   _____

2. Was it an unreasonable assumption?

   _____

   _____

3. If it was reasonable, did your conclusion logically follow?

   _____

   _____

4. How can you readjust your thinking to reduce stress in the situation?

   _____

   _____

## READING SELECTION THREE

### *Prereading Activity*: **Previewing the selection**

Preview the selection by reading the title, the boldface and highlighted text, and the first and last paragraphs. Then answer the following question: According to this article where does the solution to stressful reactions lie?

_____

_____

Now read the article carefully. As you read, be thinking about what type of personality you have and how your personality type affects the way you deal with stress.

## How Much Stress Can You Survive?

BY SUZANNE OUELLETTE KOBASA

*The answer depends on your personality*

Ask most people what they think about stress — the bugaboo of the '80s — and they're certain to tell you something bad. Stress makes you sick. It wrecks the immune system, gives people heart attacks, raises the risk of cancer. Stress runs like a truck over its helpless victims.    1

That's the popular impression left by many researchers, and by many TV and newspaper reports. And they leave us with a problem: What to do? Anyone who lives in a sizable American city, goes to school or holds a job has to deal with stress; it comes with the territory. But the antistress scare makes it seem that nothing short of retiring to rural Vermont could keep people healthy.    2

Now, however, there is a more hopeful way of looking at stress — one that's closer to reality. According to this new view, it's not just what happens to you that's important, but how you handle it. If you try to master stresses instead of feeling helpless and overwhelmed by them, they don't have to be bad for your health.    3

Over the last eight years, my colleagues and I have studied what we call "hardy" personalities: people who seem especially stress-resistant. Our research shows distinct, measurable personality traits that **buffer** the negative effects of stress. It helps explain why one executive gets severe headaches or pains in his chest, while his office neighbor weathers the same pressures in perfect health. . . .    4

*Life changes take a toll, but they don't have to make you sick*

In careful studies of hundreds of people, we've found that personality can make *the* crucial difference. For example:    5

- If you're under a lot of stress, a hardy personality may do more for your health than exercise or a strong constitution.

■ Stress-resistant people can have several Type A traits *without* a high risk of heart disease.

■ For people with high-pressure jobs, family support is less helpful than inner resources. In fact, some people are *more* likely to become sick if they have tight-knit families.

■ The same personality traits help executives, lawyers, housewives, army officers and college students — and probably the rest of us — deal with stress.

There's good news, too. If you've had trouble coping, and felt overwhelmed by life's unexpected challenges, you don't have to accept a victim's fate. There are ways to change from helpless to hardy. . . .     6

In 1975 I became interested in people who stay healthy under stress. My colleagues and I decided to look first at high-powered business executives — widely viewed as the walking wounded of the stress war. We found a group of telephone executives whose life experiences, on the standard scale, would have put them at high risk for illness — but who were still in good health. So we asked the question: What was special about them? . . .     7

We thought some people might be able to handle stress without becoming anxious and aroused in the first place — and without starting the spiral that leads to illness. So we checked out three major personality traits that seemed most likely to help:     8

1.  **Commitment** to self, work, family and other important values.

2.  A sense of personal **control** over one's life.

3.  The ability to see change in one's life as a **challenge** to master.

I saw these three "C's" — commitment, control and challenge — as the ingredients of what I called psychological *hardiness*. Hardy people should be able to face change with confidence and self-determination, and the eagerness of seeing change as opportunity. In contrast, a less hardy person could feel alienated, threatened or helpless in the face of any major challenge to the status quo.     9

### Learning to be a survivor

Hardiness is clearly a good thing. But all these studies left one crucial    10
question unanswered. Can you actually *learn* to be hardy? Or is this
aspect of personality fixed early in life?

I think it's possible to become hardier: more committed, in control    11
and open to challenge. The change can come through self-reflection. Or,
as we are learning, through teaching.

Salvatore Maddi and I took 16 executives from Illinois Bell, men    12
under high stress and starting to show such signs of strain as psychological problems and high blood pressure. Half the men participated in
weekly group meetings, led by Sal Maddi, where they studied techniques
designed to make them hardier. After eight weeks, they scored higher
on the hardiness scale and had less psychological distress than before.
Even more striking, their blood pressure—a clear measure of health—
dropped. Three months later, the benefits still held. The other eight men
who served as controls—they just kept a stress journal and met only at
the beginning and end of the eight-week period—showed no such
changes.

We plan to test group training with more people, including women and    13
non-executives. We would also like to compare our methods with meditation, relaxation training and other forms of stress management. . . .

If techniques like these really work, we have an important tool for    14
improving health. The key will not be to make our lives stress-free: that's
impossible. But it may be possible for anyone to defuse stress by learning
to be hardy instead of helpless.

## COMPREHENSION CHECK

Complete the following items by filling in the correct answer

1. Define a "hardy personality" as it is used in the context of the article.

_____

2.  Explain the three C's that constitute the hardy personality.

    _____

    _____

    _____

3.  What three factors besides the hardiness factors can be important to maintaining health in the midst of stress?

    _____

    _____

4.  How might hardiness defuse Type A behavior?  _____

    _____

5.  In what way is the idea of teaching hardiness similar to Ellis's reappraisal model?

    _____

    _____


### CHAPTER APPLICATION


You have just received a letter from a good friend who is very distressed and considering dropping out of college. In the letter she explains that her father has had an accident and is unable to work. Not only is she concerned for her father's condition, she also fears she will not be able to pay next semester's tuition. She hasn't been getting along with her roommate, and to make matters worse she is in danger of failing two of her courses.

Write a supportive letter to your friend suggesting specific approaches for dealing with her problems. Incorporate what you have learned in this chapter about understanding and coping with stressful situations.

"And they lived happily ever after" may be the end of the fairy tale, but it's not the end of the story, according to the author of "Problems and Pain." Life, he contends, is never free of problems; and the sooner we accept this notion, the better. What do you think?

## Problems and Pain

BY M. SCOTT PECK

Life is difficult. 1

This is a great truth, one of the greatest truths. It is a great truth 2 because once we truly see this truth, we **transcend** it. Once we truly know that life is difficult — once we truly understand and accept it — then life is no longer difficult. Because once it is accepted, the fact that life is difficult no longer matters.

Most do not fully see this truth that life is difficult. Instead they moan 3 more or less **incessantly**, noisily or **subtly**, about the enormity of their problems, their burdens, and their difficulties as if they were generally easy, as if life should be easy. They voice their belief, noisily or subtly, that their difficulties represent a unique kind of **affliction** that should not be and that has somehow been especially visited upon them, or else upon their families, their tribe, their class, their nation, their race or even their species, and not upon others. I know about this moaning because I have done my share.

Life is a series of problems. Do we want to moan about them or solve 4 them? Do we want to teach our children to solve them?

Discipline is the basic set of tools we require to solve life's problems. 5 Without discipline we can solve nothing. With only some discipline we can solve only some problems. With total discipline we can solve all problems.

What makes life difficult is that the process of confronting and solving  6
problems is a painful one. Problems, depending upon their nature, evoke
in us frustration or grief or sadness or loneliness or guilt or regret or anger
or fear or anxiety or anguish or despair. These are uncomfortable feelings,
often very uncomfortable, often as painful as any kind of physical pain,
sometimes equaling the very worst kind of physical pain. Indeed, it is
because of the pain that events or conflicts engender in us that we call
them problems. And since life poses an endless series of problems, life is
always difficult and is full of pain as well as joy.

Yet it is in this whole process of meeting and solving problems that  7
life has its meaning. Problems are the cutting edge that distinguishes
between success and failure. Problems call forth our courage and our
wisdom; indeed, they create our courage and our wisdom. It is only
because of problems that we grow mentally and spiritually. When we
desire to encourage the growth of the human spirit, we challenge and
encourage the human capacity to solve problems, just as in school we
deliberately set problems for our children to solve. It is through the pain
of confronting and resolving problems that we learn. As Benjamin Franklin said, "Those things that hurt, instruct." It is for this reason that wise
people learn not to dread but actually to welcome problems and actually
to welcome the pain of problems.

## JOURNAL WRITING

1.  Discuss the aspect of college life that you find most stressful. Describe
    exactly what it is that creates the stress and how you plan to alleviate or
    cope with it.

2.  Describe a situation in your life when you anticipated that something
    awful or catastrophic was going to happen but that in fact never oc-
    curred. Describe your feelings before, during, and after the experience.

3.  Dr. M. Scott Peck believes that life is made up of a series of problems
    and that you grow in wisdom and courage as you work through these
    problems. Describe an experience in your life through which you have
    grown either in wisdom or in courage, or both.

4.  Dr. Peck believes that self-discipline is the key to solving life's problems. In what ways can self-discipline help you relieve the stress you feel as a college student?

5.  Discuss the three C's described in the Kobasa article, giving specific examples of how each can help you to achieve success in college.

## CHAPTER 7

# Definitions, Examples, and Lists

After studying Chapter 7 you should be able to:

- identify definitions, examples, and lists in written passages
- underline and annotate texts effectively
- use underlining and annotating to aid comprehension and recall of text material

## CHAPTER CHECKLIST

Use the following checklist to help you plan for the text, readings, and activities in this chapter.

*Date*    *Date*
*Assigned*   *Completed*

| Assigned | Completed | |
|---|---|---|
| _____ | _____ | The importance of terminology |
| _____ | _____ | Definitions |
| _____ | _____ | Examples and explanations |
| _____ | _____ | **WARM-UP 1**: Definitions and examples |
| _____ | _____ | Simple listing or enumeration |
| _____ | _____ | **WARM-UP 2**: Lists |
| _____ | _____ | Underlining and annotating |
| _____ | _____ | **EXERCISE 1**: Underlining and annotating |

### READING SELECTION ONE

| | | |
|---|---|---|
| _____ | _____ | *Prereading Activity*: Previewing |
| _____ | _____ | **"Types of Groups"** |
| _____ | _____ | **COMPREHENSION CHECK** |

### READING SELECTION TWO

| | | |
|---|---|---|
| _____ | _____ | *Prereading Activity*: Previewing |
| _____ | _____ | **"Collective Behavior"** |
| _____ | _____ | **COMPREHENSION CHECK** |

Working with a partner, do the following:

1. List the "groups" in your school. You and your partner may have different names for the same groups.

2. Try to define each of the groups by describing the most basic thing they share in common (for example: Jocks are students who play or are very interested in athletics).

3. Under each definition, list all the characteristics that identify these people as a group (for example: types of clothing, hairstyles, etc.).

4. Discuss your notes with your classmates.

## Underlining and Annotating

As you learned in Part I, you need to become actively engaged in the reading process if you wish to increase your comprehension and recall. One way to increase involvement is to underline or highlight and annotate as you read. Although it is useful for all reading selections, this strategy is particularly well suited for passages structured by definitions, examples, and/or lists.

This marking process involves underlining, circling, and numbering key words and phrases, and summarizing key points in the margin. Learning to underline only key words and sentences and to summarize them in the margin will enable you to review your notes quickly and meaningfully. The important thing is to underline *only* key facts and ideas. Underlining too much hinders your ability to separate major from minor points when reviewing.

The following passage shows how to underline and annotate a paragraph.

This definition of groups, imprecise as it may

seem, allows us to distinguish groups from

other types of collectivities of people, which we

*nongroup =*
*collection of people*    could call nongroups. One type of nongroup,

*① aggregate =
people together
in one place*

which we will call an **aggregate** ① (or aggrega-tion), <u>consists of a number of people clustered together</u> in one place. <u>Examples</u> of aggregates might be all the <u>people in New York City</u>, or the <u>pedestrians at</u> a <u>busy intersection</u> waiting for the light to change to "walk," or all the people in North America, or the passengers on a jet from New York to San Francisco. A <u>second</u> useful <u>nongroup</u> called a **category** ② consists of a number of <u>people who have a particular characteristic in common.</u> <u>Examples</u> of categories would be all <u>females</u>, or all <u>red-haired people</u>, or all pilots, or all teenagers, or all whites.

*② catagory =
people sharing
characteristic*

**EXERCISE 1**  *Underlining and annotating*

Read the following paragraph, watching for words or punctuation that signal definitions, examples, and lists. Then underline and annotate by following the directions after the passage.

Sociologists say that a **group** exists when you have a number of people who (1) have shared or patterned interaction and (2) feel bound together by a "consciousness of kind" or a "we" feeling. "Consciousness of kind," a phrase coined by Franklin Gidding, refers to the individual's awareness of important similarities between himself or herself and certain others. This concept also refers to the awareness that the individual and other group members have common loyalties, share at least some similar values and see themselves as set apart from the rest of the world because of their memberships in this particular group. Groups vary tremendously in variety, size, and shape. A group may be as small as two people or almost infinitely large. Groups may be simple in structure or exceedingly complex; they may involve close, intimate relationships between members or more distant and infrequent personal contacts. In other words, the definition of group — patterned interaction and "we" feeling — may fit an enormous variety of situations: a family, a basketball team, a sociology class, IBM, or General Motors.

Now do the following:

1. Circle the two concepts defined in this passage.

2. Write the words or the punctuation that signal the definitions.

   _____

   _____

3. Underline the definitions.

4. Number the phrases that explain the definitions.

5. Underline the key words in the explanations.

6. Underline the three ways groups may vary.

7. Underline the examples of a "group."

8. Define a "group" by filling in the blanks below:

A group = any number of _____ who

    (1) share a patterned _____

    (2) see themselves as

        (a) having common _____

        (b) sharing similar _____

        (c) set _____ from the rest of the world

9. Write this definition in the margin next to the reading passage.

10. Write two or three examples of your own under the definition in the margin.

## READING SELECTION ONE

### *Prereading Activity*: **Previewing**

Preview the reading selection by reading the title, the introduction, and the boldface and italicized print. Then write three questions you will need to find answers for.

1. _____

2. _____

3. _____

The selection "Types of Groups," from the textbook *Sociology: Concepts and Characteristics*, is a good example of the way writers include terminology in textbooks. As you read the selection, underline and annotate by (1) circling terms, (2) underlining definitions, (3) numbering lists, (4) underlining key words in explanations and examples, and (5) paraphrasing the terms (using as few words as possible) and writing them in the margin, giving one example for each. Use the guides in the margins to help you annotate.

## Types of Groups

**BY JUDSON R. LANDIS**

*The* New York Times *has described one of the most unusual clubs in the world made up of a small number of usually serious scientists stationed at the South Pole. It is called the ''300 Club.'' Those who want to join must wait until the temperature is at least one hundred degrees Fahrenheit below zero, then strip completely nude and dash one hundred yards across the ice to a marker designating the South Pole and one hundred yards back to the scientific hut. Anyone surviving becomes a member of this very exclusive group.*

1   Social groups may be classified in many ways as the following categories illustrate. In some groups, membership is automatic and the participant has no choice; in others, the option is open and individuals may or may not join as they wish. These two types are called involuntary and voluntary groups. **Involuntary groups** might include the family one is born into or the army platoon one is drafted into. **Voluntary groups** would include any of a vast number that an individual may exercise some choice in joining: lodges, fraternities, bridge clubs, student governments, or political organizations. **In-groups** are groups that *I* belong to, that *I* identify with, that are *my* groups, while **out-groups** are groups that I do not belong to or identify with.

| Group Classification |
|---|
| 1. _____ |
| ex. _____ |
| 2. _____ |
| ex. _____ |
| 3. _____ |
| ex. _____ |
| 4. _____ |
| ex. _____ |

2   **Reference groups** are groups that serve as models for our behavior — groups we may or may not actually belong to, but whose perspectives we assume and mold our behavior after. A reference group may be made up of people one associates with or knows personally, or it may be an abstract collectivity of individuals who represent models for our behavior.

| 1. Reference group |
|---|
| _____ |
| ex. _____ |

Each individual has many reference groups. As a teacher I would have certain reference groups, as a sociologist others, as a husband others, and as a handball player still others. One's **peer group** is made up of people of relatively the same age, interests, and social position with whom one has reasonably close association and contact. A peer group may consist of a class at school, a street gang, or an occupational group such as the members of a college sociology department or a group of lawyers in a law firm. Not all the members of a peer group are necessarily friends, but the peer group exercises a major role in the socialization process. During adolescence, a peer group may be *the* major socializing agent.

Groups whose members come predominantly from one social-class level are called **horizontal groups**. Examples of horizontal groups would include almost any organization formed along occupational lines: an association of doctors, carpenters, or actors. If a group includes members from a variety of social classes, it could be called a **vertical group**. Vertical groups are more difficult to find in American society, since many divisions are made along social-class lines. A church congregation might constitute a vertical group, and in some cases an army platoon made up of draftees would include members from a variety of social classes. Groups are also categorized according to their longevity. A group brought together to perform a single, short-term task could be called a **temporary group**, whereas a longer-lasting collectivity like a family could be called a **permanent group**. Groups are defined as open or closed according to the ease of gaining membership. A white fraternity is often a **closed group** as far as a black male is concerned, but the United States army is probably a very **open group** for the same individual. Now, what type of group is the "300 Club"?

2. Peer group _____

_____

ex. _____

3

1. _____

_____

ex. _____

2. Vertical group _____

_____

ex. _____

3. _____

_____

ex._____

4. _____

_____

ex._____

5. _____

_____

ex._____

6. _____

_____

ex._____

Refer to your circles, underlinings, and annotations to complete the following items.

1. What is the topic of this selection? _____

2. The main idea of paragraph 1 is found in:
   a. sentence 1
   b. sentence 2
   c. sentence 3
   d. sentence 6

3. What is the main idea of paragraph 2? _____

   _____

4. What is the main idea of this selection? _____

   _____

5. Give one example of a "peer group." _____

6. A horizontal group would contain people from different social classes.
   a. true
   b. false

7. Is the 300 Club an "open" or "closed" group? _____

8. Is the 300 Club more apt to be a "horizontal" or a "vertical" group?

   _____

9. Give an example of a temporary group. _____

10. List five groups of which you are a member. Then classify them using the definitions from the selection.

*Group*                                    *Type*

_____                    _____

_____                    _____

_____                    _____

_____                    _____

_____                    _____

## READING SELECTION TWO

### *Prereading Activity*: **Previewing**

Preview the reading selection by reading the title, the introduction, and the boldface and italicized print. Then write three questions you will need to find answers for.

1. _____

2. _____

3. _____

Read the selection, underlining, annotating, and paraphrasing as in Reading Selection One.

## Collective Behavior

**BY JUDSON R. LANDIS**

Collective behavior is group behavior that is spontaneous, unstructured,   1
and unstable. It may be either sporadic and short-term or more continuous and long-lasting. Collective behavior is often hard to predict because
it is not rooted in the usual cultural or social norms. Spontaneous and
unstructured behavior is hard to observe or record objectively and is,
therefore, difficult to study. Ethically and practically, the researcher can-

not yell "Fire!" in a crowded theater, start a downtown riot, or produce a natural disaster and then observe how people behave. Although some artificial or laboratory-created studies of rumor and panic have been conducted, most studies of collective behavior by social scientists are after-the-fact analyses and discussions with people who happened to be involved.

These studies have revealed that collective behavior may follow reasonably consistent patterns. For example, Neil Smelser has suggested that specific conditions need to be present for collective behavior to occur: (1) *Structural Conduciveness*: Given the setting or structure of a specific group or society, a particular type of collective behavior such as panic, riot, craze, or lynching *could* happen; although the behavior would not necessarily be encouraged, it would still be possible because of historical or other structural reasons; (2) *Structural Strain*: Conditions in society place strain on people; a general feeling of deprivation or conflict is produced by such things as economic failure, hostility between races, social classes, or religion, or sudden changes in the existing order; (3) *Generalized Belief*: A set of feelings, beliefs, or rationalizations must be present to explain the cause of the strain, to create a common culture prepared for action; (4) *Precipitating Factors*: A specific event provides a concrete reason for taking action; (5) *Mobilization for Action*: The participants become organized and act; (6) *Social Control*: Factors that occur after the event has started may prevent or inhibit the effect of the above conditions from continuing and change its course.

### Crowds

An outline of the major collective behavior concepts would start with the crowd. A **crowd** is a temporary collection of people in close physical contact reacting together to a common stimulus. For example, the passengers on the flight from New York to San Francisco whose pilot suddenly decides he would like to go to the North Pole might be transformed from an **aggregation** into a crowd, or even a mob. Crowds have certain characteristics in common. **Milling** usually occurs as a crowd is being formed. In one sense milling refers to the excited, restless physical movement of the individuals involved. In a more important sense, milling refers to a process of communication that leads to a definition of the situation and possible collective action. Not long ago, a classroom I was in suddenly started shaking with the first tremors of an earthquake. Almost at once the people began turning, shifting, looking at each other, at the ceiling, and at the instructor. They were seeking some explanation for the highly unusual experience and, whether spoken aloud or not, the questions on their faces were clear: "What is it?" "Did you feel it?" "What should we do?" Buzzing became louder talking, and someone shouted, "Earthquake!!!" The students began to get up and move toward the doors. Many continued to watch the ceiling. . . . Milling may involve the long buildup of a lynch mob, or the sudden reaction in a dark and crowded theater when someone shouts "Fire!!!" Milling helps ensure the development of a common mood for crowd members.

When they are part of a crowd, people tend to be ***suggestible***. They   4
are less critical and will readily do things that they would not ordinarily do alone. This is true in part because, as members of a crowd, they are ***anonymous***. The prevailing feeling is that the crowd is responsible, not the individual. Once one becomes a member of an active crowd, it is extremely difficult to step back, to get perspective, and to evaluate objectively what one is doing. Crowd members have a narrowed focus, a kind of tunnel vision. The physical presence of a crowd is a powerful force; people almost have to separate themselves from the crowd physically before they can critically examine their own behavior. There is also a *sense of urgency* about crowds. Crowds are oriented toward a specific focus or task: "We've got to do *this*, and we've got to do it *now*!" Some form of leadership usually appears in the crowd, but, as the mood of the crowd changes, the leadership may shift quickly from one individual or group to another.

There are many different types of crowds. Some are **passive**, such as   5
those watching a building burn or those at the scene of an accident. Some are active, such as a race riot or a lynch mob. Some crowds have a number of loosely defined goals. Other crowds are focused on a specific goal. Turner and Killian distinguish between crowds that direct their action toward some external object — harassing a speaker until he leaves the platform or lynching a criminal — and expressive crowds that direct their focus on the crowd itself — cheering at a football game or speaking in tongues at a church service.

Controlling the behavior of a crowd is difficult because of the mass of people involved and the spontaneous nature of their behavior. Some methods of dealing with a potentially riotous crowd have been suggested, however: Remove or isolate the individuals involved in the precipitating incident. Reduce the feelings of anonymity and invincibility of the individuals; force them to focus on themselves and on the consequences of their actions. Interrupt patterns of communication during the milling process by breaking the crowd into small units. Remove the crowd leaders if it can be done without use of force. Finally, attempt to distract the attention of the crowd by creating a diversion or a new point of interest, especially if this can be accomplished by someone who is considered to be in sympathy with the crowd. 6

## COMPREHENSION CHECK

Fill in the partial outline below using your underlining and margin notes to aid you.

### Collective Behavior

I. Collective behavior

   A. Definition _____

      1. Example _____

   B. Necessary conditions

      1. _____

      2. _____

      3. _____

      4. _____

      5. _____

      6. _____

II. Crowds

   A. Definition _____

      1. Example _____

   B. Milling

      1. Example _____

   C. Characteristics of crowds

      1. _____

      2. _____

      3. _____

   D. Types of crowds

      1. _____

      2. _____

   E. Methods of control

      1. _____

      2. _____

      3. _____

      4. _____

      5. _____

# Summarizing

Once you have sorted out the important ideas and supporting details in a reading selection, you can summarize the information for useful feedback. A *summary* is a short, concise statement, in your own words, of the main points of a written selection. It should be about one-fourth the length of the original yet cover the main ideas and most of the important details.

Summarizing will help you to (1) monitor your comprehension, (2) review your lecture notes, (3) create organized, efficient study guides, and (4) increase recall. To summarize a reading selection, do the following:

1. Underline the topic sentence and one or two important details in each paragraph. If there is no topic sentence, write the main idea in your own words in the margin.

2. Make a brief outline using the information you have underlined and written in the margin.

3. Write an introductory paragraph stating the main point of the selection.

4. Develop paragraphs to explain each of the major ideas, choosing one or two details to support or explain each idea.

**EXERCISE 2** *Summarizing*

On a separate piece of paper write a summary of the selection "Collective Behavior" using the outline you completed in the Comprehension Check on page 211.

**READING SELECTION THREE**

### *Prereading Activity*: **Previewing a magazine article**

Preview the selection by reading the title, the subtitle, and the first and last paragraphs. Then in one sentence state the goal the author might have in writing this article.

Textbook authors use a great many signal, or clue, words to indicate definitions, examples, or lists. Journalists, on the other hand, may use fewer, more subtle signals. Reading Selection Three, "Going 'Wilding' in the City," is an article that appeared several years ago in *Newsweek* magazine. As you read the selection underline the topic sentence and key details. Watch for signals to definitions, examples, and lists. Also keep in mind what you learned about collective behavior from the previous reading selection.

---

## Going 'Wilding' in the City

**BY DAVID GELMAN WITH PETER McKILLOP**

*The power of the group can lead teens to mayhem*

On a warm April night . . . a band of . . . teenagers chased down a young 1 Wall Street investment banker out jogging by herself, rather daringly for that late hour, in Central Park. They hit the slightly built woman with fists and rocks, stabbed her head five times and then repeatedly raped and **sodomized** her. When she was found hours later she had suffered multiple skull fractures and lost most of her blood. . . .

By early accounts, the seven youths charged with the attack were 2 hardly casebook sociopaths. They were variously **vouched** for by friends, teachers and relatives as industrious, churchgoing, "shy." Individually there seemed nothing especially intimidating about them. Yet together they stood accused of an assault so wantonly vicious that, as an investigator for the Manhattan district attorney's office remarked, "even New York" was unprepared for its brutality. . . .

Originally, police say, about 35 youths, some as young as 13, had 3 gone into the park "wilding" — a variety of bash-as-bash-can gang rampage that has disrupted some of the city's public places recently. After a couple of **desultory** attempts on a male jogger and a homeless man, the group dwindled to a hard core of about 8 to 13. Ultimately, seven are believed to have participated in the rape of the woman jogger. Such expeditions usually begin spontaneously. Teenagers hanging around a housing project often have no agenda but to stir up a little excitement. "They may have said, 'Let's go wilding'," notes Franklin Zimring, director of the Earl Warren Legal Institute at the University of California, "but nobody said, 'Let's go raping'." Zimring, who conducted a 1984 study of youth homicide in New York, thinks the group may have been swayed by what he calls "government by dare — you do it because you don't want to back out."

Behavioral experts agree that in the dynamics of a group, there is    4
often at least one leader able to control the rest by playing on their need
to prove themselves. The instigator of a gang rape gains a double sense of
mastery, not only over the victim but over his **cohorts**, who feel obliged
to equal his **audacity**. There is an undeniably subtle power in the group:
it has the ability to validate and thereby **embolden** behavior. That may
be especially true of teenagers, who are particularly susceptible to pressure from peers. But the essential element is the **anonymity** group
membership confers, and thus the relative freedom from accountability.
"Basically, it's a loss of the individual's personality," says Robert Panza-
rella, a professor of police science at New York's John Jay College of
Criminal Justice. "Things he would never think of doing by himself he
does in the group." There is also a kind of division of labor, with the
chilling result that "while the action of each individual can seem relatively minor, the action of the whole may be horrific."

**Frenzied attack**: Something like that process was evident in the    5
Central Park rape. As the defendants themselves told it later, it was one of
the group, a 15-year-old, who first spotted the woman and said, "Go get
her." Another, 14, helped knock her down, then punched and kicked her.
Others, in turn, hit her with a rock, a brick and a length of lead pipe,
pinioned her legs and arms, ripped off her shirt and sweat pants, and
committed the actual rape and sodomy. "No one really knows these kids
or what was in their minds," cautions Yale's James Comer. But by their
own description there appears to have been an accelerating frenzy that is
often seen in gang rapes. Momentum builds as the assailants try to outdo
one another, in this case a momentum that carried them over the edge
into horror.

Although newspapers reported when the youths were arraigned that    6
they appeared to show no "remorse," some observers doubt that they
have yet grasped the enormity of their collective act. On the other hand,
Dorothy Lewis, a criminal psychiatrist known for her work with serial
killer Ted Bundy, warns that initial newspaper reports stressing the apparent wholesomeness of some of the group should be viewed with a
measure of **skepticism**. Lewis believes further investigation will show
that the teenagers who committed the rape were damaged in some way.
In similar cases, she says, people who commit such acts have either been
victims of abuse themselves or have witnessed terrible scenes of domestic

violence. These early experiences make the youths "unable to control their impulses," and, in essence, she thinks that is what could have happened that night in Central Park. "I see something," says Lewis, "that started out as a roaming gang, but degenerated into a **heinous, aberrant** crime."

## COMPREHENSION CHECK

Complete the following items by filling in the blank or circling the correct answer.

1. State the topic of this selection in one word. _____

2. State the main idea by explaining what the author is saying about the topic.

   _____

   _____

3. From initial reports the seven youths charged with the attack were basically law-abiding.
   a. true
   b. false

4. What is meant by the term *government by dare* in paragraph 3? _____

   _____

5. Using context to aid you, define the word *cohorts* in paragraph 4.

   _____

6. In your own words explain how the instigator of a gang rape gains a "double sense of mastery."

   _____

   _____

7. Using context to aid you, define the word *anonymity* in paragraph 4.

_____

8. In your own words explain how "the group" gives the individual freedom from accountability or blame.

_____

_____

9. We can conclude from the selection that the incident in Central Park was an isolated event that probably will never happen again.
   a. true
   b. false

10. Describe a situation in which people may be compelled by the power of the crowd to behave in a particular way.

_____

_____

_____

**COMPREHENSION EXERCISE**  *Outlining and summarizing*

Using the scrambled sentences below, complete the outline for "Going 'Wilding' in the City." Then, using your outline as a guide, write a summary of the article.

I.       ***Attack in the park*** _____

         A. _____

         B. _____

         C. _____

II.     ***Group dynamics*** _____

    A. _____

    B. _____

    C. _____

III.    ***Shared attack*** _____

    A. _____

    B. _____

IV.     ***Damaged youths*** _____

    A. _____

    B. _____

Individual young men reputed to be average teens.

An accelerated frenzy carried the assailants over the edge into horror.

Attack grew out of an evening of "wilding," or teenage bashing.

Power of the group can embolden the individuals.

All of the teens shared in the attack.

Many who commit abhorrent acts have been victims of abuse themselves.

Group membership gives the individual freedom from responsibility.

One criminal psychiatrist believes the teens are damaged in some ways.

Teenagers brutally attack and rape a young jogger.

Most groups are controlled by a leader.

**CHAPTER APPLICATION**

Choose one of your textbooks that contains a large number of terms. Read five or six pages, underlining and annotating as you did for the selections in this chapter. Then write a brief summary of the material using your markings.

**GOING BEYOND**

Roger Rosenblatt wrote this article in response to a gang rape that occurred a few years before the incident described in "Going 'Wilding' in the City." He wonders why men are capable of such behavior in a "civilized" society.

## The Male Response to Rape

### BY ROGER ROSENBLATT

Between the book reviews and the science notes, [we read of] the third     1
gang rape of the past two months. This one occurred in the Charlestown section of Boston, where seven young men have been charged with kidnapping a 17-year-old girl and raping her repeatedly for seven hours in an apartment belonging to one of the men. The incident followed the more widely publicized attack in New Bedford, Massachusetts, some weeks earlier, in which four men raped and tormented a woman for two hours on a pool table in Big Dan's bar, while onlookers cheered. That one was preceded by yet another at the University of Pennsylvania; there a young woman has charged that she was gang-raped by five to eight fraternity brothers during a party. Class distinctions need not apply. If one is tempted to construct a **hypothesis** around shiftless young Irishmen in a poor city neighborhood or the unemployed Portuguese in a depressed fishing port, sociology is obliterated by the party boys from the U. of P., no different in kind or action, just privilege. All subhumans are created equal.

Reading of such incidents, women are horrified because inevitably  2
they identify both with the victims in particular and with the entire
condition of victimization, of which gang rape may be the harshest instance. But why do men recoil so strongly? The straightforward answer
is that the vast majority of men disapprove of rape, and their disapproval
is intensified when a gang is involved. Yet the idea of gang rape is repug-
nant to men for reasons of identification as well. Few men would associate themselves with those who actually "did it to her." But quite more
than a few know what it is to be caught in the middle of an all-male show
of power and coercion, and thus to be complicit, even at the fringes, in
something their consciences abhor.

Gang rape is war. It is the war of men against women for reasons easy  3
to guess at, or for no reasons whatever, for the sheer mindless display of
physical mastery of the stronger over the weaker. In the wake of reports
from Charlestown, New Bedford and the University of Pennsylvania,
conjectures are bound to arise about the frustration of contemporary man
at the growing independence of women, and there may be some truth to
that. But men have never needed excuses to commit rape in gangs. The
Japanese in China, the Russians in Germany, the Pakistanis in Bangladesh. We read accounts of what some American soldiers did to Vietnam-
ese village girls of 13 and 14 in places like My Lai, and it seems clear that
the subject of gang rape goes a good deal deeper than modern man's
humiliation.

One psychological theory has it that these acts are homosexual ritual:  4
Men in groups desire each other, yet are ashamed of their urges, and so
they satisfy themselves by convening at a common target. Another theory
holds that there are situations where men so seek to prove their masculinity to one another that they will do anything, including murder. An
American soldier in Viet Nam described how, for no other reason than
that a comrade led the way, he shot to death a girl he had raped. Sex and
violence have an eerily close kinship as it is. Rape itself may be a form of
murder, the destruction of someone's will and spirit. No wonder those
same soldiers in Viet Nam spoke of dragging girls into the woods "for a
little boom-boom." To "bang" a woman remains part of the idiom. The
sound is a gun, the body a weapon. In a "gang bang," murder becomes a
massacre.

Upon learning such things at a distance, most men feel not only  5
**revulsion**, but also a proper urge to enact society's revenge. Lock the

bums away forever. At the same time, they can still imagine what it feels like to be present at the **atrocities**, even for the briefest instance; every life has **analogues** of its own. The essential circumstance is that of the mob, always a terrifying **entity**, whatever its goal. One thinks of lynch mobs before rape mobs, but all mobs have the same appearances and patterns, the same compulsion to tear things down or apart. The object of passion is sighted and pursued. The mob rises to a peak of pure hate, does what it does, then slinks away, its energy spent. Perhaps every mob commits rape in a way. Anybody who has ever seen a mob in action senses its latent sexuality — the collective panting, the empty ecstasy. Even at the outskirts, the voyeur participates. Eventually he may run or protest, but for at least one long moment he is helpless to move.

It is that moment of seemingly hypnotized attention most men know 6 and dread. It is a moment in which they are out of control as individuals — not merely outside the law, but out of biological order. Something stirs, an ancient reflex, as if they are dragged back through history to a starting point in evolution. The mob is a pack, its prey the female. Her difference is the instigator, her frailty the goad. Rape what you cannot have. Plunder what you can never know. Mystery equals fear equals rage equals death. It is she who stands for all life's threats, she who released animal instincts in the first place. Once aroused, why stop to reason or sympathize? The savage surfaces, prevails.

Of course, this happens only occasionally, in the heat of battle or Big 7 Dan's bar or Charlestown or the Alpha Tau Omega house, where boys were boys. But gang rape does not need to recur frequently to remind men of their own peculiar frailty. And that reminder brings terror, not the terror of the victim, to be sure, but one as benumbing in its own way; that of acknowledging one's natural potential for violence and destruction. Rape need not be involved. Was that not you, so many years ago, standing on the sidelines while that other boy was bullied in the playground? Or you in the crowd that **razzed** the old drunk in the park? Or you in the rear when they set fire to the cat? Child's play, possibly, but boy's play primarily; and the child becomes the man. If you have cast off most of the cruelty of boyhood, still some of the fascination with cruelty remains. The fascination is a form of cruelty itself, expressionless, **primeval**, a fisheye in the dark.

No, that is not you boozing it up in the Charlestown apartment, or 8 you, college boy, or you, Portuguese sailor. But isn't that you, propped neatly behind the desk, growling ever so faintly under your no-starch-in-the-collar, reading intently of all the shocking gang rapes?

At the beginning of Shakespeare's *Julius Caesar*, before Caesar's assas-   9 sination, Casca has a premonition of disaster that he reports to Cicero: "Against the Capitol I met a lion, who glared at me, and went surly by." The implication is that in every civilization, however **lofty**, a lion always roams the streets; the jungle never entirely disappears. What most men fear is a lion in the soul. Women, too, perhaps, but not in the matter of rape. That is male terrain, the masculine jungle. And no man can glimpse it, even at a distance, without fury and bewilderment at his monstrous capabilities.

## JOURNAL WRITING

1.  Is every man capable of rape given the right set of circumstances? Roger Rosenblatt suggests that although most men are appalled by the notion of rape, they have a subtle understanding of its allure because they fear what he calls "the lion in the soul." Write an essay using what you have learned about collective behavior to answer this question.

2.  Discuss the differences and similarities between individual and "gang" rape.

3.  Describe a situation in which you were influenced by the power of a group. What specifically did you do in the group situation that you might not have done had you not been a member of the group? How did you feel about your actions?

4.  There's an old saying: "You can choose your friends, but you can't choose your family." In other words, the family is an "involuntary" group that you are born into. Discuss the advantages and disadvantages of such groups. You may give examples from your own family if you wish.

5.  Describe a group you voluntarily belong to. Further classify the group by type and explain why you belong to it. What are the major benefits of membership in this group for you?

## CHAPTER 8

# Chronological Order and Narration

After studying Chapter 8 you should be able to:

- identify and comprehend selections organized by chronological order
- distinguish between a simple chronology and a narrative
- state the main idea of a narrative
- take notes in the form of a time line
- prepare a fact sheet for study
- interpret a line graph
- take objective tests

## CHAPTER CHECKLIST

Use the following checklist to help you plan for the text, readings, and activities in this chapter.

*Date* *Date*
*Assigned* *Completed*

_____  _____  Chronologies versus narrations

_____  _____  **WARM-UP**: Distinguishing between chronologies and narrations

_____  _____  **EXERCISE 1**: Previewing for chronological sequence

_____  _____  Time lines

_____  _____  **EXERCISE 2**: Creating a time line

_____  _____  Narrative illustrations

_____  _____  **EXERCISE 3**: Inferring the main idea

### READING SELECTION ONE

_____  _____  *Prereading Activity*: Note taking to get the facts

_____  _____  **"Using Alcohol and Drugs"**

_____  _____  **COMPREHENSION CHECK**

WARM-UP *Distinguishing between chronologies and narrations*

This exercise will help you understand the difference between a chronologically arranged set of facts and a narration. To complete this activity do the following:

1. On a separate piece of paper make a list of five important dates in your life. Begin with your birth and end with the day you entered college; then add any three events in between. Beside each date write a brief explanation of the event.

2. Choose one event or situation that occurred in your life that was especially meaningful to you. Describe it in detail from beginning to end using time words to make the sequence clear. (Your goal should be to make the reader understand why the event was meaningful to you.)

3. Read over what you have written for both parts of the assignment. Notice that in the first part of the activity you produced a group of facts that pertain to your life but that are not really *interrelated*. That is, you could probably substitute other interesting events for the three you chose. In the second part of the assignment your facts have a cause-and-effect relationship — each fact is dependent on another to relate the story. In other words, in the first assignment you merely arranged a group of facts chronologically while in the second you wrote a descriptive narration.

EXERCISE 1 *Previewing for chronological sequence*

Preview the following passage by scanning for and underlining the words and phrases that signal time.

> The large-scale introduction of opium to China by the British in the eighteenth and nineteenth centuries led to the Opium War of 1839-1842 and the ceding of Hong Kong to Britain.
> During the nineteenth century, opium and its alkaloids were used extensively in Western medicine. With the introduction of the

hypodermic syringe in 1853, the use of intravenous morphine became so widespread during the Civil War that addiction to it became known as the "soldier's disease."

Cocaine, isolated in 1860, was soon identified as a valuable
local anesthetic. Crude coca had been chewed by the ancient Incas
for centuries. The first reference to widespread drug addiction in
the United States, however, did not appear until the publication in
1892 of William Osler's *Principles and Practice of Medicine*. At the
time there were no controls on distribution of narcotic drugs, and it
has been estimated that in the 1880's about 3 percent of the American population was dependent on them. Narcotics were included in
baby tonics, cough medicines, soft drinks and nearly every household remedy.

# Time Lines

In addition to underlining or annotating the text, an excellent way to take
notes on chronologically arranged information is to create a time line. A
**time line** enables you to select and organize important facts and is very
useful as a study sheet at exam time.

One type of time line plots the dates horizontally across the top of the
page with the description of the events listed vertically under the dates. A
time line of this nature is useful if you simply want to gain an overview of
the information. Another type of time line plots the dates vertically and the
explanations horizontally. This method is preferable if you wish to take more
detailed notes. It is also useful as a fact sheet for reference and review.

**EXERCISE 2**     *Creating a time line*

Using the chart on page 229 make a time line of the dates and time words
you underlined in the passage in Exercise 1. Place the dates in the left-
hand column of the chart. (The first one has been done for you.) Then
describe the people, places, and events that relate to the dates.

| Time Line | | |
|-----------|---|---|
| *Dates* | *Events* | *People* |
| *18th, 19th centuries* | *Opium wars, ceding of Hong Kong to Britain* | |
| | | |
| | | |
| | | |
| | | |
| | | |

# Narrative Illustrations

The narration is a very common but diverse literary form. It may be as short and simple as the brief tale of Dee's addiction or as long and complicated as Homer's *Odyssey*. Some narrations are designed to entertain you, others to arouse your interest in a topic, and still others to inform or teach you.

In textbooks short narratives are often used as introductions or examples to create interest or to enhance the reader's ability to understand and retain the information. These short narrations are sometimes called *anecdotes*.

Notice how the following narrative introduction arouses interest and at the same time serves to illustrate the main concept of the selection:

In early February 1982, Joseph P. Barkett, a suspected drug trafficker, was arrested on Martha's Vineyard (Cape Cod) for possessing cocaine. Like most people facing drug charges, Barkett quickly planned a meeting with his lawyer, Harvey A. Silverglate of Boston.

Barkett and three others — who would later appear with him to face charges of distributing a kilo of cocaine a month — assembled in the conference room at Silverglate's Broad Street office. Other attorneys were present to discuss possible legal defenses.

But there was a fifth person at the February 24, 1982 meeting — the eventual unindicted co-conspirator — Anthony Cellilli. No one at the meeting knew that Cellilli, a pilot and courier in the drug ring, had become a government informant. Cellilli met with federal agents afterwards and was "debriefed" about the 90-minute session, which defense attorneys later argued included discussion about potential defense strategies.

The use of Cellilli to spy on the defense camp illustrates, say some legal scholars and defense attorneys, how the metaphorical "war on drugs" threatens constitutional rights. Cellilli's presence, they say, was an assault on the Sixth Amendment's protection of the attorney-client relationship.

State the main idea this introductory narrative is illustrating. (*Hint*: Reread the fourth paragraph.)

_____

_____

**EXERCISE 3** *Inferring the main idea*

Writers are not always as explicit about the main idea of a narration as in the previous example. More often the reader must infer the idea being discussed, just as one must infer the theme of a short story.

The next narration was written as the conclusion to a long article. Its purpose is to reinforce the main idea of the selection. As you read the excerpt try to infer the idea or theme the writer is illustrating with the narration. When you have finished reading, answer the questions that follow.

### From pilot to patient

Until six months ago, Jose Antonio was a fast-talking, coke-snorting pilot who ferried contraband in small planes from Colombia to the Bahamas and Panama. He is a trained engineer and had abandoned the workaday world for the flashy lifestyle of hotel suites, crisp $100 bills and, above all, plentiful drugs.

Today, he is a patient in a drug clinic where he shares a sparse dormitory with other recovering addicts. He is grateful for having "gotten out of that world alive" and eager to talk about his experiences as a cocaine runner.

"It was very alluring and amazingly easy. We would take off and land at unlit airstrips at dawn, and there was never any trouble with the police," he recalls. "Every time we came through customs, they got an automatic 100,000 pesos ($1000). I never asked what I was carrying — coke, guns, untaxed perfume. We would check into the most luxurious hotels, and we always had more cash than we could spend."

But there was a side to this high-flying life that grew more frightening as the stakes increased. First, the uncle of Jose Antonio's girlfriend was found stuffed in a trunk; then one of his bosses was shot 20 times by a rival gang. For the easygoing, 33-year-old pilot, the price of glamorous living had become too high.

At the same time, Jose Antonio was losing control of his own drug habit, needing more and more bazuko to keep up his nerve. He finally found himself alone in a Miami hotel room one night, shaking as he searched the Yellow Pages for help.

"When everything came crashing down, I suddenly saw how false it had all been," he says. "Nobody liked the underworld people I worked for; they were terrified of them. The bellhops treated us with deference and the police came to our restaurant booths to be taken care of, but they all hated us. When you have millions," he adds bitterly, "anything can be bought except trust."

1.  What is the topic of the narration? (What is it all about in one or two words?)

    _____

2.  What is the writer saying about the topic? (*Hint*: Use your answer to question 1 as the subject of your sentence and your answer to question 2 as the predicate.)

    _____

    _____

    _____

<br>

**READING SELECTION ONE**

### *Prereading Activity*: **Note taking to get the facts**

Reading Selection One is excerpted from a chapter in a health psychology textbook. Read the narrative introductory section (paragraphs 1–4). Then write one or two sentences stating the main idea.

_____

_____

_____

Now read the entire selection, by underlining and annotating as you read. When you finish, answer the questions in the Comprehension Check using only your notes. Then make a time line of the important events in the history of drinking using the chart on page 238.

## Using Alcohol and Drugs

**BY LINDA BRANNON AND JESS FEIST**

Judith was a problem drinker. Her interpersonal relationships, her teaching career, her marriage, and her health have all been adversely affected    1 by her abuse of alcohol. Her first drinking experience was at age 12, when she and several other girls "got high" on a couple of beers. During high school, she drank to the point of **intoxication** two or three times a year. In college, her drinking **escalated**, but it was still well under control. She never drank alone and confined her alcohol consumption to weekends and to parties.

Gradually, almost without her being aware of it, Judith's consumption increased to the point where she was drinking every day. Eventually she stopped going to bars, parties, and social gatherings and confined her drinking to her home. By age 30, Judith was drinking in the morning to recover from a "hangover" from the previous night. The drinking began to interfere with her job, and eventually she was released from her teaching contract. At about the same time, she developed mild liver problems and an assortment of other physical ailments.

Several times Judith tried to stop drinking. Sometimes she was successful for as long as a month. Four times she was hospitalized, always self-referred and always intoxicated at the time of admission. Hospital treatment usually consisted of a period of **detoxification**, group therapy with other alcohol abusers, and medication. The medication was for **delirium tremens**, a condition induced by alcohol withdrawal and characterized by excessive trembling, sweating, anxiety, and **hallucinations**. Twice Judith joined Alcoholics Anonymous (AA), but she quit the first time because she disliked most of the people in her group. The second time, however, she was more motivated to stop drinking. Now, at age 43, she has been abstinent for nearly five years.

Bill drinks too, but he is a nonproblem drinker. He cannot be described as a light or moderate drinker, because when he drinks he is likely to consume 8 to 10 beers in an evening. Like Judith, Bill drank sporadically during high school, about once every three or four months. While at college and away from home for the first time, he began drinking more often — one or two days every weekend. Bill, however, never escalated his drinking. He knows about the potential health consequences of alcohol because his father died at age 42 of liver cirrhosis as a result of heavy drinking. Now 33 years old and working as an engineer, Bill drinks more than he did 12 years ago. Unmarried and living alone, he never keeps alcoholic beverages in his apartment and confines his drinking to bars and parties. He never drinks alone and never feels compelled to drink.

## A brief history of drinking

Drinking fermented, alcoholic beverages dates back beyond recorded    5
history. There is evidence that most ancient cultures used beverage alcohol. Because the yeast that is responsible for producing alcohol is air-
borne, **fermentation** occurs naturally in fruits, fruit juices, and grain
mixtures. This process requires no sophisticated technology. The use of
alcohol is not something that can easily be traced; it was discovered
worldwide and repeatedly. Ancient Babylonians discovered both wine
(fermented grape juice) and beer (fermented grain), as did the ancient
Egyptians, Greeks, Romans, Chinese, and Indians. Pre-Columbian tribes
in the Americas also used fermented products.

Ancient civilizations also discovered drunkenness, of course. In sev-    6
eral of those countries, such as Greece, drunkenness was not only allowed but practically required, especially at festivals. This pattern
resembles present-day practices in the United States, where drunkenness
is condoned at weddings, birthdays, bachelor parties, other celebrations,
and holidays. Most societies condone drinking alcohol but not drunkenness, except on certain occasions.

Distillation was discovered in ancient China and refined in 8th-    7
century Arabia. Because the process is somewhat complex, the use of
distilled spirits did not become widespread until they were commercially
manufactured. In England, fermented beverages were by far the most
common form of alcohol consumption until the 18th century, when England encouraged the proliferation of distilleries to stimulate commerce.
Along with cheap gin came widespread consumption and widespread
drunkenness. However, intoxication from distilled spirits was confined
mostly to the lower and working classes; the rich drank wine, which was
imported and thus expensive.

In colonial America, drinking was much more prevalent than it is    8
today. Men, women, and children all drank, and it was considered acceptable for all to do so. This practice may not seem consistent with our
present-day image of the Puritans, but nevertheless the Puritans did not
object to drinking. Rather they considered alcohol one of God's gifts.
Indeed, in those years alcohol was often safer than unpurified water or
milk, so the Puritans had a legitimate reason to condone the consumption
of alcoholic beverages. What was not acceptable to them was drunken-

ness. They believed that alcohol should, like all things, be used in moderation. Therefore, the Puritans established severe prohibitions against drunkenness but not against drinking.

The 50 years following U.S. independence marked a transition in the  9
way early Americans thought about alcohol (Critchlow, 1986; Levine, 1980). An adamant and vocal minority came to consider liquor a "demon" and to totally abstain from its use. This attitude, however, was mostly limited to the upper and upper-middle classes. Later, abstention came to be an accepted doctrine of the middle class and of people who aspired to join the middle class. Intemperance in drinking alcohol thus became associated with the lower classes, and "respectable" people, especially women, were not expected to be heavy drinkers.

Temperance societies **proliferated** throughout the United States  10
during the mid-1800s. However, the term is a **misnomer**: The societies did not promote *temperance*, the moderate use of alcohol, but rather *prohibition*, or total abstinence from alcohol. These societies held that liquor weakened restraints; loosened desires and passions; caused a large percentage of crime, poverty, and broken homes; and was powerfully addicting, so much so that even an occasional drink would put one in danger. Figure 13.1 shows a dramatic decrease in per capita alcohol consumption in the United States after 1830, a decrease due directly to the spread of the temperance (prohibition) movement.

In response to the growing temperance movement, both the demo-  11
graphics and the location of drinking changed. Drinking became associated with the lower and working classes. Rather than being consumed in a family setting, alcohol became increasingly confined to the saloon. Popham (1978) drew a distinction between taverns and saloons. Taverns have a long history; at times they have been considered respectable family places and at other times more disreputable. Taverns often sold only fermented beverages and only rarely dispensed **distilled spirits**. They were often oriented toward serving travelers and were therefore ordinarily located in rural areas. Saloons, on the other hand, were distinctly urban, almost exclusively frequented by men, oriented toward serving liquor, and patronized largely by industrial workers. Portrayed by the temperance movement as the personification of evil and moral degeneracy, saloons served as a focus for growing Prohibitionist sentiment.

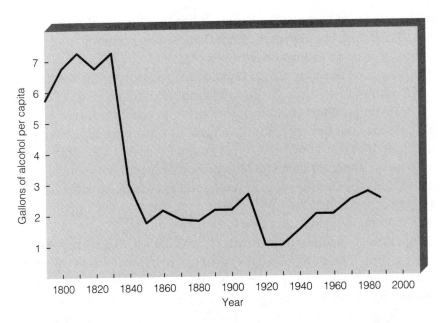

**Figure 13.1** U.S. consumption of all alcoholic beverages, 1790–1987, ages 15 and older

*Source*: From *The Alcoholic Republic: An American Tradition* (p. 9) by W. J. Rorabaugh, 1979, New York: Oxford University Press. Copyright 1979 by Oxford University Press. Reprinted by permission. Also from *Fifth Special Report to the U.S. Congress on Alcohol and Health* (DHHS Publication No. ADM 84-1291), p. 2, by National Institute on Alcohol Abuse and Alcoholism (NIAAA), 1983, Washington, DC: U.S. Government Printing Office; *Seventh Special Report to the U.S. Congress on Alcohol and Health* (DHHS Publication No. ADM 90-1656), by NIAAA, 1990, Washington, DC: U.S. Government Printing Office.

    Prohibitionists were finally victorious in 1920 with ratification of the 18th Amendment to the Constitution of the United States. This amendment outlawed the manufacture, sale, or transportation of alcoholic beverages and lowered per-capita consumption drastically (see Figure 13.1). 12

    However, the 21st Amendment repealed the 18th Amendment and ended Prohibition in 1934. Figure 13.1 shows that, after the repeal of 13

Prohibition, alcohol consumption again rose. Although the current per capita consumption of alcohol is considerably higher than during Prohibition, it is less than half the rate achieved during the first three decades of the 19th century.

COMPREHENSION CHECK

Answer the following questions using only your notes. Do not look back at the passage.

1. Why was the use of alcohol so universal even among ancient peoples?

   _____

2. Why do you think drunkenness has been widely accepted on special occasions?

   _____

3. When and why did the use of distilled beverages become widespread?

   _____

4. Why was drinking so widespread and accepted among the Puritans?

   _____

5. Why was intemperance or excessive drinking traditionally associated with the lower class?

   _____

6. What is the distinction between a tavern and a saloon?

   _____

7. What was Prohibition and how long did it last?

   _____

| Time Line: A Brief History of Drinking | | |
|---|---|---|
| Dates | Events | People |
| Prehistory | | |
| 8th century | | |
| 18th century | | |
| Colonial America | | |
| Early 1800s | | |
| Mid-1800s | | |
| 1920 | | |
| 1934 | | |

# Graphs

You will encounter many different types of charts and graphs in your college courses, the most common of which are line and bar graphs. These graphs usually depict data on two variables, one of which is plotted along a vertical line, the other along a horizontal line. Pertinent data are then charted at intervals along those lines. Information is plotted either by dots connected

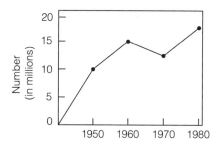 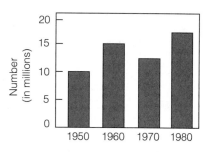

Hypothetical graduates from four-year colleges and universities

with a line (see the graph on the left, above) or with solid bars (see the graph on the right).

Look carefully at the line graph in Reading Selection One and read the description of the data depicted. Next, note the information that is plotted on the vertical line (the number of gallons of alcohol). Then note the information that is plotted on the horizontal line (years from 1790 to 1987). The bold line indicates where the statistical data from the horizontal and vertical lines would intersect. Although this figure is a line graph, solid bars could accomplish the same objective.

**EXERCISE 4**  *Reading graphs*

Answer the following questions, which relate to the graph in Reading Selection One. You may refer back to the reading if necessary.

1.  In what year were the most gallons of alcohol consumed per capita?

    How many gallons were consumed? _____

2.  In what year were the least gallons of alcohol consumed? _____

3.  During which years was consumption fairly steady? _____

4.  During what twenty-year period did the consumption of alcohol take

    the most drastic dip? _____

5.  Why do you think the consumption of alcohol never again soared to its

    previous level even after the repeal of Prohibition? _____

    _____

    _____

### *Prereading Activity*: Scanning for time signals

As you scan the selection "Smoking Tobacco," jot down the dates to create a time line similar to the one you created for Reading Selection One.

Now read the selection, filling in the time line as you did for Reading Selection One. At the end of the chapter, you will be given a short quiz on the material in the selection.

## Smoking Tobacco

### BY LINDA BRANNON AND JESS FEIST

Louise is a 49-year-old ex-smoker. She did not begin smoking until after    1
she graduated from high school and left home. Her father was a chain
smoker. Her mother, a nonsmoker, adamantly opposed all smoking.
Louise's smoking pattern closely followed that of an older brother and
sister, both of whom began smoking after leaving home and both of
whom eventually quit. At college, Louise began smoking with a group of
friends, and most of her smoking was confined to social situations.
Louise, however, was a very sociable woman and was soon smoking
more than a pack a day. At age 21, she married a nonsmoker, and eventually they had six children. During each of her pregnancies she severely
cut back on smoking, not for the health of the baby, but because it made
her intensely sick. After her youngest child started school, Louise began
a teaching career. Her job **precluded** smoking during class time, but this
restriction was not especially difficult for Louise. She smoked nearly

continuously in the teacher's lounge during her free period and was a heavy smoker in other social situations, such as visiting friends or playing bridge.

Louise never thought much about quitting until a friend tried to stop smoking on the recommendation of a doctor. To support her friend, Louise decided that she too would quit. Although the first year was difficult, she eventually lost her craving for cigarettes and has not smoked in 16 years. (Ironically, her friend's attempt was not successful, and she is currently smoking more than ever.) Louise now finds the smoking of others irritating and becomes mildly ill in the presence of secondhand smoke. 2

## A brief history of smoking

When Christopher Columbus and other early European explorers of the Western hemisphere arrived, they found that the Native Americans had a custom considered odd by European standards: They carried rolls of dried leaves, which they set afire, and then they "drank" the smoke. The leaves were, of course, tobacco. Those early European sailors tried smoking, liked it, and spread smoking and the cultivation of tobacco around the world. 3

Smoking was a habit that grew rapidly in popularity among Europe-ans, but it was not without its detractors. Elizabethan England adopted the use of tobacco, although Elizabeth I disapproved, as did her successor, James I. Another prominent Elizabethan, Sir Francis Bacon, spoke against tobacco and the hold it exerted over its users. Many objections to tobacco were of a similar nature, namely that those who could not afford it still spent their money on it because of the power it gained over its users. Because of its scarcity, tobacco was expensive: In London in 1610, it sold for an equal weight of silver. 4

In 1633 the Turkish Sultan Murad IV decreed the death penalty for smoking. From the early Romanoff empire in Russia to 17th-century Japan, the penalties for tobacco use were severe. Still the habit spread. Smoking during Mass became so prevalent among priests in the Spanish colonies that the Catholic Church forbade it. In 1642 and again in 1650, tobacco was the subject of two formal papal **bulls**, but in 1725 Pope Benedict XIII **annulled** all edicts against tobacco — he liked to take snuff. 5

The form in which tobacco has been used has varied with time and   6
country, but Brecher (1972) contended that no country that has learned
to use tobacco has ever given up the habit. Columbus found the Indians
smoking tobacco in pipes, as well as in the form of cigars. Cigarettes
(shredded tobacco rolled in paper) were not popular until the 20th century, although some appeared before the U.S. Civil War. However, cigarette use was not widespread at the time, because it was considered rather
**effeminate**. Ironically, cigarette smoking was not socially acceptable for
women either, and few women smoked during the first part of the 20th
century. It was, however, acceptable for women and men to use snuff, or
ground tobacco. Taking snuff became very popular in 18th-century England after the English fleet captured a cargo of high-quality Spanish
snuff. Taking **snuff** was widespread in all Europe as well as in America.
However, chewing shredded tobacco never became popular in Europe,
where it was considered a filthy American habit. Chewing tobacco became less popular in America after the U.S. Civil War.

The widespread adoption of cigarette smoking was aided in 1913 by   7
the development of the "blended" cigarette, a mixture of the air-cured
Burley and Turkish varieties of tobacco mixed with flue-cured Virginia
tobacco. This blend provided a cigarette with a pleasing flavor and aroma
that was also easy to inhale. Cigarette smoking became increasingly popular during World War I, and during the 1920s, the age of the "flapper,"
cigarette smoking started to gain popularity among women.

## COMPREHENSION CHECK

Reread the article underlining the dates and time words. Then complete the
time line on page 243.

# Objective Tests

Instructors often assess students' knowledge of facts through the use of
objective tests that contain multiple-choice, true-false, fill-in, and/or
matching questions.

| Time Line: Smoking Tobacco | | |
|---|---|---|
| Dates | Events | People |
| | | |
| | | |
| | | |
| | | |
| | | |
| | | |
| | | |

## Preparing for objective tests

The best way to prepare for an objective test is to create a fact sheet. If you have taken notes as described in this chapter, you have done half the work for yourself already.

### *Making a Fact Sheet*

1. Take a piece of paper and make a fold, approximately 2 inches from the left margin.

2. Read through your chapter notes. To the left of the fold, jot down the facts that you feel are important. Include all names, places, events, dates, terms, and so on.

3. To the right of the fold, write very brief phrases to explain each fact. Include only key words; do not use sentences.

4. Review your class notes, and compare them to your reading notes. Add any facts that might have been covered in class (but were not in the textbook) to your fact sheet.

### Studying the Fact Sheet

1. Read over the fact sheet two or three times, reciting the information aloud if possible.

2. Fold the paper so that only the facts are showing. Try to recall and recite the pertinent information about each fact without looking at the explanations. Check to see if you are correct. If so, go on to the next fact. If not, recite the answer two or three more times.

3. Go through the fact sheet again, placing a star next to the facts you are unable to recite.

4. Continue, repeating step 3 and crossing off the stars as you memorize each fact.

## Taking objective tests

The two major types of objective tests are multiple-choice and true-false. Your ability to do well on these kinds of tests depends first and foremost on how thoroughly you know the information. However, there are strategies you can learn to enhance your ability to make wise choices.

### Guessing Strategies

1. When two answers are similar because they have words that look alike or sound alike, one of them is often the *correct* answer.

2.  If one answer is more inclusive (covers more information), it is often the *correct* answer.

3.  When "all of the above" is included as an option, it is often the *correct* answer. However, if you are sure that one of the other options is incorrect, then "all of the above" cannot be the correct answer.

4.  Options that include "absolute determiners" such as *all, none, never,* and *always* tend to be *incorrect* answers.

### *Time Strategies*

1.  Proceed through the entire test answering the questions you are sure of first. Place a check mark next to the answers you are not sure of, and go back to them when you are finished.

2.  When you go back to the difficult questions, decide how much time you will spend on each question, leaving a few minutes to check over the entire test.

3.  Unless you will be penalized for incorrect answers, answer all the questions using the guessing techniques described above.

4.  Always read over the test to check for carelessness.

5.  Do not change your answers unless you remember information you had been unable to recall or you misunderstood the question. When you are not sure, go with your first instinct.

## CHAPTER APPLICATION 1

You will be given a multiple-choice test based on the material covered in this chapter. Study your fact sheets and commit the information to memory. When you take the exam use the time-strategy plan described here and apply as many of the guessing strategies as possible.

CHAPTER APPLICATION 2

This chapter has given you a few tips on how to prepare for and take objective tests. Although the emphasis has been on materials that involve time sequences, the strategies may be applied to almost all rhetorical structures. For this chapter application do the following:

1. Choose a course that involves the memorization of facts.

2. Pick a textbook chapter on which you will be tested in the near future and make a fact sheet of all the important information.

3. Study the fact sheet by reciting the information as necessary.

4. During the test use the time-strategy plan to ensure efficient use of your time and knowledge.

5. Use any or all of the guessing strategies as appropriate.

GOING BEYOND

While drugs seem to get the most media attention, alcohol abuse is still the most pervasive problem on college campuses. And although alcohol abuse may have been overlooked in the past, colleges today are taking action to curb the problem with a variety of programs.

## The Endless Binge

**BY JERRY ADLER WITH DEBRA ROSENBERG**

*Health: They stagger, they get sick, they get into fights and one-night stands. Who are they? The leaders of tomorrow.*

It is, approximately, the world's oldest social problem, with a **pedigree** 1 running from the drunken depravity of the medieval University of Paris through F. Scott Fitzgerald's debauched years at Princeton to . . . well, to the Bat Cave in Moorhead, Minn. This was an apartment near the campus

**Sobering Statistics**

About 16 percent of college students (male and female) are nondrinkers. The rest are drinking more than their share:

|  | Men | Women |
| --- | --- | --- |
| Drank on 10 or more occasions in the past 30 days | 24% | 13% |
| Usually binges when drinks | 43 | 38 |
| Drinks to get drunk | 44 | 35 |
| Was drunk three or more times in the past month | 28 | 19 |

of Concordia College, where last Halloween students chipped in for three kegs of beer, which they resold to more than 200 youths on an all-you-can-drink-for-$5 basis, until the Moorhead police broke up the party. Over the last two decades, public drunkenness has pretty much lost whatever **cachet** it once had in society at large, but not among students. A study published last week in the Journal of the American Medical Association examined "binge drinking" in college, defined as consuming five (for men) or four (for women) consecutive drinks. Of the large sample who were sober long enough to answer a questionnaire, 44 percent (50 percent of the men and 39 percent of the women) said they had binged at least once in the last two weeks. This was almost exactly the same percentage as a similar study found in 1980 — before, among numerous other social changes, the nationwide minimum drinking age was raised to 21.

Why should college students be so **impervious** to the lesson of the morning after? Efforts to discourage them from using drugs actually *did* work. The proportion of college students who smoked marijuana at least once in 30 days went from one in three in 1980 to one in seven last year; cocaine users dropped from 7 percent to 0.7 percent over the same period. This is just the opposite of what people expected a few decades ago; marijuana was supposed to make booze obsolete because it didn't make you throw up. Yet last Tuesday, even as he celebrated his 21st birthday at a Boston pub with his 10th drink of the night, Newbury College junior Justin Minerva was planning to cut classes and skip work in anticipation of his Wednesday-morning hangover. It was likely to be a doozy considering his taste in refreshments: tequila, beer and vodka in various combinations with Kahlua and Jägermeister. "They took me to three bars already and I'm still standing!" he boasted, although he wasn't sure for how long; his drinking buddy Scott MacDonald passed out on the streetcar tracks at the end of *his* 21st birthday party last year. "I should've been dead," MacDonald said. "I was still drunk at seven in the morning."

MacDonald, obviously, survived to drink again; not everyone is so  3 lucky. Studies have shown that two thirds of student suicides were legally drunk at the time, and 90 percent of fatal fraternity hazing accidents involve drinking. Others survive only to be murdered by their parents when they get their grades; one 1991 study found that students with D or F grade averages drink, on average, three times as much (10.6 drinks a week) as A students. Irresponsibility is not a side effect of drinking that can be eliminated through education; on the contrary, it is integral to alcohol's appeal for both men and women. "Joyce," a Stanford undergrad, plans her weekend drinking carefully, scanning bulletin boards early in the week for the best parties, or else heading to bars with friends. Then she gets so drunk she can barely make it back to her room, and goes to bed with people she admits she wouldn't look at twice if she were sober. This illustrates how the consequences of getting drunk have grown more serious. One student in five reports abandoning safe-sex practices when drunk.

Even if binge drinking is not statistically more prevalent than in the  4 past, it seems more open — spreading from, say, Prom Night to such traditionally high-minded occasions as the annual banquet of the *Yale Daily News*, which once enlisted the likes of Dwight Eisenhower as speakers. This year's guest speaker, the writer Christopher Buckley ("Thank You for Smoking"), was so revolted by his hosts' behavior that he denounced the whole affair in *The New York Times*. "Apparently the trend these days is to 'front-load,' that is, go to a party before the event and get so tanked that you will feel no pain later on," Buckley wrote. Responding, Editor in Chief Jeffrey Glasser admitted that "some people drank, and were a bit rowdy . . . but no News editor has ever been taken to the hospital after a banquet, and nobody fell unconscious at this year's event." Not everyone seems to remember it that way. "One or two people have passed out at the banquet every year for the last few years," says a former editor, Rebecca Goldsmith. "It's always less than five."

**Secondhand drinking**     Buckley was a victim of what is some-     5
times called "secondhand drinking," by analogy to secondhand smoke:
the negative effects on roommates, passersby and college property of
rampaging adolescent drunks. "We used to think that drinkers and smokers only harmed themselves," says Henry Wechsler of the Harvard School
of Public Health, one of the authors of last week's JAMA study. Drunks
make lousy roommates for anyone trying to work; the trend on many
campuses to begin partying on Thursday makes half the week unavailable for studying. Dormitory bathrooms are unspeakable.

This has given rise to the increasing popularity of "substance-free     6
dorms." "People are sick of dragging their friends home," says Cathy
Kodama, health-promotions manager at Berkeley, which established the
nonsmoking, nondrinking Freeborn Hall this year. In effect, colleges are
segregating drinkers, because they don't know how else to deal with
them. Increasing the drinking age evidently hasn't helped. Fake IDs are
tossed around like baseball cards on most campuses. Frederic Schroeder,
dean of students at the University of North Carolina's Chapel Hill campus,
believes that raising the drinking age has actually encouraged binge
drinking. A college cannot promote "moderation" in drinking if it's illegal
for most students to do it at all. "When you've got a six-pack that you're
not supposed to have in the first place," says Schroeder, "the logical thing
is to finish it."

There are no easy answers to the problem of college drinking. Some     7
of them — such as supplying Breathalyzers at parties — are actually counterproductive. "The students will compete to try to blow the top off," says
Daniel R. Herbst, health-awareness director at Washington University in
St. Louis. In one tragic but not unusual case, a University of Washington
sophomore named Jennifer Wen was walking home past a frat house one
evening in 1992 when a beer bottle came sailing out a window and hit
her in the face; the injury cost her the sight in one eye. The incident led
to a big crackdown in drinking on the Seattle campus, including a ban on
kegs and roving patrols to check on underage drinkers. Last week Wen,
now a senior, said she hasn't noticed much effect from the changes. "The
partying is the same, the attitudes are the same," she says. "Nothing's
really changed."

## JOURNAL WRITING

1.  Since the beginning of recorded history, people have used and abused alcoholic beverages, but from time to time societies have attempted to limit their use. Discuss the extent to which you feel the sale and use of alcohol should be controlled.

2.  In your opinion, what are the causes of binge drinking among college students? Do you think of this problem as a health problem? Refer to the examples in the article as well as ones from your personal experience in your discussion.

3.  The minimum drinking age has fluctuated quite a bit during the past ten years. What do you feel is an optimal age, and why?

4.  In recent years the dangers of smoking have been substantiated through extensive research. However, little consideration has been given to outlawing tobacco. Why do you think this is the case? What would you think of such a proposal?

5.  Many restaurants, buildings, and workplaces now either segregate or prohibit smokers. Airlines prohibit smoking on flights under a certain number of hours. What is your opinion on these policies?

## CHAPTER 9

# Cause and Effect

After studying Chapter 9 you should be able to:

- identify and understand cause-and-effect relationships in written prose
- map cause-and-effect relationships
- illustrate cause-and-effect relationships
- organize essay questions using direction words
- outline answers to essay questions

## CHAPTER CHECKLIST

Use the following checklist to help you plan for the text, readings, and activities in this chapter.

| Date Assigned | Date Completed | |
|---|---|---|
| _____ | _____ | Causal relationships |
| _____ | _____ | WARM-UP: Identifying effects from causes |
| _____ | _____ | Chain reactions and mapping |
| _____ | _____ | EXERCISE 1: Mapping a chain reaction |

### READING SELECTION ONE

| | | |
|---|---|---|
| _____ | _____ | *Prereading Activity*: Previewing for causal relationships |
| _____ | _____ | **"Earthly Belches Perturb the Weather"** |
| _____ | _____ | COMPREHENSION CHECK |
| _____ | _____ | COMPREHENSION EXERCISE: Outlining cause-and-effect relationships |

### READING SELECTION TWO

| | | |
|---|---|---|
| _____ | _____ | *Prereading Activity*: Mapping cause-and-effect relationships |
| _____ | _____ | **"The Villain in the Atmosphere"** |

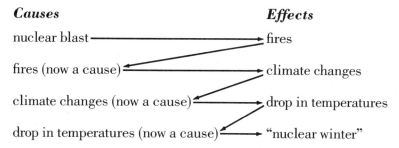

*Causes*                                        *Effects*

nuclear blast ————————————→ fires

fires (now a cause) ←————————→ climate changes

climate changes (now a cause) ←————→ drop in temperatures

drop in temperatures (now a cause) ←———→ "nuclear winter"

Again, the arrows depict the chain of causality among the various phenomena.

The use of arrows and other graphic devices to show connections among ideas, events, and so on is known as **mapping**. Mapping is an organizational strategy that helps you visualize the interrelationship of concepts and ideas. It can be used to describe main ideas and details, cause-and-effect relationships, and sequential orders. Mapping can be done in a variety of ways. The most common is to circle or box ideas and then to connect these ideas with lines and arrows.

**EXERCISE 1**   *Mapping a chain reaction*

For each of the following passages, circle any causal signal words. Then trace the cause-and-effect relationships in each chain reaction by filling in the blanks.

1.  An estimated 750 million people — one out of every six — do not have enough fertile land or money to grow their own food in rural areas or enough money to buy the food they need in cities. As a result, between 12 million and 20 million die prematurely each year from starvation, malnutrition, or normally nonfatal diseases such as diarrhea brought on by contaminated drinking water, which for people weakened by malnutrition becomes deadly.

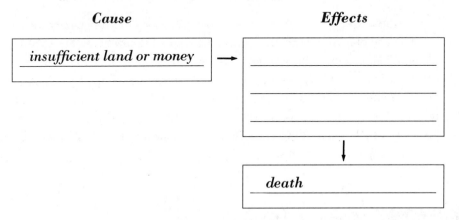

2.  Some people believe that if the present trends continue, the world will become more crowded and more polluted leading to greater political and economic instability and increasing the threat of nuclear war as the rich get richer and the poor get poorer.

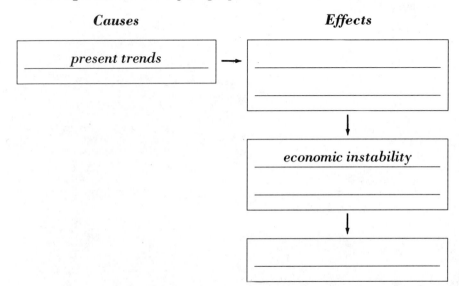

3.  Others believe that if present trends continue, economic growth and
    technological advances based on human ingenuity will produce a less
    crowded, less polluted world, in which most people will be healthier,
    will live longer, and will have greater material wealth.

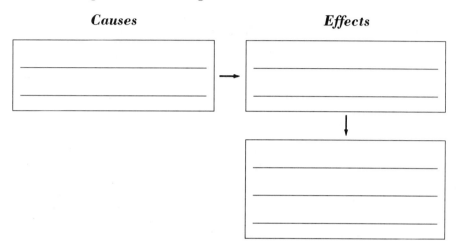

The passages you have just analyzed describe specific cause-and-effect
relationships. The next two paragraphs describe general cause-and-effect
relationships followed by specific examples that explain the relationship
more fully. Again, read the paragraphs and then map the causal relationships by filling in the blanks.

4. Concern is growing that human activities affect global climate patterns. For example, according to some scientists, increases in the average levels of carbon dioxide in the earth's atmosphere, due primarily to the burning of fossil fuels and land clearing, may trap increasing amounts of infrared radiation that otherwise would escape into space, thus raising the average temperature of the atmosphere.

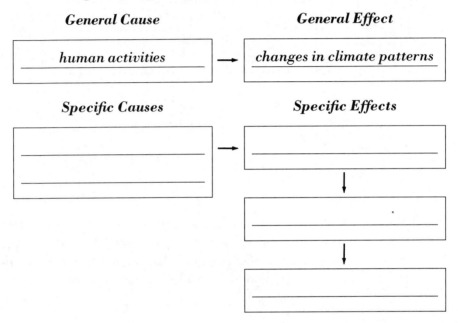

5.  Chemical pollution is a relatively new but growing threat to wildlife.
    Industrial wastes, acid deposition, and excess heat from electric power
    plants have wiped out some species of fish. . . . Slowly biodegradable
    pesticides, especially DDT and dieldrin, have magnified in food chains
    and have caused reproductive failure and egg shell thinning of impor-
    tant birds of prey such as the peregrine falcon . . . and the bald eagle.

*General Cause*                    *General Effect*

```
┌──────────────────┐        ┌──────────────────┐
│ _____ │   ───► │ _____ │
│                  │        │                  │
└──────────────────┘        └──────────────────┘
```

*Specific Causes*                 *Specific Effects*

```
┌──────────────────┐        ┌──────────────────┐
│ _____ │   ───► │ _____ │
│ _____ │        │                  │
│ _____ │        └──────────────────┘
│                  │
└──────────────────┘

┌──────────────────┐        ┌──────────────────┐
│ _____ │   ───► │ _____ │
│                  │        │                  │
└──────────────────┘        └──────────────────┘
                                      │
                                      ▼
                            ┌──────────────────┐
                            │ _____ │
                            │                  │
                            └──────────────────┘
```

### *Prereading Activity*: **Previewing for causal relationships**

Preview Reading Selection One by doing the following:

1.  Study the title. Think about the meaning of *belch*. What earthly things could belch?

2.  Read the first and last paragraphs.

3.  Skim for headings. There are two; notice that one contains a cause-and-effect signal word.

4.  Skim for names, numbers, and so on — anything that stands out from the rest of the print.

5.  Skim for cause-and-effect signal words. Underline them along with the clauses in which they are found.

This selection, taken from *U.S. News & World Report*, suggests that the pollution created by volcanic activity has an effect on the world's weather patterns. With this in mind, read the entire article and then answer the questions that follow.

## Earthly Belches Perturb the Weather

**FROM *U.S. NEWS & WORLD REPORT***

Although he had no proof, it was the ever curious Benjamin Franklin        1
who first made the connection. The Paris summer of 1783 had been
unusually cold, the sun shrouded by an almost constant fog, and Franklin — there as America's envoy to France — suggested that the Laki Volcano in Iceland might have something to do with it.

    The 50 or so volcanoes that erupt every year **spew** millions of tons of   2
dust, ash and gases into the atmosphere. By using satellites to track the
fate of this volcanic output and computer simulations that model global
climatic changes, scientists are now building the case that volcanoes are

indeed a significant — and consistently neglected — factor in establishing long-range weather patterns.

"It is not predictable yet, but we are not too far away," says Michael    3
Rampino, a professor of applied sciences at New York University.

The remote locations of many volcanoes and the lack of sophisticated    4
instruments to track volcanic clouds had in the past forced scientists to rely mostly on historical coincidence to infer a link between eruptions and weather. "We can look at volcanic records back to 1700, but it is hard to prove connections by statistics," says David Rind, a climate modeler at the Goddard Institute for Space Studies in New York.

Still, some of the connections seemed too strong to be mere chance.    5
Most dramatic was the so-called year without summer, 1816, when early frost wiped out corn and hay crops in New England and left England with average summer temperatures as much as 5 degrees below normal. It followed the eruption of a massive volcano, Mount Tambora in Indonesia, the year before. The unusual purplish sunsets that English artist Joseph Mallord William Turner captured on his easel at the time now are seen as strong confirmation that a dust cloud from the volcano in fact was responsible.

It has only been in the last few years that tools much more sophisti-    6
cated than an artist's palette and a thermometer have become available to probe the volcano-climate link. With the launch of satellites — such as SAGE in 1984 — that can directly measure particles and gases in the upper atmosphere, scientists now are able to track even minor eruptions. Ground observatories use a form of radar called lidar, which employs lasers instead of radio signals, to precisely measure the density of the clouds.

## Results differ

One important finding is that not all volcanoes are the same when it    7
comes to affecting the weather — not even volcanoes of the same explosive force. When Mount St. Helens erupted in 1980 with the force of a 10-megaton hydrogen bomb, it dumped dust throughout the Pacific Northwest but apparently left global weather patterns untouched. After the similar-sized eruption of El Chichón in Mexico in 1982, the amount of sunlight reaching some areas of the earth dropped by 2 percent while upper-atmosphere temperatures rose 7 degrees.

"Before, it was assumed that all you had to do was have a powerful    8
eruption to produce an effect," says Owen Toon, an associate fellow at
the National Aeronautics and Space Administration's Ames Research
Center in California. "Now we know it really wasn't the amount of rock
thrown up in the air that mattered."

What in fact matters most are the amount of sulfurous gas expelled    9
by a volcano and how high the gas rises in the atmosphere. Unlike dust
and ash, which make up the bulk of a volcano's output but which settle
out of the atmosphere quickly — usually within a few months — sulfur-
dioxide gas from a volcano can rise into the stable stratosphere 6 miles
above the earth. There, out of reach of the normal atmospheric-cleansing
processes such as rain, the gases are converted into sunlight-absorbing
sulfuric-acid clouds. The clouds eventually encircle the earth, and can
interfere with the normal pattern of sunlight reaching the surface for up
to two years.

Volcanoes vary considerably in the amount of sulfur they emit and in    10
the effectiveness with which they inject it into the stratosphere. Mount
St. Helens, for example, produced little sulfur and tended to blow out
sidewise, rather than straight up.

**Sifting out the answers**

Scientists suspect that eruptions near the equator cause the greatest    11
perturbation because any effect is more easily carried to both hemispheres. But how to translate these findings into hard predictions about
rain or temperature in coming seasons is tricky. "If a volcano goes off, it
is going to have an impact," says Stephen Schneider, a climatologist at
the National Center for Atmospheric Research in Boulder, Colo. The
problem is to distinguish that impact from nature's random, year-to-year
**variability** in weather.

"The general feeling is that at our current stage we can get a look at    12
how volcanoes affect the global climate over all but that regional assessments are much more uncertain," says Rind.

Schneider adds that in any case the fundamental question is "not    13
how volcanoes change the climate but how sensitive the climate is to
changes in [solar] energy," whatever the cause. Answering that question
would have far-reaching implications. It would, for example, help to
prove or disprove Carl Sagan's much debated nuclear-winter theory,

which suggests that the massive dust clouds kicked up in a major nuclear war could trigger a global ice age.

Still, a really big volcanic eruption may provide the best test. For all    14
of the new technology available to study volcanoes, though, nature hasn't been very cooperative. Recent major eruptions, such as El Chichón, were still less than one tenth the force of the 1815 Mount Tambora eruption. "We will get another big one one of these days," says Schneider. "And this time, we won't have to rely on Turner sunsets" to know what it's doing to the climate.

## COMPREHENSION CHECK

Complete the following items by filling in or circling the best answer.

1. What connection did Benjamin Franklin make in 1783?

    _____

    _____

2. When was the year without a summer? What was it like? Why does the author mention this fact?

    _____

    _____

3. What is the general cause-and-effect relationship described in this article?

    _____

    _____

4. State the main idea of the article by using your answer to item 3 to help you complete the following sentence:
    *Some scientists believe that*

    _____

    _____

5. What factors make it difficult to verify the connection between volcanic eruptions and weather patterns?

   _____

   _____

6. Using the context of the sentence to help you, write a synonym for the word *spew* in paragraph 2.

   _____

7. Using the context of the sentence to help you, write a synonym for the word *variability* in paragraph 11.

   _____

8. What important finding explains how and why the climate is actually affected by volcanic explosions? Explain.

   _____

   _____

   _____

9. Paraphrase Carl Sagan's nuclear winter theory.

   _____

   _____

   _____

10. From the article we can conclude that volcanic explosions are a threat to the continued existence of mankind.
    a. true
    b. false

**COMPREHENSION EXERCISE**   *Outlining cause-and-effect relationships*

Use the scrambled sentences below to complete the outline of the article "Earthly Belches Perturb the Weather."

I. *Volcanic eruptions may cause changes in weather.* _____

   A. _____

   B. _____

   C. *New tools for probing the volcano-climate link are available.*

      1. _____

      2. _____

II. _____

   A. *The Mount St. Helens eruption had little effect on the*

    *weather.*

   B. _____

   C. _____

      1. _____

      2. *Gas is converted into sunlight-absorbing sulfuric-acid*

       *clouds.*

      3. _____

      4. _____

III. *When, why, and how is the weather affected?* _____

   A. _____

      1. _____

B. *Regional assessments are still unclear.* _____

C. _____

   1. _____

D. _____

The amount of sulfurous gas and how high it rises seem to be the important factors.

The year without a summer, 1816, followed the eruption of Mount Tambora.

Every volcano affects the weather differently.

Ground radar, called lidar, measures the density of clouds.

The sunless summer of 1783 occurred after the eruption of the Laki Volcano.

El Chichón affected the amount of sunlight the earth received.

Volcanoes vary in the amount of sulfur they omit.

They can affect both hemispheres.

Gas rises into the stable stratosphere, 6 miles above the earth.

Clouds interfere with sunlight reaching the earth for up to two years.

Satellites such as SAGE now track volcanoes.

The question is, how sensitive is the climate to any change in energy?

Equatorial eruptions have the greatest impact on the weather.

We need a big eruption to test theories.

Carl Sagan's nuclear winter theory could be tested.

### *Prereading Activity*: **Mapping cause-and-effect relationships**

Read the following excerpt from Reading Selection Two, "The Villain in the Atmosphere," and then map the cause-and-effect relationships being described by filling in the blanks.

> Plants absorb carbon dioxide and convert it into their own tissues, which serve as the basic food supply for all of animal life (including human beings, of course). In the process, they liberate oxygen, which is also necessary for all animal life.

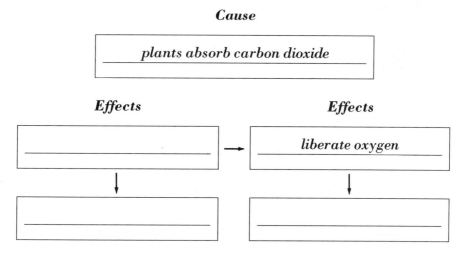

Reading Selection Two concerns the much publicized environmental problem of global warming. Isaac Asimov explains this scientific phenomenon in terms a layman can understand, and he appeals to us to do something about it. As you read the selection, watch for the various causal relationships described. When you finish the reading, you will be asked to chart the relationships on a conceptual map.

# The Villain in the Atmosphere

## BY ISAAC ASIMOV

The villain in the atmosphere is carbon dioxide.                                    1

It does not seem to be a villain. It is not very poisonous and it is   2
present in the atmosphere in so small a quantity that it does us no harm.
For every 1,000,000 cubic feet of air there are only 340 cubic feet of
carbon dioxide — only 0.034 percent.

What's more, that small quantity of carbon dioxide in the air is essen-   3
tial to life. Plants absorb carbon dioxide and convert it into their own
tissues, which serve as the basic food supply for all of animal life (including human beings, of course). In the process, they liberate oxygen, which
is also necessary for all animal life.

But here is what this apparently harmless and certainly essential gas   4
is doing to us:

The sea level is rising very slowly from year to year. The high tides   5
tend to be progressively higher, even in quiet weather, and storms batter
at breakwaters more and more effectively, erode the beaches more sav-
agely, batter houses farther inland.

In all likelihood, the sea level will continue to rise and do so at a   6
greater rate in the course of the next hundred years. This means that the
line separating ocean from land will retreat inland everywhere. It will do
so only slightly where high land abuts the ocean. In those places, however, where there are low-lying coastal areas (where a large fraction of
humanity lives) the water will advance steadily and **inexorably** and
people will have to retreat inland.

Virtually all of Long Island will become part of the shallow offshore   7
sea bottom, leaving only a line of small islands running east to west,
marking off what had been the island's highest points. Eventually the sea
will reach a maximum of two hundred feet above the present water level,
and will be splashing against the windows along the twentieth floors of
Manhattan's skyscrapers. Naturally the Manhattan streets will be deep
under water, as will the New Jersey shoreline and all of Delaware. Florida,
too, will be gone, as will much of the British Isles, the northwestern
European coast, the crowded Nile valley, and the low-lying areas of
China, India, and the Soviet Union.

It is not only that people will be forced to retreat by the millions and    8
that many cities will be drowned, but much of the most productive farming areas of the world will be lost. Although the change will not be
overnight, and though people will have time to leave and carry with them
such of their belongings as they can, there will not be room in the conti-
nental interiors for all of them. As the food supply **plummets** with the
ruin of farming areas, starvation will be rampant and the structure of
society may collapse under the unbearable pressures.

And all because of carbon dioxide. But how does that come about?    9
What is the connection?

It begins with sunlight, to which the various gases of the atmosphere    10
(including carbon dioxide) are **transparent**. Sunlight, striking the top
of the atmosphere, travels right through miles of it to reach the Earth's
surface, where it is absorbed. In this way, the Earth is warmed.

The Earth's surface doesn't get too hot, because at night the Earth's    11
heat radiates into space in the form of infrared radiation. As the Earth
gains heat by day and loses it by night, it maintains an overall temperature
balance to which Earthly life is well-adapted.

However, the atmosphere is not quite as transparent to infrared radia-    12
tion as it is to visible light. Carbon dioxide in particular tends to be opaque
to that radiation. Less heat is lost at night, for that reason, than would be
lost if carbon dioxide were not present in the atmosphere. Without the
small quantity of that gas present, the Earth would be distinctly cooler on
the whole, perhaps a bit uncomfortably cool.

This is called the "greenhouse effect" of carbon dioxide. It is so called    13
because the glass of greenhouses lets sunshine in but prevents the loss of
heat. For that reason it is warm inside a greenhouse on sunny days even
when the temperature is low.

We can be thankful that carbon dioxide is keeping us comfortably    14
warm, but the concentration of carbon dioxide in the atmosphere is going
up steadily and that is where the villainy comes in. In 1958, when the
carbon dioxide of the atmosphere first began to be measured carefully, it
made up only 0.0316 percent of the atmosphere. Each year since, the
concentration has crept upward and it now stands at 0.0340 percent. It is
estimated that by 2020 the concentration will be about 0.0660 percent,
or nearly twice what it is now.

This means that in the coming decades, Earth's average temperature 15
will go up slightly. Winters will grow a bit milder on the average and
summers a bit hotter. That may not seem frightening. Milder winters
don't seem bad, and as for hotter summers, we can just run our air-
conditioners a bit more.

But consider this: If winters in general grow milder, less snow will fall 16
during the cold season. If summers in general grow hotter, more snow
will melt during the warm season. That means that, little by little, the
snow line will move away from the equator and toward the poles. The
glaciers will retreat, the mountain tops will grow more bare, and the
polar ice caps will begin to melt.

That might be annoying to skiers and to other devotees of winter 17
sports, but would it necessarily bother the rest of us? After all, if the snow
line moves north, it might be possible to grow more food in Canada,
Scandinavia, the Soviet Union, and Patagonia.

Still, if the cold weather moves poleward, then so do the storm belts. 18
The desert regions that now exist in subtropical areas will greatly expand,
and fertile land gained in the north will be lost in the south. More may
be lost than gained.

It is the melting of the ice caps, though, that is the worst change. It is 19
this which demonstrates the **villainy** of carbon dioxide.

Something like 90 percent of the ice in the world is to be found in the 20
huge Antarctica ice cap, and another 8 percent is in the Greenland ice
cap. In both places the ice is piled miles high. If these ice caps begin to
melt, the water that forms won't stay in place. It will drip down into the
ocean and slowly the sea level will rise, with the results that I have already
described.

Even worse might be in store, for a rising temperature would manage 21
to release a little of the carbon dioxide that is tied up in vast quantities of
limestone that exist in the Earth's crust. It will also **liberate** some of the
carbon dioxide dissolved in the ocean. With still more carbon dioxide,
the temperature of the Earth will creep upward a little more and release
still more carbon dioxide.

All this is called the "runaway greenhouse effect," and it may even- 22
tually make Earth an uninhabitable planet.

But, as you can see, it is not carbon dioxide in itself that is the source 23
of the trouble; it is the fact that the carbon dioxide concentration in the

atmosphere is steadily rising and seems to be doomed to continue rising. Why is that?

To blame are two factors. First of all, in the last few centuries, first 24 coal, then oil and natural gas, have been burned for energy at a rapidly increasing rate. The carbon contained in these fuels, which has been safely buried underground for many millions of years, is now being burned to carbon dioxide and poured into the atmosphere at a rate of many tons per day.

Some of that additional carbon dioxide may be absorbed by the soil 25 or by the ocean, and some might be consumed by plant life, but the fact is that a considerable fraction of it remains in the atmosphere. It must, for the carbon dioxide content of the atmosphere is going up year by year.

To make matters worse, Earth's forests have been disappearing, slowly 26 at first, but in the last couple of centuries quite rapidly. Right now it is disappearing at the rate of sixty-four acres per minute.

Whatever replaces the forest — grasslands or farms or scrub — pro- 27 duces plants that do not consume carbon dioxide at a rate equal to that of forest. Thus, not only is more carbon dioxide being added to the atmosphere through the burning of fuel, but as the forests disappear, less carbon dioxide is being subtracted from the atmosphere by plants.

But this gives us a new perspective on the matter. The carbon dioxide 28 is not rising by itself. It is people who are burning the coal, oil, and gas, because of their need for energy. It is people who are cutting down the forests, because of their need for farmland. And the two are connected, for the burning of coal and oil is producing acid rain which helps destroy the forests. It is *people*, then, who are the villains.

What is to be done? 29

First, we must save our forests, and even replant them. From forests, 30 properly conserved, we get wood, chemicals, soil retention, ecological health — and a slowdown of carbon dioxide increase.

Second, we must have new sources of fuel. There are, after all, fuels 31 that do not involve the production of carbon dioxide. Nuclear fission is one of them, and if that is deemed too dangerous for other reasons, there is the forthcoming nuclear fusion, which may be safer. There is also the energy of waves, tides, wind, and the Earth's interior heat. Most of all, there is the direct use of solar energy.

All of this will take time, work, and money, to be sure, but all that  32
time, work, and money will be invested in order to save our civilization
and our planet itself.

After all, humanity seems to be willing to spend *more* time, work, and  33
money in order to support competing military machines that can only
destroy us all. Should we begrudge *less* time, work, and money in order
to save us all?

## COMPREHENSION CHECK

Complete the following items by circling or filling in the best answer.

1. The topic of this selection is:
   a. the greenhouse effect
   b. carbon dioxide
   c. the environment

2. The main idea of the selection is:
   a. A slow warming of the Earth will eventually cause the major bodies
      of water to rise, thus reducing the land masses and potential food
      sources.
   b. Carbon dioxide concentration in the atmosphere is steadily rising
      and will continue to rise if something isn't done.
   c. Global warming, caused by an increase of carbon dioxide in the
      atmosphere, could be disastrous to human life if we do not take steps
      to stop it.

3. The Earth maintains an overall temperature balance because:
   a. carbon dioxide allows the heat to escape at night
   b. Earth's heat radiates into space at night
   c. the opaque quality of carbon dioxide prevents too much heat from
      escaping into the atmosphere at night

4. It is warm inside a greenhouse because the glass:
   a. absorbs heat
   b. radiates heat
   c. allows sunlight in and holds heat in

5. Using the context of the sentence to help you, give a synonym for the word *plummets* in paragraph 8. _____

6. Using the context of the sentence to help you, give a synonym for the word *transparent* in paragraph 10. _____

7. Briefly explain what is meant by the "runaway greenhouse effect." ____

   _____

   _____

   _____

8. Briefly explain why the sea level is steadily rising. _____

   _____

   _____

   _____

9. What are the two possible effects of the rising sea level?

   a. _____

   b. _____

10. From this selection we can conclude that life on Earth will eventually cease to exist.
    a. true
    b. false

COMPREHENSION EXERCISE   *Mapping cause-and-effect relationships*

Use your answers to the Comprehension Check to help you complete the conceptual map of the selection "The Villain in the Atmosphere" on page 277.

READING SELECTION THREE

### *Prereading Activity*: **Previewing for and mapping causal relationships**

Preview Reading Selection Two by reading the title, the *first* paragraph, and the cartoon (the cartoon that originally accompanied this article appears at the beginning of this chapter, on page 254). When you finish, on a separate piece of paper make a map of the cause-and-effect relationship described in the first paragraph.

Now read the entire article to discover the proof on which the theory described in paragraph 1 is based. Then complete the Comprehension Check that follows.

## Where Have All the Dinos Gone?

**FROM *U.S. NEWS & WORLD REPORT***

Of all the mysteries of the dinosaurs, none has generated more specula-   1
tion than why the beasts vanished some 65 million years ago. Increasingly, the evidence points to an explanation that's literally out of this world: A giant meteor or comet that crashed into the earth, blasting huge clouds of debris aloft. With sunlight choked off for months, plant life would have dwindled, robbing the dinosaurs of their chief food supply. Small omnivorous mammals could have gotten by with scavenging.

# Conceptual Map: Global Warming

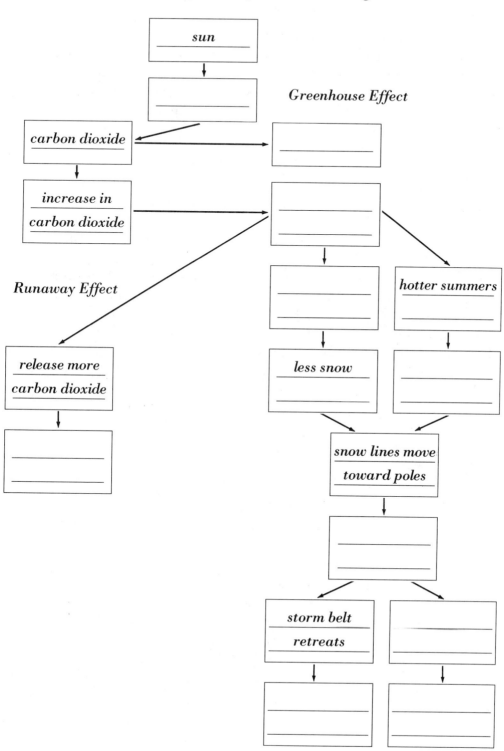

The impact theory was suggested seven years ago by physicist Luis  2
Alvarez of Lawrence Berkeley Laboratory, who found high concentrations of the element iridium in clay throughout the world, deposited just
when the dinosaurs vanished. Iridium is rare on earth but is richly concentrated in comets and meteors. That suggested an impact occurred, and
that its force was enough to eject a dust cloud that settled over the globe.

Now researchers at the U.S. Geological Survey in Denver have bol-  3
stered Alvarez's theory. Bruce Bohor and co-workers examined the crys-
tal structure of quartz particles from the similar clay deposits at seven
sites. In every instance, the quartz showed signs of being struck by an
enormous shock wave. The only other places such shocked quartz is
found are known meteor-impact craters and underground nuclear-test
sites.

Volcanic eruptions also give off high concentrations of iridium, and  4
had been suggested as an alternative explanation for Alvarez's discoveries.
But volcanoes pack too little punch to shock quartz grains. A meteor 6
miles across, on the other hand, striking the earth at 45,000 miles per
hour, would release as much energy as several billion atomic bombs. The
resulting prehistoric nuclear winter could have sent the dinosaur to
oblivion.

## COMPREHENSION CHECK

Complete the following items by filling in or circling the best answer.

1. What is Alvarez's theory called? _____

2. State the connection on which he based his theory. (*Note:* This is
   tricky, because he gives the effect *first.*) Map your answer by filling in
   the blanks.

| _____ | → | _____ |
|----------------|---|-----------------|

3. Fill in the following blanks to explain how researchers have bolstered the impact theory.

| | |
|---|---|
| _____ | → |

4. What other explanation has been given for the concentration of iridium?

   _____

5. The topic of this selection is:
   a. dinosaurs
   b. the impact theory
   c. iridium deposits
   d. a giant meteor

6. State the main idea of this selection by filling in the blanks in the following sentence:

   Alvarez's theory that a _____ _____ ultimately caused the extinction of the dinosaurs is based on the discovery that _____ of _____ were deposited throughout the world at about the same time.

7. Using the context of paragraph 1 to help you, define *omnivorous*.

   _____

8. Using the context of paragraph 2 to help you, define *eject*.

   _____

9. What do you think the main idea of the cartoon is?

   _____

   _____

10. How does Alvarez's impact theory relate to Carl Sagan's nuclear winter theory?

_____

_____

# Essay Exams

Whereas certain of the rhetorical structures — such as chronologies and narratives — are more likely to be closely identified with objective tests, causal relationships are likely to become more important in essay exams. Preparing for essay exams is more complicated than preparing for objective tests because merely knowing the facts does not necessarily equip you to answer an essay question. When studying for an essay exam, you must first assess the relative importance of the *concepts* presented by both the instructor and the textbook. Then you need to study the specific details that *support* those concepts. Studying for an essay exam thus involves selection, organization, and preparation.

## Selection

A good place to start is with your class notes. Begin by comparing major concepts, or ideas, covered by the instructor with those emphasized in the text. All topics that the instructor used as the focus of a lecture or class discussion should be considered possible test material. You can determine which concepts the text emphasized by rereading the introductory material at the beginning of each chapter and the summary at the end, and by noting the major headings and subheadings. In addition, consider the discussion or review questions at the end of the chapter and note which ones the instructor also covered. Draw your potential topics from the material that received the most coverage from both the instructor and the text, unless the instructor informs you that the material will come from only one source.

## Organization

The next step is to create possible exam questions. Essay questions usually contain specific "direction" words that indicate how many parts the question has and how the answer should be organized — that is, the *rhetorical structure*. Consider the following sample essay question, in which the direction words are underlined.

> Explain how photochemical smog occurs and what might be done to prevent it.

In this example "explain how . . . occurs" asks you to show *cause and effect*, and "what might . . . prevent" suggests a *problem-and-solution* structure.

When studying for an essay exam, you need to create questions that use direction words and then organize your answers based on the particular structure the direction words dictate.

---

**EXERCISE 2**  *Direction words and rhetorical structures*

Following is a list of possible rhetorical structures by which essay questions may be organized. It is followed by ten essay questions, in which some of the common direction words are underlined. For each question write the structure(s) by which you might organize the question. Remember that when the essay question contains a number of parts, it may be necessary to use more than one structure.

| | |
|---|---|
| definitions | sequence or chronological order |
| lists | cause and effect |
| examples | comparison and contrast (Chapter 10) |
| problem and solution | evaluation or justification (Chapter 11) |

1. Trace the progress of the population control projects in China and India.

2. Identify three environmental pollutants, and give examples of their effects on plant life.

   _____

3. Define ecosystems, list the major types, and describe the major environmental threat to each.

   _____

4. List the major types of resources, and explain how they are in danger of being depleted.

   _____

5. Evaluate the advantages and disadvantages of using solar energy for heating.

   _____

6. Relate the major effects of air pollution on human health.

   _____

7. Trace the progress of the EPA in establishing antipollution regulations in the United States.

   _____

8. Describe the major types of pesticides, and evaluate the advantages and disadvantages of using them.

   _____

9. Compare population growth in the United States during the past 100 years with that of India, and illustrate your comparison graphically.

   _____

10. Explain the reasons endangered species become endangered.

   _____

**EXERCISE 3**  *Direction words*

Exactly what do the direction words direct you to do? Following is a list of direction words. See if you can match the words to the directions they represent by placing the letter for each definition in the appropriate blank.

_____    1. trace         a. discuss similarities and differences

_____    2. identify      b. discuss the good and bad features

_____    3. define        c. discuss points in chronological order

_____    4. describe      d. draw or picture or diagram and label parts

_____    5. relate        e. discuss reasons

_____    6. list          f. name and describe

_____    7. compare       g. discuss who, what, when, where, how

_____    8. explain       h. explain the meaning

_____    9. evaluate      i. number facts 1, 2, 3

_____  10. illustrate     j. show the connection between

**EXERCISE 4**  *Creating essay questions*

Create two essay questions for each of the reading selections in this chapter. The first question has been done for you to serve as a model.

"Earthly Belches Perturb the Weather"

1. *Explain how volcanic eruptions affect the environment.* _____

2. _____

"Hard Facts About Nuclear Winter"

3. _____

4. _____

"Where Have All the Dinos Gone?"

5. _____

6. _____

## Preparation

To prepare answers for your questions, you need to locate the important concepts in the text by using the headings and subheadings as guides. Once you have selected the concepts and created your questions, your next step is to organize an outline of the supporting details using facts found under the specific subheadings. The following sample essay answer outline, which is built around the headings from a text chapter on endangered species, demonstrates this technique.

### *Question*

Explain why endangered species are in danger of becoming extinct.

### *Answer outline*

*Introduction*    Increasing numbers of plant and animal species are becoming endangered for the following reasons. (You might include statistics on numbers of extinct and/or endangered species.)

*Body of essay*

**A.** Habitat Disturbance or Loss
(list the details that explain the cause-and-effect relationship between habitat loss and extinction)

**B.** Commercial Hunting
(list pertinent details)

**C.** Predator and Pest Control
(list pertinent details)

**D.** Medical Research and Zoos
(list pertinent details)

**E.** Pollution
(list pertinent details)

    **F.** Alien Species
       (list pertinent details)

    *Conclusion*   (Summarize the characteristics of extinction-prone species.)

## CHAPTER APPLICATION

Choose a course in which you are usually given essay exams, and work with a classmate to prepare materials for a future exam by doing the following:

1. Each of you create two essay questions either from class notes or from the textbook.

2. Write an answer outline for each question using main headings to list key points and subheadings to locate supporting facts.

3. Share your questions and answers so that both of you have four questions with answer outlines.

4. After the exam discuss the usefulness of this procedure.

## GOING BEYOND

When we burn gas, oil, or coal to produce electricity or to move vehicles, we do so at the expense of clean air. Although many alternative sources of power exist, until recently they have been considered too impractical, inefficient, or expensive for mass use.

    "Running Cars on Plain $H_2O$" describes ways in which scientists are perfecting the use of chemistry rather than fuel combustion to power everything from cars to buses to office buildings.

# Running Cars on Plain H$_2$O

## BY SHARON BEGLEY WITH MARY HAGER

*Fuel cells produce energy without pollution. They'll even become affordable.*

The amazing part isn't that the bus shuttling passengers between terminals at Los Angeles International Airport is powered by what amounts to a chemical perpetual-motion machine: it runs on a fuel cell, a sort of battery that never needs recharging. Nor is it that the 553-room Hyatt Regency in Irvine, Calif., gets electricity from a fuel cell, too, which is not only quiet enough to sit beside the tennis court but doesn't emit as much as a molecule of smog-making pollution. Nor is the amazing thing that 50 more fuel cells are or soon will be churning out electricity at places like California's Folsom prison, a computer center in New Jersey, the Plaza hotel in Osaka, Kaiser Permanente hospitals and Kraft Foods in Buena Park, Calif. Fuel cells are indeed "a remarkable technology," says consultant Curtis Moore, coauthor of the recent book on environmentally sound technology called "Green Gold." "But the most remarkable thing is, nobody knows about them."    1

That will change. "The demand for clean energy [for transportation as well as energy] will drive the technology," says David Ramm, CEO of International Fuel Cell (IFC). Burning oil, gas or coal produces electricity; burning gasoline moves vehicles. But combustion sends pollution out the tailpipe or up the smokestack. Fuel cells, in contrast, produce electricity not by combustion but by chemistry. They combine hydrogen (typically, as a gas or from methanol or natural gas) with oxygen from the air to produce electricity, water . . . and nothing else (diagram). They emit essentially no pollution. They date from 1839, when a British lawyer-cum-inventor, Sir William Grove, came up with the principle, but they remained only lab curiosities until NASA put them aboard the Gemini and Apollo capsules to provide electricity and potable water. Now they're coming down to Earth:    2

- Vehicles: California and some Eastern states require that an increasing percentage of cars sold, starting in 1998, produce no tailpipe emissions. Burning *anything*—gasoline, methanol, natural gas or other "alternative fuel"—produces some emissions. The only way to get to zero is with electricity. Although "electric" has    3

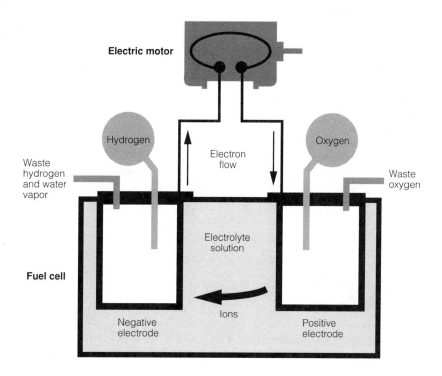

become synonymous with "battery powered," a fuel cell would give a car more zip and power, could operate a heavier vehicle (like a truck or bus) and would never need recharging. It could refuel at a landfill (garbage dumps emit methane, a rich source of hydrogen) or with a canister of natural gas, also a hydrogen source. Fuel cells make possible the dream of running a car on water: separate water into $H_2$ and O and, presto — car fuel. A bus made by Ballard Power Systems, with a 500-amp, 57-volt fuel cell by H Power — a New Jersey-based fuel-cell manufacturer — started taking passengers around LAX this month. Daimler-Benz already has a prototype fuel-cell Mercedes. The biggest hurdle: reducing the cost from $2,000 per kilowatt to $50. But Alan Lloyd of the Southern California Air Pollution Control District thinks that will come: "The question is not if, but when."

■ Electricity: In California, ten 200-kilowatt fuel cells from IFC are   4 providing power to hotels, hospitals and offices. And there's no reason fuel cells must be confined to single-building uses. The

Tokyo Electric Power Co., the largest private power company in the world, installed an 11-*mega*watt unit in 1990. Energy Research Corp. is constructing a $40 million fuel-cell power plant in Santa Clara, Calif.; by next summer, it should be providing two megawatts to the city. Fuel cells have to get cheaper if they're going to displace traditional sources of energy. They now generate a kilowatt for about $3,000; IFC's Ramm predicts that within four years the price will drop to $1,500 (five cents a kilowatt-hour). That would make fuel cells competitive with electricity from oil, coal or gas. And then fuel cells would be even more like a perpetual-motion machine: all the electricity you want without a speck of pollution.

## JOURNAL WRITING

1. Comment on the statement, "The history of life is enormously more quirky than we imagined." In your answer, identify at least three factors that could alter the balance of nature, and explain their effects.

2. For many years scientists have hypothesized about the relationship between volcanic eruptions and the weather. Explain the problems in researching this question and describe what has been learned.

3. Explain the term "runaway greenhouse effect." Do you think this "effect" is as serious as Isaac Asimov suggests? Evaluate some of the possible solutions. Specifically, how effective do you think the solutions such as those described in the article "Running Cars on Plain $H_2O$" might be?

4. We can do many things to help maintain the balance of life on Earth. For example, many people recycle certain materials or campaign for clean air, water, and so on. Describe what you do, or could do, to assure an inhabitable Earth for future generations.

5. When we review the history of the Earth, it is apparent that species and civilizations have come and gone. Describe what the Earth might be like in terms of ecology by the year 3000.

## CHAPTER 10

# Comparison and Contrast

After studying Chapter 10 you should be able to:

- use comparison and contrast to make decisions
- identify and analyze readings organized by comparison and contrast
- recognize different methods of comparison and contrast
- chart details in a comparison-and-contrast selection
- organize a comparison-and-contrast essay

## CHAPTER CHECKLIST

Use the following checklist to help you plan for the text, readings, and activities in this chapter.

*Date* *Date*
*Assigned* *Completed*

_____  _____  Comparing and contrasting

_____  _____  WARM-UP: Charting similarities and differences to make decisions

### READING SELECTION ONE

_____  _____  *Prereading Activity*: Previewing for comparison and contrast

_____  _____  **"Private Versus Public Goods"**

_____  _____  COMPREHENSION CHECK

_____  _____  COMPREHENSION EXERCISE: Taking comparison-and-contrast notes

_____  _____  Two methods of organizing comparison and contrast

### READING SELECTION TWO

_____  _____  *Prereading Activity*: Previewing for the main idea

_____  _____  **"The Isms: Socialism, Communism, Capitalism"**

_____  _____  COMPREHENSION CHECK

_____  _____  COMPREHENSION EXERCISE: Taking comparison-and-contrast notes

In Chapter 10 you will learn to use the organizational structure of comparison and contrast (1) to organize information while reading and taking notes and (2) to facilitate and improve the decision-making process.

**WARM-UP**  *Charting similarities and differences to make decisions*

There are many ways to chart similarities and differences. One common method involves using three or four columns. The first column lists the categories or features being compared and contrasted, such as size, price, color, value, form, and location. The remaining columns list the specific features of each of the items being compared or contrasted.

With this chart structure in mind, pretend you are looking for an apartment for yourself and two friends, and do the following (or compare cars or some other item of your choice):

1.  Using a newspaper, locate three apartments you might like to rent.

2.  Fill in the first column of Apartment Rating Chart I by listing the features you need to consider (cost, condition, location, number of rooms, and so on).

| **Apartment Rating Chart I** | | | | | |
|---|---|---|---|---|---|
| | | | | Rating | | |
| Features | Apartment 1 | Apartment 2 | Apartment 3 | Apt. 1 | Apt. 2 | Apt. 3 |
| | | | | | | |
| | | | | | | |
| | | | | | | |
| | | | | | | |
| | | | | | | |
| | | | | | | |
| | | | | | | |
| | | | | | | |
| | | | Total | | | |

3.  List the characteristics of each apartment in the second, third, and fourth columns.

4.  Now rate each description 1, 2, or 3, depending on your preference for that feature. For example, suppose the first feature is cost. Apartment 1 is $500, apartment 2 is $450, and apartment 3 is $600. Therefore you rate apartment 2 a "1" (your first choice), apartment 1 a "2" (your second choice), and apartment 3 a "3" (your last choice). Do the same for the rest of the features.

5.  Add up the ratings for each apartment. The apartment with the lowest total (the most 1's and 2's) would be your first choice. (*Note*: Because this process assumes that characteristics are of equal value, however, you also need to consider which characteristics are most important to you.)

Another way you might compare the three apartments is to list advantages and disadvantages of each choice. Using the features in the chart you just completed, fill in Apartment Rating Chart II.

| Apartment Rating Chart II | | | |
|---|---|---|---|
|  | *Apartment 1* | *Apartment 2* | *Apartment 3* |
| Advantages |  |  |  |
|  |  |  |  |
|  |  |  |  |
|  |  |  |  |
| Disadvantages |  |  |  |
|  |  |  |  |
|  |  |  |  |
|  |  |  |  |

Still another way to chart similarities and differences is to make a chart like Apartment Rating Chart III. This method might be used when you are comparing and contrasting only two items. To complete this chart, do the following:

1. Look at Apartment Rating Chart II and narrow your choice to two apartments.

2. Place all the "like" characteristics in the middle column.

3. Place the "unlike" characteristics under the appropriate apartment. For example, if both had four rooms, you would write "four rooms" in the middle column. If one had a garage or a porch, you would write "garage" or "porch" under that apartment. If both had modern kitchens but only one had a dishwasher, you would write "modern kitchen" in the middle column and "dishwasher" under the appropriate apartment.

4. Compare the entries for the two apartments. Clearly, the one with the most features would be the more desirable apartment.

| Apartment Rating Chart III | | |
|---|---|---|
| *Apartment 1* | *Both Apartments* | *Apartment 2* |
| | | |
| | | |
| | | |
| | | |
| | | |
| | | |
| | | |
| | | |

*Prereading Activity*: **Previewing for comparison and contrast**

Preview Reading Selection One by reading the title, the first paragraph, and the first sentence of each paragraph. Scan for and underline the comparison-and-contrast signal words. When you finish, write a sentence explaining what you think the selection is about.

_____

_____

The following comparison-and-contrast selection taken from an introductory economics text is a good example of how authors combine rhetorical structures in textbooks. As you read, notice that although the selection focuses on contrasting two things, the author also uses two other structures that you have studied in this text. When you have finished, complete the Comprehension Check and the Comprehension Exercise.

## Private Versus Public Goods

**BY PHILIP C. STARR**

Just what is it that causes a market-price system to produce a good or    1
service or to neglect it? The answer, as you might guess, has to do with whether or not there is any profit in producing and selling the good or service.

   Economists will argue that if a good is a private good the market-    2
price system will provide it. A **private good** is a good that is produced by a seller and sold to a buyer with no one else involved. Virtually everything you buy in a store, from tubes of toothpaste to cassette tapes, are private goods. Private goods have two noteworthy attributes: (1) The product is divisible: it can be sold unit by unit to buyers; and (2) people who cannot afford to buy it are excluded from the transaction. . . .

On the other hand, **public goods** are neither divisible nor can the ₃ purchase of them include some people and exclude others. Economists often use a lighthouse as an example of a public good. There is no way the light from the lighthouse can be divided up and sold unit by unit to individual buyers. And there is no way ships passing by the light can be excluded from seeing it. Who would ever want to pay for seeing the light when everyone around could see it whether they had paid or not?

If, therefore, the good is indivisible and there is no price that will ₄ exclude nonpayers who want to use the light from using it, there is an absence of any possible profit in the enterprise that might motivate entrepreneurs to produce it. If groups of people such as ship owners want a lighthouse, they will have to persuade their local, state, or federal government (by voting) to provide it. The government will then tax ship owners (and probably others) to provide the lighthouse. . . .

What are some public goods? National defense is one. Although ₅ many people may disagree with military strategies, the maintenance of an armed force must be presumed to be a public good. There is no way the defense provided by an army can be said to give you any more defense than it gives someone else. The good is indivisible; none are excluded.

## COMPREHENSION CHECK

Complete the following items by filling in the blank or circling the correct answer.

1. Paragraph 2 is organized by definition, example, and simple listing. What textual signals indicate each of these structures?

   a. definition _____

   b. example _____

   c. simple listing _____

2. Paragraph 3 is organized by:
   a. sequence
   b. definition and example
   c. comparison and contrast

3. The main structure of the selection is:
   a. sequence
   b. definition and example
   c. listing
   d. comparison and contrast

4. The main idea of the selection is:
   a. Public goods are different from private goods.
   b. A public good will not be produced by the market-price system because it does not render a profit.
   c. Private goods will be sustained by the market-price system because they can be sold unit by unit.

5. In your own words explain the difference between a "divisible" and an "indivisible" good.

   _____

   _____

6. A lighthouse is an example of:
   a. a divisible good
   b. an indivisible good

7. Define the word *good* as it is used in this selection.

   _____

   _____

8. Define the word *service* as it is used in this selection.

   _____

   _____

9. Who pays for public goods? _____

10. Give examples of a public good and a private good not mentioned in the selection.

    a. public good _____

    b. private good _____

**COMPREHENSION EXERCISE**    *Taking comparison-and-contrast notes*

Complete the following chart using the information given in Reading Selection One.

|  | *A Private Good* | *A Public Good* |
|---|---|---|
| Who provides it? |  |  |
| Who uses it? |  |  |
| How can it be sold? |  |  |

Now, for the two examples you gave as answers to item 10 in the Comprehension Check, answer the questions on the following chart.

|  | *Good 1* _____ | *Good 2* _____ |
|---|---|---|
| Private or public? |  |  |
| Who provides it? |  |  |
| Who uses it? |  |  |
| How can it be sold? |  |  |

# Two Methods of Organizing Comparison and Contrast

If you were to outline the first three paragraphs of Reading Selection One, "Private Versus Public Goods," it would look something like this:

A. Produce or neglect?

B. Private good

   1. divisible

   2. exclusive

C. Public good

   1. indivisible

   2. inclusive

As the outline shows, the author uses two paragraphs to make the comparison: One paragraph describes private goods, the other public goods. Note that with this method of making a comparison (we'll call it method A), each subject is discussed separately. Method A often involves two paragraphs, as in "Private Versus Public Goods," but it may also be written using one long paragraph. Method A begins with a statement about one of the subjects, describes details pertaining to that subject, and then, using a comparison-and-contrast word, introduces the second subject. It then goes on to describe details pertaining to the second subject.

Another method of making a comparison (method B) involves integrating the two subjects within a single paragraph. This method begins with a topic sentence that describes both subjects and then uses transitional words as it relates the details of both subjects either within single sentences or in a series of sentences. If the selection "Private Versus Public Goods" had been organized by method B, the outline might have looked something like this:

A. Produce or neglect?

B. Private and public goods

   1. divisible and indivisible

   2. exclusive and inclusive

In actual practice writers generally will mix these methods, especially in longer selections.

### *Prereading Activity*: **Previewing for the main idea**

Preview Reading Selection Two by reading the title, the introductory paragraph, and the two headings. Then write one sentence predicting the main idea.

_____

_____

Throughout history economic systems have fallen into three broad categories depending on the method they employ to answer three key questions about goods and services: What? How? For whom? The three categories are traditional systems, command/planning systems, and market-price systems. Societies with ***traditional* systems** find the answers to the three questions by copying the decisions made by previous generations. The best examples of traditional systems are seen in tribal communities. In the ***command/planning* systems** the three questions typically are answered by the central government. ***Market-price* systems** are based on the bargaining that occurs between buyers and sellers. Reading Selection Two, excerpted from an economics text, describes the basic economic systems that have emerged out of these categories in recent history.

## The Isms: Socialism, Communism, Capitalism

**BY PHILIP C. STARR**

The division of societies into traditional, command/planning, and market-price economic systems spans the entire course of history, but in the last century the world has become divided into two great economic and political camps representing socialism and capitalism. (In this discussion we are going to overlook the World War II versions of Nazism and fascism; these systems were capitalistic but were under the control of dictators Adolf Hitler and Benito Mussolini.)   1

As you read this discussion, you will find that the distinction between  2
socialism and capitalism often becomes blurred, particularly when we
try to pin a label on any one country. Nevertheless, there are important
differences. In each case it is helpful to ask two questions: (1) Who owns
the factories? (2) Who decides the answers to the three questions?

Under **socialism**, the government owns and operates the major in-  3
dustries of the country. Consequently, the government also decides — in
those major industries — the answers to the three questions. There are
almost as many **variants** of socialism as there are countries. In France
and Italy, many of the major industries are nationalized. In the Soviet
Union and the People's Republic of China they *all* are. In the United
States, there are municipally owned airports and utilities and federally
owned projects like the Tennessee Valley Authority and Hoover Dam.
Sweden is often called socialistic because of its extensive welfare programs, but more property there is privately owned than in the United
States.

Note that socialism does not imply dictatorship. Socialism can exist in  4
democratic countries as well as authoritarian ones. The main reason for
socialism's existence is that socialists hope to overcome capitalism's two
major problems: (1) the unequal distribution of income and wealth, and
(2) the uneven course of economic growth with periods of boom or bust.
For that reason, socialist countries, whether democratic or not, tend to
have a high (relative to capitalism) degree of economic planning and
government regulation.

Communism is a form of socialism that is the dream of many social-  5
ists. **Communism** holds that the people themselves — not the government — own the means of production. In a communist state, everyone
works at what he or she can do best. There is no system of wages or profits
needed to spur people to work. Everyone simply takes from what is
produced whatever he or she needs to live comfortably. No government
or bureaucracy supervises what the people do. Consequently, communism is considered an ideal, still to be realized, by those who believe in it.

**Capitalism** has three aspects, as follows:  6

1.  The institution of private ownership is generally accepted. Facto-
    ries, land, goods, and services are privately owned by individuals
    or groups of individuals like stockholders.

2. Most people are free to pursue their own economic self-interest, that is, to work for personal gain. For this reason, capitalism is often called the *free enterprise system;* most people are free to choose their own occupations.

3. Because people are motivated by self-interest, they compete with one another to get ahead, to make a better product, to control markets in order to obtain a larger profit. The struggle for larger profits leads (usually, but by no means always) to a high degree of competition among businesses.

The description we have just given is of pure capitalism — capitalism without tax laws, licenses to buy, government ownership of some enterprises (city-owned airports), and myriads of government regulations. But that is clearly not the capitalism that exists in twentieth century America. Economists frequently call our system *mixed capitalism.* That means our system is a mixture of free, privately owned enterprise with government **intervention.**

## COMPREHENSION CHECK

Complete the following items by circling or filling in the best answer.

1. The subject of the selection is:

   a. economics

   b. socialism versus capitalism

   c. three basic types of economic systems

2. The main purpose of the selection is:

   a. to explain the differences between socialism, communism, and capitalism

   b. to outline the advantages and disadvantages of three market systems

   c. to show the advantages of capitalism over socialism

3. The main idea of the selection is:

   a. The basic difference between socialism, communism, and capitalism lies in who owns the factories and who decides the answers to the three basic economic questions.

   b. There are many differences between socialism, communism, and capitalism.

   c. Socialism, communism, and capitalism are examples of command/planning and market-price economic systems.

4. What do socialists see as the two major problems with capitalism?

   a. _____

   b. _____

5. Socialism usually exists in countries ruled by dictators.

   a. true

   b. false

6. One of the basic elements that distinguishes capitalism from other systems is that of competition.

   a. true

   b. false

7. Using the context of paragraph 3, define the word *variants*.

   _____

8. Using the context of paragraph 6, define the word *intervention*.

   _____

9. You can conclude from the selection that most communist countries are also dictatorships.

   a. true

   b. false

10. You can conclude from this selection that:

    a. A mixed system is the best economic system.

    b. There are very few countries whose economic systems fit neatly into one of the three types.

    c. Communism will always be only an ideal, and never a reality.

**COMPREHENSION EXERCISE** *Taking comparison-and-contrast notes*

The selection "The Isms: Socialism, Communism, Capitalism" is organized using what we called method A, or block comparison. Sometimes it is more difficult to understand a comparison organized by this method than by method B, which presents the material point by point. Making a chart that separates the details by points can help to make the ideas clearer. Separate the major points of comparison and contrast in the selection by filling in the chart below.

|  | *Socialism* | *Communism* | *Capitalism* |
|---|---|---|---|
| Who owns businesses? |  |  |  |
| Who answers the three questions? |  |  |  |
| What drives the economy? |  |  |  |

### *Prereading Activity*: **Comparing living costs**

Have you ever visited a city, another state, or even another part of your own state, and noticed how the prices of particular items are higher or lower than where you live? For example, breakfast in a small-town diner may cost about $5, whereas even in a small, unpretentious restaurant in New York City the same breakfast could cost as much as $10. Likewise, a studio apartment in New York City could easily cost $1,100 a month; a comparable apartment in another city or town might only cost $600 or $700.

If you were offered a job paying $30,000 a year in a small rural town, and another job in New York City paying $50,000, where would you be better off financially, in New York or in the rural town?

Following is a list of standard living expenses. Discuss the lists with your classmates and determine an approximate cost for each of the items in the vicinity of the college. Then choose another location that one or more students are familiar with and compare the cost of the expenses.

| *Expense* | *Cost near College* | *Other Location* |
|---|---|---|
| two-bedroom apartment | _____ | _____ |
| insurance on a new car | _____ | _____ |
| sales tax | _____ | _____ |
| gallon of gasoline | _____ | _____ |
| haircut | _____ | _____ |
| lunch in a restaurant | _____ | _____ |
| movie | _____ | _____ |
| pound of hamburger | _____ | _____ |
| gallon of milk | _____ | _____ |
| loaf of bread | _____ | _____ |

Discuss why the costs of particular items may differ in the two locations, and where you would prefer to live and why.

In Reading Selection Three the author uses a comparison to explain an economic concept. As you read the comparison, consider what the author is saying about standards of living in different countries and how they relate to the GNP.

---

# What Is a Less Developed Country?

## BY PHILIP C. STARR

Several phrases are used to describe countries that are poorer than others: 1 underdeveloped countries, third world countries, sometimes even fourth or fifth world countries. Economists have no specific criteria or explicit definitions of such terms. A nation's position is usually determined by dividing its GNP by population (per capita GNP)* so that there is a ladder of countries from rich to poor — from $21,920 per person per year in the United Arab Emirates to $110 per person per year in Ethiopia in 1984.

We know that GNP says little about the quality of life [in a country]. 2 Moreover, a per capita GNP figure conceals the distribution of income within a nation. For example, per capita GNP in Brazil was about $2000 a year in 1984, but 30 million of Brazil's 133 million people had average annual incomes of only $77.

### The trouble with comparing per capita GNPs

When we use per capita GNPs to compare countries, we find our- 3 selves trapped by numbers that offer little help in describing real differences in standards of living. Not only is GNP an imperfect measure of welfare or progress within a country . . . , it has even less meaning when used for comparison among countries. Two examples will clarify this point.

In a poor, less developed country . . . like Tanzania, with a per capita 4 GNP of $210 per year, the $210 figure is imperfect because it is based primarily on cash transactions. But much of Tanzania's production and consumption typically involves little or no cash. The people in Tanzania's villages feed themselves out of their own production. Therefore, in most

---

*Gross National Product is an estimate of the dollar value of the goods and services produced (in a country) in one year.

cases per capita GNP figures in poor countries understate their true incomes. Of course, that doesn't mean such people are rich. We could double the numbers, and these people would still be **abjectly** poor by any standard.

In another example, let's look at the comparative lifestyles of Americans and New Zealanders. In the fall of 1978, New Zealand's per capita GNP was about half that of the United States. But it would be very foolish to conclude that New Zealanders' standard of living was half that of the average American. Fresh food prices were generally half of the U.S. prices, so that with much lower wages, the New Zealanders are just as well, or better off than Americans. Housing costs (rents and home purchase prices) were also about half of ours. Education, medical care, and retirement pensions were all provided from a highly progressive schedule of income taxes. In one specific case, a highly skilled New Zealander construction worker retired from his job at age 60. At the time of retirement, he earned $3.80 per hour—by our standards an abysmally low wage after a lifetime of work. Nevertheless, he owned a home and automobile free and clear, had $50,000 in the bank, and began a pension of 80 percent of his highest earnings. He and his wife were comfortable and content, traveled overseas occasionally, and had no financial worries. However, New Zealanders also have to contend with high prices of imported products like automobiles. 5

So how does one evaluate these differences in lifestyles: Can one say that Americans are better off than New Zealanders or vice versa? The question is impossible to answer. Nevertheless, the GNP per capita method of comparison among different countries is the method most commonly used. 6

In one attempt to improve on the GNP per capita measure, economists devised an index called the Physical Quality of Life Index (PQLI). The PQLI is a composite of a nation's life expectancy, infant mortality, and literacy. The index is 97 for Sweden, 94 for the United States, 35 for Bangladesh. The index reveals the weaknesses of looking only at GNP per capita. GNP per capita in Saudi Arabia is a healthy $10,530 (1984), but its PQLI is only 28. . . . 7

Complete the following items by filling in or circling the best answer.

1. According to this selection what is a "less developed country"?

   _____

2. Give two reasons GNP is a deceptive measure of a country's economic situation.

   a. _____

   b. _____

3. Explain why GNP figures in many poor countries are not real indications of their standard of living.

   _____

   _____

4. What measures are used to determine the Physical Quality of Life Index?

   _____

5. The main idea of the selection is:
   a. New Zealanders are better off than Americans even though their GNP is lower.
   b. The true indication of standard of living is the PQLI.
   c. GNP is not a good indicator of standard of living because it doesn't consider quality of life.
   d. Evaluating true quality of life in a particular country is difficult because it is determined by many factors other than the GNP.

6. Based on the context, define the word *abjectly* in paragraph 4.

   _____

7. What explanation can you give for the great discrepancy between Saudi Arabia's GNP and its PQLI? (*Hint*: Consider your answer to item 2.)

_____

_____

8. The PQLI in the United States is 94. How might this figure be deceptive?

_____

_____

9. By placing an **X** under the name of the appropriate country in the following chart, indicate where the items in the left-hand column would be more expensive, and where possible, specify how much greater.

|  | *United States* | *New Zealand* |
|---|---|---|
| GNP | _____ | _____ |
| food | _____ | _____ |
| housing | _____ | _____ |
| income taxes | _____ | _____ |
| income | _____ | _____ |
| imports | _____ | _____ |

10. Based on the completed chart, in which country would you be financially better off? Why?

_____

_____

_____

**COMPREHENSION EXERCISE**    *Outlining for comparison and contrast*

Complete the outline for the article "What Is a Less Developed Country?"

I. _____

    A. *Development is determined by dividing GNP by population*

        1. _____

        2. _____

           a. *Example: Brazil GNP was $2000, but 30 million of*

              *133 million people average only $77 per year*

II. *Problems with comparing per capita GNPs*

    A. _____

    B. _____

        1. *Tanzania*

           a. _____

           b. *GNP understates true incomes*

        2. *American lifestyle versus that of New Zealand*

           a. _____

           b. _____

           c. *Education, medical, retirement, etc. provided from*

              *highly progressive schedule of income taxes*

           d. _____

        3. *Difficult to evaluate whether Americans or New Zealanders are better off*

C. _____

1. _____

2. *Saudi Arabia is example of weakness in using GPA*

---

## CHAPTER APPLICATION

Choose a textbook from one of your classes and skim the last few assigned chapters to locate a passage, or passages, organized by comparison and contrast. Look for chapter headings and signal words that indicate the comparison or contrast of two items, ideas, or events. Take notes on the passage by creating a chart similar to those you have designed or filled in previously in this chapter.

---

## GOING BEYOND

On a scale of 1 to 10, how would you rate your satisfaction with life? The selection "Minds of States" describes the results of an interesting study in which researchers asked this question to thousands of people from nineteen countries. Before reading the article, study the chart that accompanies it to see how others from your country rated their lives. Then read the selection to determine why.

---

## Minds of States

**BY JOSHUA FISCHMAN**

Swedes are more content than Spaniards, Greeks more **disgruntled** 1 than the Irish. More than anything else, it seems, happiness depends on the country you live in.

    Political scientist Ronald Inglehart and opinion researcher Jacques- 2 René Rabier combed 10 years of public-opinion surveys in 19 countries to find out how satisfied people were with the quality of their lives. They

| Life Satisfaction in Nineteen Countries (1974–1983) | | |
|---|---|---|
| Country | Average Satisfaction (0 = Very dissatisfied, 10 = Very satisfied) | Gross National Product per capita (1979) |
| Denmark | 8.03 | $ 8,470 |
| Sweden | 8.02 | 10,071 |
| Switzerland | 7.98 | 9,439 |
| Norway | 7.90 | 8,762 |
| Netherlands | 7.77 | 7,057 |
| N. Ireland | 7.77 | 3,560 |
| Ireland | 7.76 | 3,533 |
| Finland | 7.73 | 5,814 |
| Luxembourg | 7.64 | 7,754 |
| U.S.A. | 7.57 | 10,765 |
| Britain | 7.52 | 4,972 |
| Belgium | 7.33 | 7,978 |
| W. Germany | 7.23 | 9,507 |
| Austria | 7.14 | 6,311 |
| France | 6.63 | 8,619 |
| Spain | 6.60 | 2,830 |
| Italy | 6.58 | 4,191 |
| Japan | 6.39 | 7,244 |
| Greece | 5.85 | 2,881 |

discovered that differences in personal contentment within a country were very small, regardless of social or economic circumstances. However, the differences between countries were quite strong, and they remained so over the 10-year period.

One obvious explanation for these differences — the problem of translating "satisfaction" from one language to another — does not explain why French-, German- and Italian-speaking Swiss all expressed similarly high satisfaction with their lives, higher, in fact, than the French, Germans or Italians.

3

Another likely explanation, differences between the wealth of na-    4
tions, accounts for some of the **disparities**, but not all. Greece, Spain
and Italy are relatively poor, and they rank at the bottom of the satisfaction list, while the well-off Scandinavian countries place at the top. But
Northern Ireland, with a level of contentment identical with that of the
Netherlands, has a per capita income only half as high. The French are
more than twice as rich as the Irish, but appear much less pleased with
their lot in life. And the United States, with the highest per capita income,
places right in the middle in terms of fulfillment.

"Could it possibly be true that the Italians experience life as burden-    5
some on the whole, while the Swiss, living literally next door, find it
enjoyable?" the researchers wonder. "Could fate be so unkind as to doom
entire nationalities to unhappiness?"

The real difference, Rabier and Inglehart suggest, lies not in the lan-    6
guage or the pocketbook, but in the culture. "Quite possibly, these cultures differ in the extent to which it is permissible to express unhappiness
and dissatisfaction with one's life." In other words, we all have very
different ideas about what happiness is, and judge our lives accordingly. . . .

**JOURNAL WRITING**

1.  Consider the culture in which you have spent most of your life. What
    do people in your culture value most? Family? Religion? Education?
    Work? Possessions? Money? Beauty? Leisure? Freedom? Wisdom?
    Health? Something else? Evaluate your lifestyle. In what way does the
    economic system under which you live or have lived affect your lifestyle
    and your ability to enjoy the things that you value?

2.  If you could live anywhere in the world, where would you prefer to live,
    and why?

3.  Compare and contrast the advantages and disadvantages of a capitalist
    society.

4.  Competition is an ideal that is valued in capitalist societies. Evaluate your attitude toward competition. How does your attitude affect your ability to interact in the work world?

5.  One of the major flaws of capitalism is that it creates an unequal distribution of the wealth. Many believe that the inequality in the United States is growing — that is, that the rich are getting richer and the poor are getting poorer. Discuss why you think this might be happening.

CHAPTER 11
**Issue and Debate**

CHAPTER 12
**Research Studies and
Statistical Data**

# PART III

# Critical Thinking and Research

W hich house would you prefer to live in: house 1, 2, 3, or 4?

Although each house may be beautiful in its own way, one house may appeal to you more than another. But is there an objective "truth" as to which of these houses is more beautiful, or is there only opinion: your opinion, my opinion, and the opinions of others who view these houses?

Where do personal preferences or opinions originate? Is each personal preference equally valuable? If ten people agreed that the second house was the most desirable, but you disagreed, who would be right?

Part III encourages you to think about "truth." Is everything equally true or are there degrees of "truth"? Is everything that cannot be conclusively proven true, untrue? These are questions you will consider as you read the last two chapters of this text. Parts I and II were about reading, writing, and study strategies that require you to *think* about what and how you learn. Part III is about *thinking strategies* that enable you to make better decisions about your reading, writing, and learning.

## CHAPTER 11

# Issue and Debate

After studying Chapter 11 you should be able to:

- identify an issue in a reading selection
- identify a writer's position on an issue
- map the positions in an argument
- distinguish facts from opinions
- evaluate the validity of arguments

## CHAPTER CHECKLIST

Use the following checklist to help you plan for the text, readings, and activities in this chapter.

*Date* *Date*
*Assigned* *Completed*

_____ _____ What is an issue?

_____ _____ WARM-UP: Stating an issue

_____ _____ EXERCISE 1: Identifying the issue

_____ _____ EXERCISE 2: Identifying a writer's position or viewpoint

_____ _____ EXERCISE 3: Taking a position or point of view

_____ _____ EXERCISE 4: Fact versus opinion

### READING SELECTION ONE

_____ _____ *Prereading Activity*: Scanning for signal words

_____ _____ **"Death"**

_____ _____ COMPREHENSION CHECK

_____ _____ COMPREHENSION EXERCISE 1: Mapping the arguments

_____ _____ COMPREHENSION EXERCISE 2: Summarizing the arguments

### READING SELECTION TWO

_____ _____ *Prereading Activity*: Evaluating arguments

_____ _____ **"For the Death Penalty"**

Issues are all around us: in the media we watch, read, and listen to; in the words of our friends and family; in our jobs, schools, and personal lives. Our minds are constantly bombarded by arguments designed to prove to us what others have reasoned to be true. If you are to make rational, logical decisions about this barrage of information around you, you must be able to distinguish when and how someone is trying to persuade you. In Chapter 11 you will learn to identify an issue, determine point of view, distinguish between facts and opinions, and evaluate the soundness of arguments.

**WARM-UP**    *Stating an issue*

Each of the following statements represents a topic, not an issue. Convert the topics into questions that present issues. As you attempt to create the issues, consider the arguments on both sides. Later you will be asked to take a position on one of the issues. The first one has been done for you to serve as a model.

1.  Prisons in the United States are overcrowded.

    *Should we consider alternatives to imprisonment to alleviate*

    *overcrowding?*

2.  Some states uphold the use of the death penalty.

    _____

3.  Crime victims have the right to justice.

    _____

4.  Prisoners are allowed furloughs in many states.

    _____

5.  Prisoners' wishes are given consideration in the sentencing process.

    _____

For sample question 1, for example, you now have a controversial question to which you might answer yes or no. You could take a position in favor of alternatives, stating that (1) incarceration is extremely costly to taxpayers, (2) many offenders are not dangerous to the public and can be monitored by surveillance devices and techniques, and (3) for white-collar criminals, public service is more appropriate. Or you might take a position against the alternatives, stating that (1) crimes committed by criminals who are not incarcerated are costly to society in terms of money and human suffering, (2) smart criminals find ways around surveillance devices and techniques, and (3) those who commit crimes of any kind should have to suffer in some way.

**EXERCISE 1**    *Identifying the issue*

Not all issues are posed as questions, but critical readers should be able to identify controversial statements and transform them into appropriate questions. For each of the following newspaper headlines, state the issue in the form of a question. Again, the first one has been done for you to serve as a model.

1.  "Furlough Fallout — 'Punish, Don't Treat'"

    Issue: *Should prisoners be released on temporary furloughs?*

2.  "The Slow Pace on Death Row"

    Issue: _____

3.  "Doing Hard Time Fairly"

    Issue: _____

4.  "Victims' Rights Cut into Our Real Rights"

    Issue: _____

**EXERCISE 2**  *Identifying a writer's position or viewpoint*

The way people feel and think about a controversial issue is called their position or "point of view." You can identify writers' viewpoints by examining their choice of words as well as the reasons they give to support their arguments.

Reread each headline in Exercise 1 and make a prediction as to whether the accompanying article is for or against the issue. Explain your prediction. Once again, the first one has been done for you.

1.  *The author is probably against furloughs because the title states "Punish, don't treat." This infers a belief that people should suffer for their crimes.*

2.  _____

    _____

    _____

3.  _____

    _____

    _____

4.  _____

    _____

    _____

5.  _____

    _____

    _____

EXERCISE 3   *Taking a position or point of view*

Read the following narration, "Death by the Highway," taken from the text *The American System of Criminal Justice.*

# Death by the Highway

## BY GEORGE F. COLE

### *Gregg* v. *Georgia*, 428 U.S. 153 (1976)

As they stood trying to hitch a ride from Florida to Asheville, North    1
Carolina, on November 21, 1973, Troy Gregg and his sixteen-year-old
companion, Sam Allen, watched car after car whiz past. Finally, as they
were beginning to lose hope, one came to a stop, the door was opened,
and they entered and were off. Fred Simmons and Bob Moore, both of
whom were drunk, continued toward the Georgia border with their passengers. Soon, however, the car broke down. Simmons purchased another, a 1960 Pontiac, using a large roll of cash. Another hitchhiker,
Dennis Weaver, was picked up and then dropped off in Atlanta about
11 P.M. as the car proceeded northward.

In Gwinnett County, Georgia, just after Simmons and Moore got out    2
of the car to urinate, Gregg told Allen, "Get out, we're going to rob them."
Gregg leaned against the car to take aim at the two men, and as they were
climbing up an embankment to return to the car, he fired three shots.
Allen later told the police that Gregg circled around behind the fallen
bodies, put the gun to the head of one and pulled the trigger, and then
quickly went to the other and repeated the act. He rifled the pockets of
the dead men, took their cash, and told Allen to get into the car. Then
they drove away.

The next morning the bodies were discovered beside the highway. On    3
November 23, after reading about the discovery in an Atlanta newspaper,
Weaver — the other hitchhiker — called the police and described the car.
The next afternoon Gregg and Allen, still in Simmons's car, were arrested
in Asheville. A .25-caliber pistol, later shown to be the murder weapon,
was found in Gregg's pocket. After receiving the *Miranda* warnings,
Gregg signed a statement in which he admitted shooting and then rob-

bing Simmons and Moore. He justified the slayings on the grounds of self-defense.

Georgia uses a two-stage procedure in which one jury decides ques-  4
tions of guilt or innocence and a second jury determines the penalty. At the conclusion of the trial, the judge instructed the jury that charges could be either **felony** murder or nonfelony murder, and either armed robbery or the lesser included offense of robbery by intimidation. The jury found Gregg guilty of two counts of armed robbery and two counts of murder. At the penalty stage, the judge instructed the jury that it could not authorize the death penalty unless it first found that one of three aggravating circumstances was present: (1) that the murder was committed while the offender was engaged in committing two other capital felonies; (2) that Gregg committed the murders for the purpose of acquiring the money and automobile; (3) that the offense was outrageously and **wantonly** vile, horrible, and inhuman, and showed the depravity of the mind of the defendant. The jury found the first and second circumstances to be present and returned verdicts of death on each count.

The sentence was affirmed by the Supreme Court of Georgia in 1974.  5
Gregg appealed to the U.S. Supreme Court, arguing that imposition of the death penalty was cruel and unusual punishment in violation of the Eighth Amendment.

## Decision

On July 2, 1976, the Supreme Court upheld the Georgia law under  6
which Gregg had been sentenced. In a widely split opinion, seven of the justices said that capital punishment is not inherently cruel and unusual and thus upheld the laws in those states where the judge and jury had discretion to consider the crime, the particular defendant, and **mitigating** or aggravating circumstances before ordering death.

Now divide into groups of four, with each person assuming one of the following roles:

Troy Gregg's lawyer

Fred Simmons' wife

a juror at Gregg's trial

the Supreme Court justice who heard the appeal

Discuss what punishment you think is appropriate for Troy Gregg, and why. (*Note*: Before discussing the issue, write down a few supporting arguments for your position. Try not to let your own personal opinions interfere with those of the person whose role you are assuming.)

**EXERCISE 4** *Fact versus opinion*

A writer's point of view represents his or her opinion, which may or may not be based on facts. The more facts a writer uses to support the opinion, the more valid the argument. In order to evaluate a writer's arguments, you must be able to distinguish between reasons that are factual and those that are strictly opinion.

Read the following introduction to a controversial article on capital punishment from the *Roanoke Times and World News* of March 13, 1984.

> James David "Cowboy" Autry is scheduled to die of lethal injection before sunrise Wednesday in Huntsville, Texas. He says he wants to die in public — with television cameras in attendance. Wisely, Texas prison officials have vetoed the idea.

What issue do you think this article will discuss?

_____

Next, read the following sentences from the article, and for each statement write F if it is a fact and O if it is an opinion.

_____ 1. If executions serve as deterrents, then there's a very logical argument that they should be done publicly.

_____ 2. Attempts at demonstrating a statistical relationship between capital punishment and the incidence of capital crime have been inconclusive.

_____ 3. The point is not whether capital punishment prevents future crimes, but whether it is a proper and fitting penalty for crimes that have occurred.

———    4.    An argument can be made that the state of Texas imposes death sentences too readily for crimes that do not reach the ultimate depths of human depravity.

———    5.    Its [Texas's] death-row population outnumbers that of any other state except Florida. . . .

———    6.    An individual's death should be private.

———    7.    A televised execution would turn the solemn occasion into a morbid sideshow for those who exult in the macabre.

Now, state whether you think the writer is for or against the issue and explain why. Does his or her argument rest more on fact or opinion?

_____

_____

_____

_____

## READING SELECTION ONE

### *Prereading Activity*: **Scanning for signal words**

Scan Reading Selection One and underline the signal words that indicate the author is using the issue-and-debate structure for the issue of capital punishment.

Reading Selection One is a chapter excerpt from the text *American Corrections*. It discusses the death penalty and the manner in which it is applied in the United States. As you read the excerpt, note the author's point of view, and use signal words to help you follow his argument.

## Death

### BY TODD R. CLEAR AND GEORGE F. COLE

More than 2,000 **incarcerated** persons are awaiting execution in thirty-    1
three of thirty-seven death penalty states, yet since 1976, when the Supreme Court upheld Georgia's capital punishment law, the number of
executions has been less than twenty-five in any one year. From 1930
through 1967, in contrast, more than 3,800 men and women were executed in the United States, 199 of them in 1935, the deadliest year. The
slow rate at which death sentences are being carried out today provoked
the displeasure of Chief Justice Burger in 1983, at the time of the death of
Robert Sullivan, who had been able to delay the carrying out of his
sentence for ten years while appeals wound their way through the courts.
Today about two hundred new death sentences are given out each year
and the number of states where capital punishment is permitted continues to mount, yet executions remain few. Is this situation the result of a
complicated and time-consuming appeals process or a lack of will on the
part of political leaders and of a society that is perhaps uncertain about
the taking of human lives? Is the death penalty consistent with the Eighth
Amendment's prohibition against cruel and unusual punishments?

In the 1972 case of *Furman* v. *Georgia*, the Supreme Court ruled for    2
the first time that the death penalty, as administered, constituted cruel
and unusual punishment, thereby voiding the laws of thirty-nine states
and the District of Columbia. Every member of the Court wrote an opinion, for even the majority could not agree on the legal reasons to support
the ban on the death penalty. Three of the five members of the majority
emphasized that judges and juries had used their discretion with regard
to imposition of capital punishment in such an **arbitrary**, **capricious**,
and **discriminatory** manner that the penalty constituted cruel and unusual punishment. Justices Thurgood Marshall and William Brennan
argued that capital punishment **per se** was cruel and unusual, in violation of the Eighth Amendment.

Although headlines declared that the Court had banned the death    3
penalty, many legal scholars felt that state legislators could write capital

punishment laws that would remove the arbitrariness from the procedure and thus pass the test of constitutionality. By 1976 thirty-five states had enacted new legislation designed to meet the faults cited in *Furman* v. *Georgia*. These laws took two forms. Some states removed all discretion from the process by mandating capital punishment on conviction for certain offenses; other states provided specific guidelines for judges and juries to follow in deciding whether death is the appropriate sentence in a particular case. The new laws were tested before the Supreme Court in June 1976 in the case of *Gregg* v. *Georgia*. The Court struck down the **mandatory** death penalty provisions of the new laws but upheld those that required the sentencing judge or jury to take into account specific aggravating and mitigating factors in deciding which convicted murderers should be sentenced to death. Many state legislatures, citing public opinion polls showing that a great majority of citizens favored the death penalty for murder, quickly revised their laws to accord with those of Georgia. By 1983 thirty-eight states had enacted such laws.

On 17 January 1977 Gary Mark Gilmore was executed by a firing   4 squad within the walls of the Utah State Prison for the crime of murder. Worldwide attention focused on Gilmore's case because it was the first time capital punishment had been carried out in the United States in almost ten years, because bizarre circumstances surrounded it (Gilmore had demanded that the death sentence be carried out), and because it was entangled with the moral and legal considerations of the issue. Since Gilmore's death, executions have continued at a slow but quickening pace. Two Americans were put to death in 1979 and 1982, five in 1983, and twenty-two in 1984. Thirteen minutes of electricity were required to kill John Evans in Alabama because of a malfunctioning chair. In December 1982 the execution in Texas of Charlie Brooks, Jr., fueled the debate, for the state used a drug overdose to bring about his death. The death of James D. Autry (whose codefendant plea-bargained a prison term and was on parole) was stayed by Justice Byron White in 1983 minutes before poison was to begin flowing into his veins. Over the appeals for clemency by the pope and the Catholic bishops of Florida, Robert Sullivan was executed in November 1983.

Debate over the legal and moral issues of capital punishment contin-  5 ues. Some people believe that the death penalty should be carried out to support the objectives of **deterrence** and deserved punishment. Others say that the death penalty has virtually no effect on reducing the crime rate, is always administered in a discriminatory fashion, inevitably results in the execution of an innocent, and is morally wrong. The question of proportionality arises when some offenders are sentenced to death while others — even partners in crime — who have committed the same offense receive prison terms. Critics who raise this issue argue that the death penalty is imposed by means of a macabre lottery in which a few are chosen for execution and the overwhelming majority are chosen for incarceration. Is this fair?

Reacting to strong public support for the death penalty, politicians    6 have called for executions, but in most states the appeals process has delayed implementation of the sanction. Some governors appear to be unwilling to shoulder this responsibility. There is increasing evidence that the justices of the Supreme Court are becoming impatient with the slowness of the death sentence appeals process. Justice William H. Rehnquist has criticized his colleagues for providing capital offenders "numerous procedural protections unheard of for other crimes" and "for allowing endlessly drawn out legal proceedings." Justice Lewis F. Powell, Jr., told judges of the Court of Appeals for the Eleventh Circuit that the American system of justice was irrationally "permissive" in the way lawyers for death row clients exploited constitutionally guaranteed due process. As he said, slowness "undermines public confidence in our system of justice." Perhaps, because the appeals process is slow, it is only a matter of time before executions in the United States become more frequent; but it may also be that although the public responds affirmatively to the symbolism of the death penalty, it does not fully support implementation of the decrees. If fewer than 10 of the more than 1,500 death sentences handed down since 1977 have been carried out, can it be argued that the manner in which the death penalty is carried out is as arbitrary as *Furman* v. *Georgia* said the manner of its imposition was?

## COMPREHENSION CHECK

Complete the following items by circling the best answer or by filling in the blanks.

1. The role of paragraph 1 is to present background information in order to enhance your understanding of the issue. The main idea of this paragraph is:
   a. The death sentence is being carried out too slowly.
   b. The number of states that permit the death sentence is growing.
   c. The death penalty violates the Eighth Amendment.
   d. The number of executions remains low in spite of an increase in the number of states that permit capital punishment.

2. In what famous case was capital punishment abolished?

   _____

3. On what grounds did the Supreme Court rule capital punishment unconstitutional?

   _____

   _____

4. Explain the two ways in which individual states dealt with the ruling of the *Furman* v. *Georgia* case.

   a. _____

   _____

   b. _____

   _____

5. Give two reasons people favor the death penalty.

   a. _____

   b. _____

6. Give two reasons people oppose the death penalty.

   a. _____

   b. _____

7. Using the context of the surrounding sentences to help you, define the phrase *per se* in paragraph 2.

   _____

8. Using the context of the paragraph, define the word *mandatory* in paragraph 3.

   _____

9. The author thinks that the public is unsure of its feeling about implementing the death sentence.
   a. true
   b. false

### COMPREHENSION EXERCISE 1    *Mapping the arguments*

Writers use a number of approaches when presenting issues. For example, they might present both sides objectively without imposing a particular point of view. They can present both sides of the argument but make clear their point of view, or bias. Or they can present only the arguments to support their own point of view, or bias.

In order to better understand the approach the writer has used and to follow the arguments, it is helpful to create a visual map that lists the arguments given for each side of the issue. Using the following chart, map the arguments in the reading selection "Death."

### *"Death"*

A. Issue: Is the death penalty consistent with the Eighth Amendment's prohibition against cruel and unusual punishment?

B.  Background: (State the present dilemma in the U.S. judicial system with regard to capital punishment.)

_____

_____

_____

C.  Possible positions

Yes _____    No _____

*Supporting Arguments*

1. _____    1. _____

   _____       _____

2. _____    2. _____

   _____       _____

3. _____    3. _____

   _____       _____

**COMPREHENSION EXERCISE 2**  *Summarizing the arguments*

Once you have mapped the positions, it is very easy to summarize an article written in the issue-and-debate structure. On a separate piece of paper write a summary of the excerpt "Death" using only your notes and the map from Comprehension Exercise 1. To complete your summary, do the following:

1.  Write an introductory paragraph stating the issue (possibly in the form of a question) and the most relevant background information.

2.  Write a paragraph in which you state one of the positions and the basic arguments for that position.

3. Write another paragraph in which you state the other position and its arguments.

4. Write a brief conclusion in which you state the outlook for the issue: Does the issue seem to be heading toward a positive or negative · resolution?

## *Prereading Activity*: **Evaluating arguments**

When evaluating arguments, we must examine whether the reasons given to support them are factual or merely opinions of the author. If they are opinions, we must then consider whether they are logical and sound by asking: Do they make sense? Do they in fact support the arguments? Skim the reading selection and try to get a sense of how opinionated the author is.

Reading Selection Two is taken from a feature section of the criminology textbook *American Corrections*. As you read the selection, try to distinguish the facts from the opinions.

## For the Death Penalty

**BY E. VAN DEN HAAG**

Arguments for and against the death penalty are either moral or **utilitar-**   1
**ian**. Morally, I believe that anyone who takes another's life should not be encouraged to expect that he will outlive his victim at public expense. Murder must forfeit the murderer's life, if there is to be justice.

**Abolitionists** disagree, believing that society has no right to take the   2
life even of a murderer, that only God does — although many abolitionists do not believe in God and constitutionally have confined belief in Him to the private sphere, thus precluding any legal reliance on His justice.

However, in my view moral "arguments," whether for or against the   3
death penalty, are not arguments but expressions of feeling. But feelings certainly are no less important than arguments. I simply do not share the

abolitionist feeling that no crime can be horrible enough to deserve death. I would cheerfully have executed Hitler or Stalin, given the chance. I favor executing persons who acted as they did, albeit **microcosmically**.

Variations of the abolitionist moral argument suggest that the death 4 penalty may be applied discriminatorily and disproportionately or that innocents may be executed. Yet, even if somehow abolitionists could be absolutely certain that none but the guilty are executed, and without discrimination or capriciousness, they would want to abolish the penalty anyhow. Wherefore, the discrimination and mistake arguments are a sham. Further, innocents are unintentionally victimized not only by the courts but also by traffic, by construction in the streets, which abolitionists would retain because it is useful. I think justice is, too. And discrimination is not **inherent** in the death penalty but in its discriminatory distribution, which can be, and is being, corrected.

But is it useful? The death penalty cannot revive the victim of murder. 5 Can it help protect the living? I believe that some murders can be deterred.

Common sense, lately bolstered by statistics, tells us that the death 6 penalty will deter murder, if anything can. People fear nothing more than death. Therefore, nothing will deter a criminal more than the fear of death. Death is final. But where there is life there is hope. Wherefore, life in prison is less feared. Murderers clearly prefer it to execution — otherwise, they would not try to be sentenced to life in prison instead of death (only an infinitesimal percentage of murderers are suicidal). Therefore, a life sentence must be less deterrent than a death sentence. And we must execute murderers as long as it is merely possible that their execution protects citizens from future murder.

I have occasionally asked abolitionists if they would favor the death 7 penalty were it shown that every execution deters, say, 500 murders. The answer to this admittedly **hypothetical** question, after some dodging, has always been no. This instructive answer demonstrates that abolitionists want to abolish the death penalty regardless of whether it deters. The nondeterrence argument they use is a sham, too. It is fair to conclude that they would rather save the life of a convicted murderer than that of any number of innocent victims. In their eyes, the sanctity of the life of the murderer exceeds that of any future murder victims.

I must leave it to abolitionists to defend their values. They seem 8 indefensible to me.

**COMPREHENSION CHECK**

Following is a list of statements from the selection "For the Death Penalty." Place an F in front of those that are facts, and an O in front of those that are opinion.

_____    1. Murder must forfeit the murderer's life, if there is to be justice.

_____    2. Society has no right to take the life even of a murderer . . . only God does . . .

_____    3. No crime can be horrible enough to deserve death.

_____    4. Abolitionists . . . suggest that the death penalty may be applied discriminatorily and disproportionately or that innocents may be executed.

_____    5. Even if . . . abolitionists could be absolutely certain that none but the guilty are executed, and without discrimination or capriciousness, they would want to abolish the penalty anyhow.

_____    6. Discrimination is not inherent in the death penalty but in its discriminatory distribution . . .

_____    7. The death penalty cannot revive the victim of murder.

_____    8. Some murders can be deterred.

_____    9. Death is final.

_____    10. Life in prison is less feared [than death].

**COMPREHENSION EXERCISE 1**    *Summarizing and mapping the arguments*

Of the reasons presented in Comprehension Check, half were facts and half were opinions. Now let's examine which side of the argument they support. To do this, use the following chart to map the facts and opinions from "For the Death Penalty" as well as any additional arguments in the selection.

### *"For the Death Penalty"*

A.  Issue: _____

B.  Background: _____

_____

_____

_____

C.  Possible positions

Yes _____         No _____

### *Supporting Arguments*

1.  _____         1.  _____

2.  _____         2.  _____

3.  _____         3.  _____

4.  _____         4.  _____

5.  _____         5.  _____

6.  _____         6.  _____

---

**COMPREHENSION EXERCISE 2**  *Determining validity*

Once you have separated the facts from the opinions, you must examine the logic of the opinions. Then you must determine whether the facts and opinions actually support the argument. If the facts and opinions are both logical and pertinent, they can be considered valid.

Let's examine the validity of the facts and opinions given to support the arguments in "For the Death Penalty." For each of the following statements from the reading, explain any errors in the reasoning. Then decide whether the statement supports the argument. The first two have been done for you to serve as models.

1. Murder must forfeit the murderer's life, if there is to be justice.

   *This opinion supports the argument that the death sentence is*

   *justifiable but is flawed reasoning because there are other ways*

   *to serve justice. We might ask, what is justice?*

2. Society has no right to take the life even of a murderer . . . only God does . . .

   *This opinion supports the argument that the death sentence is*

   *not justifiable but is flawed because not all people believe in the*

   *existence of a Supreme Being. Even among those who believe in a*

   *deity, there are contradictory opinions regarding man's right to*

   *take a life.*

3. No crime can be horrible enough to deserve death.

   _____

   _____

   _____

   _____

4. Abolitionists . . . suggest that the death penalty may be applied discriminatorily and disproportionately or that innocents may be executed.

   _____

   _____

   _____

   _____

5. Even if . . . abolitionists could be absolutely certain that none but the guilty are executed, and without discrimination or capriciousness, they would want to abolish the penalty anyhow.

_____

_____

_____

_____

6. Discrimination is not inherent in the death penalty but in its discriminatory distribution . . .

_____

_____

_____

_____

7. The death penalty cannot revive the victim of murder.

_____

_____

_____

_____

8. Some murders can be deterred.

_____

_____

_____

_____

9. Death is final.

_____

_____

_____

_____

10. Life in prison is less feared [than death].

_____

_____

_____

_____

## READING SELECTION THREE

### *Prereading Activity*: **Stating an opinion**

In certain cultures it is not only accepted but expected that if you or your loved ones are wronged, you must personally avenge yourself by punishing the culprit. On a separate piece of paper, write a brief paragraph describing your opinion on this cultural expectation.

Reading Selection Three consists of two editorials that demonstrate different perspectives on the same topic. Both discuss the issue of vigilantism, or taking the law into your own hands, but only the first one, from the *Miami Herald*, presents the issue without bias. Its purpose is to encourage the reader to examine the issues and contemplate the possible consequences of the various positions. The second editorial, from the Manchester, N.H., *Union Leader*, is designed to make the opinions of the editor unequivocally clear and to persuade others to embrace those opinions. Read the two editorials carefully, applying what you have learned in this chapter about distinguishing facts from opinions, summarizing arguments, and so on. Then complete the Comprehension Checks for each editorial.

## Two Editorials on Vigilantism

### FROM THE *MIAMI HERALD*

Anyone who ever has ridden on New York's subways can empathize. The  1
express train from the Bronx was clattering along beneath Manhattan.
Alone sat a middle-aged man, presumably minding his own business.
Four teen-age punks gathered round him. They asked him the time. They
asked for a match. They asked for $5.

They carried long-handled screwdrivers, though it is not known if  2
they threatened him with them. Accounts vary as to precisely what happened next; eyewitnesses say that the man pursued the youths after an
unspecified interval, and found them in another subway car. The youths
say that they always were together with the man in one subway car.

"Yes, I have $5 for each of you," the man said as he stood, according  3
to the teen-agers. He pulled a revolver from his waistband and methodically shot each of them, three in the chest, one in the back. A dozen other
riders dove for cover. The gunman threatened no one else. He even paused
to converse briefly with the halted train's conductor, then leaped into the
dark tunnel and escaped.

The gunman immediately became a folk hero, precisely because so  4
many people do empathize with his plight and even admire his response.
He became the embodiment of the modern urban soul who, as the movie
*Network* put it, is "mad as hell and I'm not going to take it any more."

On Monday, nine days after the shootings, Bernard Hugo Goetz, 37,  5
surrendered to police in Concord, N.H. He asserts self-defense, that he
"did nothing wrong," that "I'm sorry for what happened, but it had to be
done."

Did it? Much depends on facts not now clear. Were the punks threat-  6
ening him up to the moment of shooting, forcing him to defend himself,
or had the hassling ended before he hunted down his tormentors? Such
details could make the difference legally.

What about morally? The gunman took the law into his own hands,  7
but many would argue that where he was, there is no law. Some 12,000

felonies were reported in New York's subways last year; fewer than 1,000 resulted in jail sentences. Those numbers add up to utter failure of the city's criminal-justice system.

The subway gunman dispensed vigilante justice. He appears to have gone beyond self-defense to immediate, severe retribution. One wounded teen-ager remains in critical condition, paralyzed from the waist down. Vigilantism cannot be **condoned**. The dangers of vigilante violence are as fearsome as those of unchecked predators in the streets. Innocent bystanders can be shot. 8

Similar episodes could happen in any big American city. People will defend themselves if they cannot reasonably rely upon government to protect them. The law-abiding would prefer civilized justice, but when individuals feel that their only real choice is between being a victim or being a vigilante, many will prefer the latter. That is the challenge to America's criminal-justice systems. If they do not provide better justice and protection to the law-abiding, then America's cities will descend further into **anarchy**. 9

**FROM THE MANCHESTER, NEW HAMPSHIRE, *UNION LEADER***

Crime's victims are society's biggest losers. 1

*The nation's courts have done everything possible to hamstring law enforce-* *ment agencies, minimize punishment and protect the rights of criminals — to the* *extent that it is virtually impossible for a victim to get a fair shake.* 2

In Pershing County, Nev., residents have donated $7,500 and must raise a total of $60,000 to prosecute an accused sex fantasy killer — but they would rather see taxes raised to finance the trial than risk having the accused killer tried in California where he almost certainly would escape the death penalty if convicted. 3

The realities of crime, and the frequent lack of punishment, cause many otherwise law abiding citizens to cheer when a victim strikes back. The case of the father of a 12-year-old kidnap victim who shot his son's suspected abductor in the head in a crowded airport last Friday night is a perfect example. Who, other than the courts, which will insist the father be rigorously prosecuted, can feel any real sympathy for the alleged kidnapper, who threatened to kill the child and subjected the father, mother and child to incredible mental anguish? By all societal standards, the 4

father was wrong: But his frustration with "justice" is entirely under-
standable to any rational citizen in modern society.

*Victims pay; criminals seldom suffer the pain, both physical and psycholog-* 5
*ical, they force upon those whose rights they almost freely violate.*

*And the fault rests squarely on the courts and, to an only moderately lesser* 6
*extent, on legislators for their abject failure to insure that punishment is swift,*
*certain and commensurate with the crime committed.*

New Hampshire is no exception.    7

When was the last brutal murderer executed? When was the last 8
chronic criminal given a life term that meant life in prison, rather than
parole in a mere handful of years? When, indeed, were escalating mandatory minimum sentences employed to insure that repetitive offenders — career criminals — preying on society, received the punishment
they had earned? Where is justice when a vicious killer like Edward
Coolidge can be facing parole, long before serving his full sentence for a
heinous crime? What father, in similar circumstances today, would not
feel compelled to take the law in his own hands to prevent a recurrence
of New Hampshire's Coolidge travesty?

## COMPREHENSION CHECK 1

Complete the following items about the *Miami Herald* editorial by filling in
the blank or circling the best answer.

1. The first few paragraphs provide background on the subway incident.
   In your own words explain what happened.

   _____

   _____

2. This editorial raises a number of issues. What is the first issue raised
   (in paragraph 6)?

   _____

   _____

3. What issue is raised in paragraph 7?

   _____

   _____

4. Which sentence in paragraph 8 states an opinion?

   _____

   _____

5. Which sentence in paragraph 8 is a fact?

   _____

   _____

6. What is the main idea of this selection?

   _____

   _____

7. Using the context of paragraph 8, define *condoned.*

   _____

   _____

8. Using the context of paragraph 9, define *anarchy.*

   _____

   _____

9. We can infer from this selection that the editorial's main focus is more law enforcement than vigilantism.
   a. true
   b. false

10. Although the editorial does not take a stand on the issue of vigilantism itself, it does present an opinion. What is it?

   _____

   _____

## COMPREHENSION CHECK 2

Complete the following items about the *Union Leader* editorial by filling in
the blanks.

1.  What is the main issue presented in this editorial?

    _____

    _____

2.  What examples does the editorial use to prove that crime victims feel
    frustrated by their treatment? Do these examples prove that justice is
    not served? (*Hint*: Consider what you have learned about facts and
    opinions.)

    _____

    _____

3.  According to the editorial, who is responsible for the injustice ren-
    dered to the victims? Do you agree? Why or why not?

    _____

    _____

    _____

4.  According to the editorial, what steps must be taken to ensure that
    justice is truly served?

    _____

    _____

5.  What assumption does the editorial make about the function of crimi-
    nal justice that serve as the basis of its argument?

    _____

    _____

## CHAPTER APPLICATION 1

Bernard Goetz was eventually cleared of all charges except illegal posses-
sion of a handgun. Do you think that justice was served? Choose one of the
scenarios below to create a dialogue that presents your opinion on the issue
of vigilantism.

> a dialogue between Goetz and his victims
>
> a dialogue between a news reporter and five members of the jury

## CHAPTER APPLICATION 2

Write a letter to the editor of your local newspaper stating your opinion on
any one of the issues discussed in this chapter. In writing your letter, be
sure to do the following:

1.  Create a map stating the issue, the important background knowledge,
    and the two positions. List the arguments for both sides.

2.  Decide which side of the issue you support; then write an introductory
    paragraph stating the issue and making your position evident.

3.  Write two or three paragraphs stating your reasons, supporting them
    with facts and examples whenever possible. Present some of the oppos-
    ing arguments in order to clarify and accentuate your own.

4.  Write a concluding paragraph predicting a possible resolution to the
    issue.

## GOING BEYOND

Sometimes, in order to win a conviction in a particular criminal case, the
prosecutor will offer one of the defendants a "plea bargain" — his or her
testimony against another defendant in exchange for a lesser or suspended

sentence. The author of "Getting Away with Murder" discusses some of the pros and cons of this policy.

## Getting Away with Murder

BY JACK LEVIN

*For some accused, ''snitching'' means beating the rap*

This was to be Kelly Keniston's big break in journalism. For four straight   1
months she corresponded with Douglas Clark, the man known as the "Sunset Strip Killer," while he was serving time on San Quentin's death row. According to the State of California, in 1980 Clark and a female accomplice had murdered and mutilated at least seven people. Some of the victims were adults, others were juveniles. Some were prostitutes and one was a male. All were slain in an unusually brutal manner including **decapitation**.

Keniston's plan was simple. She would meet the convicted killer, gain   2
his confidence, pump him for information and then write an article about him for a major magazine. But Keniston never penned the story that was to launch her journalistic career. Instead, in October 1984, she married Douglas Clark and became an advocate not only for her husband but also for "returning integrity to the American concept of justice."

To this day, Kelly argues that her husband is innocent; that he was   3
victimized by a **shoddy** legal defense and by a secret plea bargain with the woman whom the prosecution claimed was his accomplice. That woman, Carol Bundy, originally of Lowell, Massachusetts, was able to convince the court by her testimony that Douglas Clark was the main culprit in their killing spree and that mesmerized by his charm, she merely went along for the ride to please her lover. Despite assurances to the jury that the District Attorney would go for the death penalty, Carol Bundy received a parolable sentence; Doug Clark is scheduled to die in the gas chamber.

Whether her husband is guilty or innocent, Kelly Keniston's mission   4
directs attention to the use of a controversial procedure in the prosecution of certain killers, especially serial killers. In order to secure a conviction, one of the defendants is convinced by the prosecuting attorney to turn

state's evidence in return for a lesser sentence. From the prosecution's standpoint, it makes good sense to convict at least one defendant on the word of another, rather than to convict no one at all. But this advantage is not always properly weighed against its potential for abuse. How much credibility should the court give to the testimony of an accomplice who is eager to escape the gas chamber or a lifetime behind bars? To what extent does a plea bargain with accomplices actually promote lying and perjury? The importance of such questions is highlighted by the fact that some 30 percent of all serial murders are committed by teams of assailants — usually brothers, cousins, friends or co-workers. If they are caught and tried, one defendant often ends up informing on another.

The extreme absurdity as well as logic of this kind of snitching can be      5
seen in the case of the Zebra killers — members of a Black Muslim cult called the Death Angels who, during 1973 and early 1974, killed 14 and injured eight on the streets of San Francisco. In the absence of an eye-witness account, the Zebra killers may never have come to justice. But based on the testimony of one of their own members, Antony Harris, four defendants were found guilty and sentenced to life in prison. Under oath, Harris described the slayings in detail and identified the killers by name. In return he received a grant of **immunity**.

The use of informants by prosecuting attorneys under bizarre circum-      6
stances is well illustrated by the case of the Johnson brothers, who during the 1970s operated a million-dollar crime ring in the tri-state region of Pennsylvania, Maryland and Delaware. To silence some of their disloyal accomplices who were scheduled to testify to the FBI, the Johnson brothers committed mass murder. During the summer of 1978 they shot to death six members of their gang.

In 1980, Bruce, Norman and David Johnson were tried, found to be      7
guilty of murder and given life sentences. Their conviction depended a good deal on securing the cooperation of gang members who were willing to "snitch." For example, in return for his testimony, the gang's hit man, Leslie Dale, received 10 to 40 years. Another gang member, Richard Donnell, got a sentence of one to three years concurrent with a term he was already serving.

In the Sunset Strip killer case, one defendant, Douglas Clark, was a    8
man; the other, Carol Bundy, was a woman. The prosecution chose to
plea bargain with the female rather than the male defendant, to use Carol
Bundy's version of the crimes against Douglas Clark.

This is nothing new. In fact, there seems to be a consistent willingness    9
for juries, prosecuting attorneys and citizens generally to side with female
defendants who stand accused of committing **heinous** crimes. In 1958,
for example, Charlie Starkweather and Carol Fugate went on an eight-
day killing spree across Nebraska and Wyoming that resulted in the
slaughter of 10 innocent people. Jurors heard testimony that implicated
both defendants. Yet only Charlie Starkweather went to the electric chair.
His partner, Carol Fugate was released from prison in 1976 and is now a
housewife living in Michigan.

By lightening the burden on our courts, plea bargaining may be    10
generically essential to the criminal justice system as we know it. In cases
of serial murder, however, bargaining with one defendant against another
can only be justified as a tactic of last resort. Most serial killers are sociopaths. They lack conscience and empathy. They have no feelings of remorse. But serial killers do excel at manipulating other people. They are
exceptionally convincing liars who skillfully lure their victims into their
trap and if apprehended, skillfully defend themselves in court.

Is Douglas Clark an expert liar or an innocent man? He remains on    11
death row, still waiting for his case to be reviewed and hoping to have his
conviction overturned. And his wife Kelly continues to agitate. She has
proclaimed her husband's innocence on television programs across the
country including "People Are Talking" in Baltimore, Pittsburgh, San
Francisco and Boston. She has established the Information Clearing-
house on Criminal Justice in San Rafael, California, whose quarterly
newsletter contains information and editorials concerning the death penalty, prosecutorial immunity and related issues. Kelly also writes articles
but they don't get printed in major magazines. After all, who will believe
a writer who is also the wife of the Sunset Strip Killer?

## JOURNAL WRITING

1. Utilizing some of the opinions you have developed about criminal justice during your study of this chapter, write an essay giving your position on the issue of plea bargaining. Begin by stating your opinion in a clear, informative introduction. Then develop and support your opinion with sound and logical arguments. In your conclusion explain the direction you see this issue taking in the future.

2. A great many Americans believe that we need to "get tough" on criminals. Some propose that we make prisons tougher. Give your impression of American prison conditions and discuss how, if at all, they should be changed.

3. If you were the mayor of a large city, what measures would you take to reduce crime?

4. In the past few years a number of highly provocative criminal cases have been televised. Construct a persuasive essay giving your opinion on the role of the media in criminal cases.

5. Some people welcome the opportunity to do jury duty; others dread it. How do you feel about it, and why? Do you think all citizens should have to serve on juries?

# Research Studies and Statistical Data

After studying Chapter 12 you should be able to:

- specify how scientists search for truth
- identify flaws in research
- understand tables and graphs that illustrate findings
- identify how a research study is designed

**CHAPTER CHECKLIST**

Use the following checklist to help you plan for the text, readings, and activities in this chapter.

| Date Assigned | Date Completed | |
|---|---|---|
| _____ | _____ | The search for knowledge |
| _____ | _____ | WARM-UP: Postulating theories |
| _____ | _____ | Research methods |
| _____ | _____ | EXERCISE 1: Choosing a research method |
| _____ | _____ | EXERCISE 2: Finding flaws |
| _____ | _____ | EXERCISE 3: Constructing tables and graphs |
| _____ | _____ | Locating information on research |
| _____ | _____ | EXERCISE 4: Previewing technical vocabulary |

## READING SELECTION ONE

| | | |
|---|---|---|
| _____ | _____ | _Prereading Activity_: Previewing textbook material |
| _____ | _____ | **"Sexual Differentiation"** |
| _____ | _____ | COMPREHENSION CHECK |
| _____ | _____ | COMPREHENSION EXERCISE 1: Examining the research |
| _____ | _____ | COMPREHENSION EXERCISE 2: Charting research data |

## READING SELECTION TWO

| | | |
|---|---|---|
| _____ | _____ | _Prereading Activity_: Sex roles |
| _____ | _____ | **"Biology Influences Sex Roles"** |

Date       Date
Assigned   Completed

_____  _____   COMPREHENSION CHECK

_____  _____   COMPREHENSION EXERCISE: Examining the research

**READING SELECTION THREE**

_____  _____   *Prereading Activity*: Your family

_____  _____   **"When Siblings Are *Unlike* Peas in a Pod"**

_____  _____   COMPREHENSION CHECK

_____  _____   CHAPTER APPLICATION 1

_____  _____   CHAPTER APPLICATION 2

_____  _____   GOING BEYOND: "Where Have All the Smart Girls Gone?"

_____  _____   JOURNAL WRITING

# The Search for Knowledge

How much does social pressure affect one's behavior?

What effect does passive smoke have on the nonsmoker?

Is there a correlation between alcohol use and chronic depression?

Are top executives more prone to heart disease than blue-collar workers?

Are crime victims victimized by the legal system?

Are people in the former Soviet Union happier than people in America?

Has your curiosity been aroused by some of the reading selections in the previous chapters? Would you like to know more about these topics? If so, you need to know how to go about finding answers to these questions — that is, how to acquire knowledge.

In the physical and social sciences "knowledge" is based on evidence that can be confirmed by observable **data**. This evidence comes from statistical data that has been gathered through experiments, surveys, and clinical or field observations. Once the data is compiled, it is critically evaluated to determine patterns or relationships of cause and effect, or **correlations**. If correlations are positive, scientists can then theorize why the relationships occur.

For example, in the study described in Going Beyond on page 389, the researchers conducted a ten-year study to determine whether male and female high school valedictorians were equally successful in the world after high school. They found that even though the female valedictorians outperform their male counterparts in college, "two-thirds of the women had begun to lower their career aspirations by their sophomore year." They also found that fewer women go on to pursue doctoral degrees, and in the work world they work at lower levels. The question is, Why? One theory is that some schools "teach girls to act helpless, sit quietly and find math and science difficult." Another theory is that girls maintain their aspirations, but the work world simply does not offer them the opportunities to fulfill them.

Which theory is correct? Both? Neither? In an attempt to arrive at the "truth," researchers turn these theories into **hypotheses** — theories to be tested. For example, we could hypothesize that the reason girls achieve less is that they receive less parental support regarding education and career choices. We could then design a study to research that hypothesis. Finally, we would have to determine if the new data supported the hypothesis. If the correlation were consistently positive, then the hypothesis could be considered a valid theory.

This process of moving from specific data to general theory is called **inductive** research; moving from theory to data is called **deductive** research. Viewed this way, science becomes an ongoing search for "truth."

Chapter 12 describes the basic methods social scientists use to arrive at "truth." It teaches you to interpret and evaluate the results of scientific findings and suggests ideas for improving your own research skills.

**WARM-UP** *Postulating theories*

What theories can you derive for the following correlations or relationships? The first one has been done for you to serve as a model.

1. *Correlation*: A large percentage of single mothers are also poor and undereducated. (Why?)

   *Theory*: <u>**Poor, undereducated women have less access to information concerning birth control methods.**</u>

   (Can you think of another theory?) _____

   _____

2. *Correlation*: Women cope with stress better than men do.

   *Theory*: _____

   _____

3. *Correlation*: Male siblings fight with one another more than do female siblings.

   *Theory*: _____

   _____

4. *Correlation*: Identical twins bear very similar behavioral traits even if they were not raised in the same environment.

   *Theory*: _____

   _____

5. *Correlation*: Men prefer younger women, while women prefer older men.

   *Theory*: _____

   _____

6. *Correlation*: Stepchildren are more likely to be abused than natural children.

   *Theory*: _____

   _____

# Research Methods

Basically, three general methods are used to conduct research: experiments, surveys, and observations. In addition, a fourth method — historical research — draws on data obtained from all three primary methods.

## Experimentation

**Experiments** involve manipulating **variables** — characteristics, behaviors, or events — under controlled conditions in order to test theories of cause and effect. For example, if you wanted to test the hypothesis that girls are more patient than boys, you might conduct an experiment wherein students in a particular classroom were asked to wait an extra five minutes before going to lunch and recess each day. You would then observe the effects of the delay on the children to determine how and if the boys' reactions were different from the girls'.

The advantage of experimentation is that it can simulate situations for a large numbers of **subjects** — participants in the experiment — in a way that is not possible in real life. However, experimental research has three basic drawbacks. First, the conditions of the experiment may involve unfair, even unethical treatment of the subjects. (Why should some students miss five minutes of their lunch break?) Second, because the conditions are artificial, the subjects may act differently than if they were in an ordinary environment. (If the students are told they are part of an experiment, they may "act out" because they feel they must do something.) Third, unknown, extraneous variables may affect the behavior of several members of the experimental group. (The students may be required to spend fifteen minutes in the lunchroom when they only need ten minutes to eat; therefore they really don't object to spending the extra five minutes in their classroom.)

## Surveying

**Surveys** involve a set of standardized questions asked of a large number of people, either orally through interviews or over the telephone, or by way of pencil and paper. A survey may use a **cross-sectional sample** — a random group of people at a particular time. Or it may be applied **longitudinally** to a specific sample of people over a number of years. The advantage to the survey is that it can be applied to a variety of topics using large numbers of people. The disadvantages are that it can only be used in the social sciences and it is subject to social and personal biases. For example, people refrain from giving answers that place them in an unfavorable light. Therefore we would have to be skeptical of data from a survey that asked men how often (if ever) they coerced women into sexual activity.

## Observation

**Observation** involves watching people in their natural environments. Usually the researcher chooses one or two factors to observe, and sometimes even becomes part of the group in order to have access to the environment. This type of research is used to determine how people act, rather than how they *say* they act. For this reason observation is preferable to the survey because it diminishes the possibility of subject **bias**. It does not, however, eliminate researcher bias. Because most researchers set out to prove their hypothesis, they may tend to give more attention to those responses that support their view, and might unintentionally overlook negative responses. Another disadvantage is that observation is often limited to a small, statistically nonrepresentative sample.

## Historical research

Another type of research, **historical research**, involves compilation of statistical data on a specific topic of interest. For example, studies of marriage records over the past fifty years might be used to indicate various trends, such as how social or economic variables affect marriage age.

**EXERCISE 1**    *Choosing a research method*

What methods might be used to research the following hypotheses, and why? Again, the first one has been done for you to serve as a model.

1. *Hypothesis*: Males are naturally more aggressive than females.

   *Method*: <u>**observation or experiment**</u>

2. *Hypothesis*: Men prefer women who are not as smart as they are.

   *Method*: _____

3. *Hypothesis*: Children who are firmly disciplined as children will be more conforming as adults than those whose parents were lenient.

   *Method*: _____

4. *Hypothesis*: The gender-role development of children is affected by the highly stereotyped male and female characters in children's literature.

   *Method*: _____

5. *Hypothesis*: When it comes to love, opposites attract.

   *Method*: _____

6. *Hypothesis*: Male students are more likely to misbehave in a classroom of all boys.

   *Method*: _____

**EXERCISE 2**   *Finding flaws*

One of the major problems scientists face in searching for "truth" is lack of control over the factors that influence correlations. As a result, achieving "absolute truth" is rarely possible, particularly in the social sciences. In reading technical journals and textbooks that contain research findings, we must learn to examine critically the procedures and findings in order to uncover **flaws** — weaknesses in design or procedure — that affect the **validity**, or truth, of the experiment.

Read the following studies looking for flaws in procedure or conclusions. Give at least two reasons the findings in each study could be faulty.

*Study 1*: Researchers wish to conduct a survey to determine whether men or women are happier in their marriages. Using census lists from five major American cities, they randomly mail surveys to 2,000 married couples in each city.

1. _____

2. _____

*Study 2*: Researchers wish to determine whether individuals who have strong religious beliefs develop higher moral standards than those with little or no religious faith. They set up an experiment in which wallets with $300 (counterfeit) are left in the lunchroom of a large professional building over a period of many months. The people who find and return the wallets are then told of the experiment and asked if they are willing to be interviewed regarding their religious training and beliefs.

1. _____

2. _____

*Study 3*: Researchers wanted to know whether first-born males achieve higher levels of success than those born at different positions in a family. They conducted case studies of fifty families with at least two males, one of whom was the first born. The families ranged in size from two to six, and the number of boys and girls in each family varied.

1. _____

2. _____


**EXERCISE 3** *Constructing tables and graphs*

In order to simplify presentation of data, researchers often summarize their findings in the form of tables or graphs. Both methods are suitable for explaining percentages related to a single variable, as well as for describing comparative data. Some data may lend itself better to one method or the other, but often the two types may be used interchangeably.

Figure A and Table B show imaginary data based on the fictitious studies in the Warm-Up activity. Study the graph and the table carefully. Then, using the "blank" models on page 363, construct a table to describe the data contained in Figure A and a bar graph to depict the data shown in Table B.

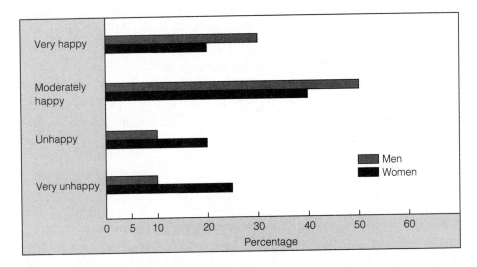

**Figure A**  Marital Happiness of Men and Women

| Table B | Educational Success of First-Born Males | |
|---|---|---|
| *Highest Level of Education* | *First-born Males* | *Second-born or Later* |
| Graduate degree | 20% | 10% |
| Bachelor's degree | 40% | 30% |
| Associate's degree | 15% | 20% |
| High school diploma | 24% | 37% |
| High school dropout | 1% | 3% |

**Table A    Marital Happiness of Men and Women**

**Figure B**  Educational Success of First-Born Males

# Locating Information on Research

There are two common types of research articles: (1) those that explain and discuss the original empirical evidence of a study and (2) those that summarize and review the study in light of previous research. Newspapers and magazines abound in summaries of research data from every field, and many textbooks incorporate explanations of studies directly into their texts.

The best source of accurate, complete data on research, however, may be found in technical journals, which are written for and by professionals in the field. Numerous indexes to these journals and periodicals, offering information on a wide range of academic topics, are available in your college library. Many are available on computer databases, which can be accessed with the help of your librarian. If you would like more information on indexes and how to use them, see Appendix C.

## EXERCISE 4    *Previewing technical vocabulary*

Research articles are often difficult to read because scientists use technical vocabulary, or jargon as it is called. Before we read an example of a study from a technical journal, let's review some of the vocabulary we have encountered thus far in this chapter.

Define the following words by skimming the first part of this chapter to locate the words. Then use context clues to determine their meaning.

sample: _____

subject: _____

data: _____

hypothesis: _____

findings: _____

variable: _____

bias: _____

correlation: _____

survey: _____

cross-sectional sample: _____

extraneous variable: _____

longitudinal study: _____

*Prereading Activity*: **Previewing textbook material**

Preview the reading selection by skimming the title, the first paragraph, and the headings. Then answer the following question as best you can: How are researchers attempting to explain the differences between men and women?

_____

_____

Reading Selection One is an example of how textbooks incorporate research data into their texts. As you read, notice that certain statements are followed by parenthetical notations. These indicate the author and date of the research finding under consideration.


## Sexual Differentiation

### BY METTA SPENCER AND ALEX INKELES

Men and women are different. Biology differentiates their physical forms   1
and cultural norms in every society differentiate their roles. These differences pose an interesting question: How much is biological, and how much is cultural? Are gender roles really roles? Can we treat them as optional parts in the play of life? If we do not like the script society hands

out, can we throw it away and rewrite our lines? Or are we bound by nature to play our parts in a certain way? Psychologists, biologists, **anthropologists**, and **sociologists** are all working to discover the balance between cultural and biological forces.

### Sex versus gender

In understanding the social roles of men and women, it is helpful to make a distinction between gender and sex. **Sex** refers to the two biologically differentiated categories, male and female. It also refers to the sexual act that is closely related to this biological differentiation. **Gender**, on the other hand, refers to the expected dispositions and behaviors that cultures assign to each sex. Although biology provides two distinct and universal sexes, cultures provide almost infinitely varied gender roles. Each man is pretty much like every other man in terms of sex — whether he is upper class or lower class, black or white, Chinese or Apache. **Gender roles**, however, are a different matter. The rights and obligations, the dispositions and activities, of the male gender role are very different for a Chinese man than for an Apache man. Even within a given culture, gender roles vary by class, race, and subculture. In addition, of course, individuals differ in the way they act out their expected roles. Some play an exaggerated version of the manly man, whereas others display few of the expected characteristics.

2

Social scientists are more interested in gender roles than in sex. They want to know about the variety of roles that have been assigned to women and men and, more particularly, about what accounts for the variation. Under what circumstances do women have more or less power, prestige, and income? What accounts for the recent changes that have occurred in gender roles in our society?

3

### Cross-cultural evidence

There is wide variability in gender roles across societies. Cross-cultural research shows that the behaviors we normally associate with being female and male are by no means universal. Among the New Guinea Arapesh, both sexes are expected to be gentle and giving, subordinating their own needs to those of others. Their neighbors, the Mundugumors, are fierce, combative, and aggressive. Both sexes exhibit what we would call **compulsive** masculinity. The Tschambuli, a third culture of New Guinea, adhere to gender roles opposite to what is expected in

4

our society: Dominance in women is the norm; men are expected to be more passive, emotional, and dependent (Mead, 1935). In some societies, men rather than women wear makeup and spend hours preening themselves.

These societies demonstrate that it is possible to structure a society 5 with gender roles different from our own. Human "nature" appears to be quite plastic, and culture molds us in many different ways. It is also important to note the universals, however: In all cultures childcare is a female responsibility, and in all cultures women have less power than men.

Physically, women are different from men; in terms of social status, 6 they are inferior. In spite of the fact that women do substantial amounts of work in all societies, often supplying much of the food as well as taking care of stock, children, and households, women universally have less power and less value. A simple piece of evidence is parents' almost universal preference for male children. Table 12.1 includes data on sex preference for six nations.

## Table 12.1   Cross-Cultural Differences in Sex Preference

*Most cultures have a strong preference that a new baby be a boy. This preference is even stronger for firstborn children.*

"When a family has several children, both sons and daughters equally, and a new child is coming, is it preferable that the new child be a boy, either one, or a girl?"

|  | Boys | Girls | Either | Boy/Girl Ratio |
|---|---|---|---|---|
| Argentina | 33% | 3 | 63 | 11/1 |
| Chile | 56 | 5 | 39 | 11/1 |
| India | 78 | 5 | 17 | 16/1 |
| Bangladesh | 91 | 2 | 8 | 46/1 |
| Israel (non-Europeans) | 44 | 4 | 52 | 11/1 |
| Nigeria | 67 | 2 | 31 | 34/1 |

SOURCE: A. Inkeles and D. M. Smith, 1974.

If children are to be born, then women of course must be the ones to    7
bear them. Culture cannot redistribute this particular role. Subsequent
care of the child, however, is not so clearly a biological **imperative**.
Nevertheless, all societies, including our own, have viewed this as a female responsibility. The last few years have seen increased emphasis on
fathers' involvement with their children, and some modest shifts in childcare responsibility have occurred. The increase in the proportion of fathers changing diapers, however, has been overshadowed by the increase
in the number of children being raised by single mothers. The major
responsibility for childcare in most American households rests with the
mother.

Differences in childcare responsibility have enormous consequences    8
for women's roles in society. Although a woman may have only one or
two children and see the last one into school before she is 30, her responsibility for their health, their homeroom cookies, their scouting uniforms
and drama costumes, and so on will continue. As a result, even with very
low fertility levels, women's attention is frequently diverted from the
larger world of commerce and politics to the smaller world of home and
children. This is a major reason why women are not equal to men in
status and power.

Although childcare is a barrier to achievement outside the household,    9
it would be a mistake to view it simply as a weight around women's
necks. Substantial evidence indicates that women embrace the mother-
hood role; they enjoy interaction with infants and small children (Rossi,
1984). Although most mothers will feel overburdened and resentful at
least occasionally, especially if they are single parents or participate in the
labor force, it is a role that brings rewards as well as obligations.

*Determinants of women's status.*    There are no known societies where    10
women have more power than men, but important variations exist from
society to society in the amount of women's power and status. In some
societies, their status is very low, whereas in others it approaches equality.
Three key factors determine women's status in any society: (1) the degree
to which women are tied to the home by bearing, nursing, and rearing children; (2) the degree to which economic activities in a society
are compatible with staying close to home and caring for children; and

(3) the degree of physical strength necessary to carry on the subsistence activities of the society.

Until the sharp fertility declines of the last 200 years, the first factor   11
showed relatively little variability: Most women in most societies were more-or-less continually tied close to home by pregnancy and subsequent responsibility for nursing and rearing children. The degree to which women could participate in the economic life of their society and contribute to subsistence depended substantially on the second and third conditions. When economic activities required little physical strength and could be carried on while caring for children, women made major contributions to providing subsistence for their families and communities (Chafetz, 1984).

As a result of these factors, women have the highest status in hunt-   12
ing and gathering and in simple **horticultural** societies (Quinn, 1977). In these societies, the major subsistence activities (gathering and simple hoe agriculture) are compatible with women's child-related roles, and women may be responsible for as much as 60–80 percent of a society's subsistence (Blumberg, 1978). Moreover, their economic activities make them an active part of their community and increase their likelihood of being involved in community and group decisions.

These three factors help explain most of the important differences in   13
women's status across societies, and they allow us to understand why women's status was low during industrialization but now shows signs of rising. Industrialization moved work away from home and made it difficult for women to be economically productive while bearing and rearing children. Reduced fertility, however, has allowed women to leave the household and increase their participation in society's economic and public life. As a result, the status of women is improving. Nevertheless, men remain substantially advantaged in status and power. In the rest of this chapter, we discuss the reasons this is so and the prospects for change.

## Labor force participation

In 1987, 94 percent of men compared with 72 percent of women aged   14
25–54 were in the labor force. This discrepancy reflects differences in American norms about appropriate behavior for men and women.

## Table 12.2   Changes in Labor Force Participation

*Little change has occurred in men's occupational role: We expect men to work and nearly all of them do. In the last 30 years, however, there have been dramatic increases in women's labor force participation, especially for mothers with young children.*

|  | MEN | WOMEN | |
|---|---|---|---|
|  | *25–54** | *25–54* | *Married with Children under 6* |
| 1960 | 95.7% | 42.7% | 18.6% |
| 1965 | 95.5 | 45.0 | 23.3 |
| 1970 | 95.9 | 50.2 | 30.3 |
| 1975 | 94.3 | 55.1 | 36.6 |
| 1980 | 94.0 | 63.6 | 45.1 |
| 1987 | 93.6 | 71.8 | 53.6 |

SOURCES: U.S. Bureau of the Census, Statistical Abstract of the United States, 1986 (tables 660, 675) and 1979 (tables 645, 662); U.S. Department of Labor, Employment and Earnings, April 1987.

*Figures for the age group 25–54 were calculated by averaging participation rates for three age groups, 25–34, 35–44, and 45–54.

In 1900, only about 5 percent of married women worked outside the home. By 1940, the proportion had increased to just 15 percent. In every decade since, however, there have been dramatic increases (see Table 12.2). The largest increases have been in the percentage of mothers of young children in the labor force. There are a variety of reasons for these increases. Married women work for a higher standard of living, for insurance against the possibility of divorce, for career continuity in a work life likely to last 30 to 40 years, and for a socially valued and respected role. Unmarried women, of course, also work because of a simple need to support themselves and their children. Since later age at marriage and high divorce rates have increased the proportion of women in this category, this factor plays a part in increasing the overall participation rate of women.

Changing norms about labor force participation have had little impact  16
on male roles. Men have been and are still expected to support their
families through their work. Men who aren't in the labor force between
the ages of 25 and 60 are likely to receive informal negative sanctions
unless they have a very good excuse, such as a serious handicap. Even
having a lot of money isn't considered an adequate excuse for not
working.

The major changes have been in women's roles. Just 25 years ago,  17
the majority of the American public considered it wrong for women with
children to work; now only a minority feel this way. Labor force participation is still more of an option than an obligation for women, however,
and women are far less likely than men to be sanctioned by their friends
and neighbors for their inability to support their families. They will,
however, be sanctioned if their employment results in neglect of their
children's or husband's needs. American norms make it clear that, although employment is an acceptable option, their families should be
women's primary obligation.

## COMPREHENSION CHECK

Complete the following items by filling in the blank or circling the best
answer.

1. In your own words, explain the difference between sex and gender.

   _____

   _____

2. Sociologists are more interested in gender than sex.
   a. true
   b. false

3. Men and women:
   a. take on the same roles in all societies
   b. differ in their ability to care for children
   c. are always unequal in status
   d. assume different roles and statuses in different cultures

4. The main idea of the section "Labor Force Participation" is:
   a. The number of women in the work force has increased dramatically since 1900.
   b. Men's roles have not changed even though labor patterns have.
   c. Although labor patterns have changed, male and female roles are substantially the same.

5. The main idea of the selection is:
   a. Men and women are basically different.
   b. There are many cultural, social, and economic factors that determine the social roles of men and women.
   c. Scientists are interested in finding out more about the factors that differentiate men from women.

6. Using the context of the sentence, define *imperative* in paragraph 7.

   _____

7. Using the context of paragraph 12, define *horticultural*.

   _____

8. According to Mead's research, is male and female behavior a result of nature or nurture?

   _____

   _____

9. According to Table 12.1, which country has the greatest preference for male babies? Which country looks most favorably on female babies?

   _____

10. Based on Table 12.1, what inference can you make concerning the status of women in Israel?

_____

**COMPREHENSION EXERCISE 1**  *Examining the research*

Complete this exercise by filling in the blanks.

1. Examine the research finding by Mead (paragraph 4). What method or methods of research do you think were used to obtain these data? Explain.

_____

_____

_____

2. What possible flaw do you find with this study? Explain.

_____

_____

_____

3. The authors of this selection state that in all cultures women have less power than men. To support this statement they use data that indicate cultural preferences in the sex of a new baby (see Table 12.1). What method of research do you think was probably used to obtain these data, and why?

_____

_____

_____

4. Do you think this information really supports the statement that in all cultures women have less power than men? Explain.

_____

_____

_____

5. According to Quinn and Blumberg, women have highest status in hunting and gathering and simple horticultural societies (see paragraph 12). Explain why this may be so.

_____

_____

_____

6. What application might this finding have to the status of women in the United States today?

_____

_____

_____

**COMPREHENSION EXERCISE 2**  *Charting research data*

Construct a chart that compares and contrasts the information on male versus female behavior among tribes in New Guinea. (Review Chapter 10 if necessary.)

### *Prereading Activity*: Sex roles

For each pair of activities below, circle the one you would prefer.

| | | |
|---|---|---|
| attend a movie | or | attend a sporting event |
| study communication | or | study business |
| wait in line at a good restaurant | or | find a less popular place to eat |
| ask for directions | or | read a road map |
| play a board game | or | play a video game |

Are men naturally more aggressive than women? Are women naturally more nurturing than men? The following selection discusses the role of biological versus environmental influences in the determination of sex (gender) roles. As you read the selection, think about your preferences in the prereading activity.

## Biology Influences Sex Roles

**BY TIM HACKLER**

Recent research has established beyond a doubt that males and females    1
are born with a different set of "instructions" built into their **genetic code**. Science is thus confirming what poets and parents have long taken for granted.

Studies at Harvard University and elsewhere show that marked dif-    2
ferences between male and female baby behavior are already obvious in the first months of life. Female infants are more oriented toward people. Girls learn to recognize individual human faces and to distinguish between individual voices before male babies of the same age. By four months, a female infant is socially aware enough to distinguish between photographs of familiar people. Girls learn to talk earlier than boys; they articulate better and acquire a more extensive vocabulary than boys of a comparable age. They also begin to smile earlier than boys. . . .

Male infants, on the other hand, are more interested in *things*. At four    3
months a boy will react to an **inanimate** object as readily as to a person.
Given the choice between a mother's face and a bright geometric object
hanging over his crib, the boy, unlike the girl, will just as frequently
babble at the inanimate object as at his mother. A few months later he
will begin trying to take it apart. When boys and girls of pre-elementary-
school age are asked to manipulate three-dimensional objects, boys over-
whelmingly out-perform girls. Boys also show more rough-and-tumble
play than girls — as almost any parent can attest — and tend to explore
away from their mothers earlier and more often. Stanford psychologists
Karl Pribram and Dianne McGuinness conclude that women are "com-
municative" animals and men are "manipulative" animals.

But to what extent are these sex differences learned, and to what    4
extent are they genetically determined?

Until recently it was widely assumed that most human behavior    5
could be explained by "socialization." In the heredity versus environment argument — sometimes phrased as nature versus nurture — environment was considered of overwhelming importance in determining
human behavior. To suggest that any human behavior could even remotely be compared to the instinctive behavior that we see in animals
was dismissed as barbarian. Indeed, extreme environmentalists remain
committed to the idea that mankind is unlike all other animal species by
insisting that heredity has nothing to do with the difference in the ways
males and females act and think. If boys and girls were brought up in
exactly the same way, they contend, then all behavioral differences between men and women would evaporate. . . .

In most animal species, and in all **primate** species, males are more    6
active, exploratory, and aggressive than females. The primate species
**Homo sapiens** is no exception. In no human culture ever studied has
the female been found more aggressive than the male. The argument that
parents tolerate aggression in boys but discourage it in girls, and that
therefore aggression is not genetically determined, but culturally taught
does not stand up to recent evidence linking aggression specifically to the
male hormone testosterone.

Numerous studies have shown that when testosterone is adminis-    7
tered to pregnant laboratory animals, the female offspring show an in-

crease in the incidence of rough-and-tumble play and a decrease in the tendency to withdraw from threats and approaches of other animals.

In a famous decade-long series of studies at Johns Hopkins University, Drs. Anke Ehrhardt and John Money demonstrated that the same phenomenon seemed to be true for human beings as well. . . .    8

We have already seen that one of the most pronounced differences between men and women (a difference already present in the first months of life and continued through adulthood) is that women show verbal superiority, while men show "spatial superiority," a quality that shows up in such tasks as map reading, solving mathematical problems, and perceiving depth.    9

Researchers have found that this sex difference in skills apparently has something to do with the organization of the brain. It has been known for a decade that the two **cerebral hemispheres** of the brain are functionally different, and that in the large majority of individuals, the left hemisphere specializes in verbal tasks, while the right hemisphere specializes in spatial perception. It is only recently, however, that neuropsychologists have noticed that males and females differ in their tendencies to use these hemispheres.    10

Dr. Sandra F. Witelson of McMaster University in Hamilton, Ontario, was among the first to show that males tend to specialize in use of the spatially oriented right hemisphere, while females tend to use their left and right hemispheres about equally, thus implying a relatively greater usage of the linguistically oriented left hemisphere. . . .    11

It bears repeating that all of the sex differences described here represent differences *on the average.* That is to say a minority of women will be found to be more interested in "masculine" pursuits than the average man, and vice versa, Also, there is some evidence that the more creative the individual, the more he or she tends to include both typically male and female behavior in his or her personality. Finally, no experts suggest that the culture in which we live is unimportant in shaping male and female behavior; indeed it is probably more important than genetic considerations.    12

It does seem certain, however, that the extreme environmentalist explanation for behavior, which has been so dominant in political and academic thought for the past few decades, is no longer **tenable**. Males and females may, in fact, be marching to the beat of a different drummer. . . .    13

The most commonly offered explanation for these differences is that   14
such a division of skills had survival value for our ancestors, when men
were specialized for skills involved in hunting, and women were specialized for skills involved in rearing children and tending to domestic tasks.
(There is some evidence that women may have invented pottery, and it is
almost certain that in most cultures they tended to the sewing. This is
reflected today in the fact that women are able to perform better at manual dexterity tasks involving fine finger coordination than men.) Even
though such division of tasks may have less survival value today than for
our ancestors, such specialization has, to some extent, found its way into
our genes, since mankind existed in a hunter/gatherer state for the first
99 percent of his history.

## COMPREHENSION CHECK

Complete the following items by circling the best answer or filling in the
blanks.

1. The topic of this selection is:

   a. differences in sex roles

   b. nature versus nurture

   c. biological influences on sex roles

2. In your own words, state the main idea of the selection.

   _____

   _____

3. According to the author, which of the following is true?

   a. Boys prefer playing to talking.

   b. As babies, girls are more social than boys.

   c. Girls do not like rough-and-tumble play.

4. According to the selection, testosterone makes female offspring of laboratory animals more aggressive.

   a. true

   b. false

5. According to the environmentalists, heredity has little to do with the way men and women behave.

   a. true

   b. false

6. Use the context of paragraph 3 to define the word *inanimate*.

   _____

   _____

   What type of context clue is offered in this paragraph?

   _____

7. Using the context of the entire selection, write a synonym for the word *tenable* in paragraph 13. _____

8. You can infer from this selection that baby boys prefer inanimate objects to their mothers.

   a. true

   b. false

9. From the research presented in this selection, you can conclude that in general:

   a. Men should be better at sports than women.

   b. There should be no difference in athletic ability between men and women.

   c. Women should be better at sports than men.

10. The author of this selection has concluded from the research presented that:

     a. The differences in men's and women's behavior are completely biological.

     b. The differences in men's and women's behavior are the result of evolutionary adaptation.

     c. Men and women are different but equal.

## COMPREHENSION EXERCISE    *Examining the research*

Complete this exercise by filling in the blanks.

1. The research cited in paragraph 2 describes children's behavior at a very young age. The inference is that differences between males and females exist from birth. What flaw do you see in using this study to prove that differences are not environmental? Explain.

    _____

    _____

    _____

2. In paragraph 6 the author states that "in no human culture ever studied has the female been found more aggressive than the male," yet Margaret Mead's study of the people of New Guinea suggests differently. How might you explain this discrepancy?

    _____

    _____

    _____

3. What does the experiment with lab animals and testosterone prove in terms of male versus female behavior?

   _____

   _____

   _____

4. Does Dr. Sandra Witelson's research findings that men tend to specialize in use of the right hemisphere of the brain while females tend to use both the left and right hemispheres equally actually prove that women are naturally better communicators than men? Why or why not?

   _____

   _____

   _____

5. If the explanation for male-female differences has evolutionary roots, how might the present trend toward unisexuality affect male and female behavior in the future?

   _____

   _____

   _____

## READING SELECTION THREE

### *Prereading Activity*: **Your family**

Before reading the selection, on a separate sheet of paper write briefly about your family: the number of children, their sexes and ages, and so on. How are you different from or similar to the other members of your family? If you are an only child, compare yourself to your parents or perhaps to a close cousin.

The research described in Reading Selection Three may hold a possible answer to the nature versus nurture question. Before reading, activate your knowledge of the topic by reviewing what you learned from the first two reading selections.

## When Siblings Are *Un*like Peas in a Pod

**BY ALISON BASS**

*How they turned out may stem in large part from differences in how their parents treated them*

Mark Twain was a bit of a hell-raiser as a boy, always getting into scrapes that frustrated and exasperated his long-suffering mother. His younger brother, Henry, was the opposite, a sweet, **docile** child who did everything that was expected of him.     1

In "The Adventures of Tom Sawyer," Twain made delightful use of this difference between **siblings**, portraying Tom as even more of a hellion than he had been, and casting Tom's half-brother Sid as the kind of righteous goody two-shoes that every spirited child loves to hate.     2

The 19th century author and humorist was focusing on a phenomenon that continues to baffle psychologists today: why siblings, who share 50 percent of their parents' genes and are raised in the same family, sometimes grow up to be so different.     3

In Twain's day and through most of this century, psychologists considered such differences an **anomaly**, and families usually wrote off an especially unusual sibling as the "black sheep." Then in the last decade, some researchers looked to newly discovered variations in inherited traits as the primary explanation. Nature had to be responsible, they reasoned, given how similarly children in the same family were nurtured.     4

But now researchers are discovering that there is no single environment in the home. Instead, there are disparate environments for each child, and the differences can have a surprisingly profound influence on     5 each one's personality, interests and eventual occupation. Researchers suspect, for instance, that subtle differences in the way parents respond to their children can have a major impact on a child's sense of self-worth and development.

"The data from adoption and family studies all converge on the same  6
conclusion," said Robert Plomin, a developmental psychologist at Pennsylvania State University, in a recent interview. "Kids experience very different environments within the same family."

Genetic variations appear to underlie some of the initial differences  7
between children, Plomin and other researchers believe, but may not explain as much about development as had been thought. Psychologists suspect that differences in parental treatment, the way siblings interact, and the impact of chance events will turn out to be the major factors in shaping each child's world.

"I would bet that the major differences have a lot to do with chaos  8
and chance—the way parents treat a particular child and idiosyncratic experiences," Plomin said. "A kid has a certain experience at a certain period of time, and that little nudge has a cascading effect."

Plomin's favorite example is Charles Darwin. He was groomed by his  9
parents for a career in the clergy or medicine—like his brother, Erasmus—but Darwin's life took a radical turn because an astute uncle, on the spur of the moment, drove him 30 miles to meet a certain Captain Fitzroy. Fitzroy, the captain of the ship Beagle, was looking for a botanist to accompany him on a year long trip around Cape Horn, and Darwin, although inexperienced, was invited along. That voyage set him on his historic path toward discovering how species evolve.

Researchers are also finding that factors once thought to loom large  10
in distinguishing siblings have far less significance. Birth order and family size, for instance, turn out not to be as important as the way children perceive they are treated by their parents or influences they encounter outside the family.

"In terms of intelligence and adult outcome, we've found that birth  11
order, family size, and spacing of children don't account for more than 2 percent of the variance between siblings," Plomin noted. "It's surprising to realize how little they explain."

At the core of the **micro-environment** theory are data from studies   12
of identical twins reared in the same family. Many of these twins, although they were identical genetically, had sharply contrasting life experiences. In one ongoing study of 35-year-old twins in Sweden (part of
a large study group of 10,000 twins), preliminary results show very different patterns between siblings. In some cases, for instance, one twin became an alcoholic while the other downed at most a drink or two a week.

The twins themselves generally ascribed their differences to their en-   13
vironment, not to variations in inherited traits. One pair said the alcoholic
twin just fell in with a group of friends who drank a lot.

In a long term study of schizophrenic patients, researchers found that,   14
of those who were identical twins, only 30 percent of the twin siblings
also developed schizophrenia, a sign these twins were experiencing different environments within a family.

"You have genetically identical individuals who are similar by only   15
30 percent," Plomin noted. "Nothing else can explain that large a difference other than environment."

### Adoptee comparisons

Recent studies also show that environments within a family can affect   16
how children develop as much as if they were raised in different families.
In studies of biologically related and adoptive families ranging in socio-
economic status from working to upper middle class, researchers found
that most children experience "functionally equivalent" environments.
In other words, the differences between children adopted in infancy by
families with vastly different backgrounds were no larger than the differences between siblings born to the same family.

"Upper middle-class brothers who attend the same school and whose   17
parents take them to the same plays, sporting events, music lessons and
therapists, and use similar child-rearing practices on them, are little more
similar in personality measures than they are to working-class or farm
boys, whose lives are totally different," wrote Sandra Scarr, a co-author
of this study and psychologist at the University of Virginia, in the July
1987 issue of Behavioral and Brain Science.

"It doesn't seem to matter much whether you're being reared by the   18
Bernsteins or the Smiths — as long as you're not being neglected, abused
or extremely disadvantaged," Scarr said in a recent telephone interview.

Of far greater importance, Scarr and other researchers say, are differ-    19
ences within a family, and some of the largest developmental differences
may come from relatively minor variations in how parents treat each
child. Most parents will not admit that they treat children differently; in
a recent study, however, one-third of all siblings said they noticed discrep-
ancies in the way their parents treated them.

"Kids can be very sensitive to pretty subtle cues — like the fact that a    20
parent laughs at one kid's jokes more often or looks at his brother more
often," said Plomin, who did the study. "And a relatively small difference
in treatment may make a big difference in development."

One of the most compelling is 19th century British writer Charles    21
Dickens. Although Dickens' destitute parents allowed his sister Fanny,
who was musically gifted, to attend the Royal Academy of Music on
scholarship, they made Dickens work in a factory starting at age 13 to
supplement the family's income.

Some of Dickens' biographers have suggested that his acute jealousy    22
of his sister set the stage for his later problems with women. Dickens
himself said his years of hardship as a factory worker shaped much of his
later novels, particularly "David Copperfield."

Although Dickens' parents may have treated their children differently    23
out of financial need, psychologists say many parents unconsciously favor one child over another because he or she reminds them of themselves
or of someone else they admire or hate. Or one child might have traits
that the parent dislikes in himself.

Robert Brooks, director of outpatient child psychology at McLean    24
Hospital in Belmont, recalls one parent who confided she was furious
over her 7-year-old daughter's inability to handle new situations easily
and had become very intolerant of the daughter's shyness. In therapy, the
mother recognized that she had also been very shy in childhood and was
trying to prevent her child from experiencing the pain she went through.

"As parents, we bring some of our own baggage from the past into    25
our roles as parents," Brooks noted. "And many parents find it easier to
be with some children than others."

Too often, psychologists say, parents don't recognize the "poor fit"    26
between themselves and their child and try too hard to mold a child into
something he or she is not.

Researchers are also finding that the relationship between brothers    27
and sisters can have a profound effect. The American writer Henry James
was dramatically influenced by the fact that he was the younger brother
of William James, an outgoing and intellectually impressive boy who
went on to become a distinguished philosopher and psychologist.

According to biographer Leon Edel, Henry James withdrew at an    28
early age into the world of books and imagination, turning himself into
an acute observer of social events, rather than compete directly with his
popular older sibling.

"For Henry, life in the James family was a state of inexhaustible    29
younger brotherhood," Edel wrote in his 1985 biography. So Henry,
"making himself small and quiet among the other Jameses, turned into
the depths of himself to fashion a fictional world based on the realities
around him in which elder brothers are vanquished, fathers made to
disappear, mothers put into their place."

Chance events also may have a strong impact on making one child's    30
experience in a family different from another. Often, siblings grow up
with different neighbors, different teachers and different friends, all of
whom can turn a child's attitudes and interests in new directions.

Even children who attend the same school and have the same teach-    31
ers experience different realities, Scarr noted, for the simple reason that
they are genetically different in temperament. Because many teachers
expect children from the same family to behave similarly, it can be particularly difficult for temperamentally different siblings to measure up to
their expectations.

Both teachers and parents need to be more aware of the potentially    32
enormous differences between siblings in the same family, specialists say.

"The United States gives great lip service to the concept that children    33
should be treated individually, but there is an awful lot of stereotypical
handling — at home and in the schools," said Dr. Stella Chess, a child
psychiatrist at the New York University School of Medicine. "The concept
that children from the same family can be very different is not that well
accepted."

Complete the following items by filling in the blanks.

1.  According to the researchers, what three major factors account for the differences among siblings raised in the same family?

    a. _____

    b. _____

    c. _____

2.  According to this selection, what percentage of the variance among siblings is caused by: birth order? By family size? By spacing?

    _____

3.  Explain what is meant by the statement "The major differences [in siblings' development] have a lot to do with chaos and chance."

    _____

    _____

    _____

4.  What conclusion can be drawn from the fact that the differences between adopted and natural children in a family are not greater than the differences between the natural children themselves?

    _____

    _____

    _____

5. According to this selection, parents often treat children differently without even realizing it. Explain how you think this might happen.

_____

_____

_____

## CHAPTER APPLICATION 1

In this chapter you have learned a great deal about the influences of nature and environment on the human personality. Write an essay stating your opinion on this topic. Integrate information from the selections you have read with examples from your own experience.

Remember to do the following:

1. Write an interesting introduction that in some way conveys the main point you wish to make.

2. Organize your paragraphs using one or more of the rhetorical structures you have studied in this text: cause and effect, comparison and contrast, definition, example, and list.

3. Include a conclusion that sums up the main idea of the essay.

## CHAPTER APPLICATION 2

Using one of the journal indexes in your college library, locate a research article on a topic of your choice. In your own words:

1. Paraphrase the hypothesis being tested.

2. Summarize the subjects, methods of research, and procedures used.

3. Explain the conclusions reached by the researchers.

4. Evaluate the conclusions by discussing possible flaws in the study.

GOING BEYOND

When it comes to professional success among men and women, environment seems to play a greater role than nature. "Where Have All the Smart Girls Gone?" is an interesting report of a study that found that, more than intelligence, the school a girl attends affects her ultimate success in life.

## Where Have All the Smart Girls Gone?

BY MARY CONROY

Picture two high school **valedictorians**, one boy and one girl, marching to the strains of "Pomp and Circumstance." They may walk side-by-side at high school graduation, but seven years later, the woman is likely to lag far behind.    1

That's what psychologist Terry Denny of the University of Illinois has discovered. Seven years into a 10-year study of valedictorians, Denny finds that two-thirds of the women had begun to lower their career aspirations by their sophomore year of college. Even though female valedictorians outperform men in college, few of the women go on to pursue doctoral degrees. And in the work world, women valedictorians perform at lower levels than men do.    2

Denny and researcher Karen Arnold find the record frightening. "We're losing the talents of some of our best women," Arnold says, "and if this is happening to those who have everything going for them, who have every conceivable credential, one can only imagine the handicaps and barriers that women in general face."    3

Denny and Arnold found that the women who did continue their performance had a supportive college environment. They were far more likely to have had significant interaction with faculty and professionals in their fields. In addition, they had been given many chances to test their abilities in a nurturing environment.    4

The work by Denny and Arnold complements many other studies. There is a large body of research showing how schools at every level teach girls to act helpless, sit quietly and find math and science difficult.    5

Even girls who reach adolescence with egos intact face a real chal-    6
lenge. At that age, peer pressure to conform combines with their need to
be popular. Suddenly, assertive girls act demure, worried that talent will
scare boys away.

Offering mentors is one way to support girls, and many students are    7
turning to women's colleges for such encouragement. Alumnae of these
schools say they were free to take risks and learned that women's leadership is as natural as breathing and nearly as important. According to
Myra Sadker, dean of the School of Education at American University
and an expert on school sexism, "When girls go to single-sex schools,
they stop being the audience and become players."

Although many girls' schools and women's colleges either closed or    8
went coed during the '70s, the majority of the survivors find applications
booming. Parents who once sent their daughters to be protected are
now sending them for leadership experiences they're unlikely to get anywhere else.

That experience pays off later in the work world. Research from the    9
Women's College Coalition has found that, compared with graduates of
coed schools, alumnae of women's colleges are:

- Six times more likely to be on the boards of Fortune 500
  companies.

- Seven times more likely to be named as one of *Good Housekeeping*'s outstanding women graduates.

- Two times more likely to pursue doctoral degrees.

- Six times more likely to be on *Business Week*'s list of top corporate
  women.

The argument isn't all one-sided, however. Some researchers say that    10
graduates of women's colleges perform so well because they come from
higher socioeconomic groups. In addition, many girls adamantly refuse
to attend single-sex schools. Most of them find that coed schools help
develop essential social skills. Others say women can't compete with men
unless they learn how in coed schools.

But Sadker isn't so sure. "It's like young corn in a field," she says. "If    11
you don't water it and nourish it, it'll never grow into a bumper crop."
And who would even think of planting in soil full of rocks?

## JOURNAL WRITING

1. The Denny and Arnold study suggests that girls are more likely to be successful if they attend an all-girls college. However, other researchers feel women must learn to compete with men, and for this reason suggest that a coed environment is more beneficial. Write an essay giving your opinion on this issue.

2. Write an essay discussing the influence of nature versus nurture with regard to gender roles. Use experiences from your own life to support the theory that men and women are naturally different. Then cite experiences that would support the environmental theory.

3. The idea that biology determines one's personality is one of the most controversial among researchers. Choose one of your own personality traits (or one of someone close to you) and evaluate whether you believe this trait to have been biologically or environmentally determined. Use examples to support your evaluation.

4. Women have traditionally been less valued than men. Describe how men and women are valued in your culture. Is this changing? If so, how and why?

5. In the prereading activity for "When Siblings Are *Un*like Peas in a Pod," you compared yourself with a family member. Using information from the article, explain what you believe to be the reasons for the differences or similarities.

# Additional Readings for Review

E ach chapter in Parts I, II, and III of *Reading and Learning Across the Disciplines* emphasizes a specific reading or study skill. Although each of these skills is reinforced in subsequent exercises throughout the book, Part IV provides an additional reading and skills exercise for each of the twelve chapters. The readings in Part IV complement the theme of each chapter and may be used either to reinforce and apply skills as you progress through the book or to test your mastery at the end of the course.

## *Prereading Activity*: **Identifying context clues**

Below are a number of sentences from the selection "The Language Detectives: How They Found the Tribe That Gave Us Words." For each sentence (1) underline the parts that provide clues to the meaning of the italicized word, (2) attempt to define the word without using the glossary, and (3) indicate the type of context clue used.

1.  What tribe first spoke that mother tongue that hatched this *brood* of cousin languages?

    a. definition _____

    b. type of context clue _____

2.  We might think of these ancestors as only wandering *nomads* had we not found their word for "plow" . . .

    a. definition _____

    b. type of context clue _____

3.  When, fanning out, *migrating* branches of the tribe met the thunder of ocean surf, each gave this new marvel a separate name.

    a. definition _____

    b. type of context clue _____

4.  One branch was to push Slavic up to the *polar* sea, another was to bring Latin down to the Mediterranean . . .

    a. definition _____

    b. type of context clue _____

5. The ideas *enshrined* in these words are not the least of the inheritance from that long-forgotten tribe — an inheritance more ancient than the wall of Troy and probably more enduring than the pyramids.

   a. definition  _____

   b. type of context clue  _____

## The Language Detectives: How They Found the Tribe That Gave Us Words

**FROM** *STRANGE STORIES, AMAZING FACTS*

Tracing missing persons can take much patient detective work. But a special kind of "private eye" can trace the missing ancestors of whole peoples by studying the clues buried in words.     1

These **philologists**, as the language detectives are called, have traced the word trail back from peoples in Europe, India, South Africa, the Americas, and the Pacific islands to a tiny, nameless, and forgotten tribe that roamed central Eurasia 5,000 to 6,000 years ago, before the dawn of written history.     2

### Word clues

For a long time scholars puzzled over the striking similarity of words in different languages. In Dutch, *vader*; in Latin, *pater*; in Old Irish, *athir*; in Persian, *pidar*; in the Sanskrit of distant India, *pitr*. These words all sounded alike and meant the same thing — "father."     3

How did it happen that widely separated peoples used such closely related sound symbols? The problem baffled **linguists** for years, the more so because "father" was but one of a host of such coincidences. Toward the end of the 18th century it dawned on scholars that perhaps all these words stemmed from some common language.     4

### The language law

At last a brilliant German, Jacob Grimm — joint collector with his brother Wilhelm of *Grimm's Fairy Tales* — and other scholars of his time worked out a "law" of language changes. Their discoveries showed that the changes that take place as a language develops and spreads are regular     5 and consistent enough to permit enlightening comparisons between languages and to allow the earlier stages of these languages to be reconstructed.

Once the pattern of change was clear, scholars could see that the many 6
words for "father" all pointed back to an original, *pater*. Also, "water" in English, *wasser* in German, *hydor* in Greek, *voda* in Russian (vodka is "little water"), *udan* in Sanskrit, and even *watar* in the language of King David's captain, Uriah the Hittite—all could have come only from an original *wodor*. Using the law, they could trace the origin of countless words.

Philologists have evolved an entire ancient vocabulary. They labeled 7
this early speech "Indo-European" because it had Indic and European branches. There is a Latin branch, from which stems Italian, Spanish, Portuguese, French, and Rumanian. There is a Germanic branch, which includes English, German, Danish, Dutch, Swedish, and Norwegian. The Celtic branch includes Welsh, Irish, and Breton. The Slavic includes Russian, Polish, Czech, Bulgar, and Serb.

In addition, Indo-European languages include Lithuanian, Persian, 8
Greek, Armenian, and a score of dialects in India that have sprung from ancient Sanskrit.

What tribe first spoke that mother tongue that hatched this **brood** of 9
cousin languages? Today we know a good deal about these dawn people, even though archeologists have uncovered not a single crumbling wall nor any pottery that we can be sure was theirs.

**How they lived**

Our speech ancestors had domesticated the "cow," *gwou*, which gave 10
them "milk," *melg*. From this strain they also bred "oxen," *uksen*, which were joined together by a "yoke," *yug*. They also knew sheep (their *owa* became English "ewe"), which must have been tame, for from their "fleece," *pleus*, they got "wool," *wlana*, which they had learned to "weave," *webh*, into cloth and then "sew," *siw*, into garments.

We might think of these ancestors as only wandering **nomads** had 11
we not found their word for "plow," which was *ara*. Because of Latin *arare* ("to plow"), we speak in English of land that is arable—capable of cultivation.

What did they plant? Their word *grano* gives English "grain." One 12
kind of *grano* may have been light in color, for their word for "white,"

*kweit*, coming down through Old Germanic *hweits*, gave us the English "wheat."

These speech ancestors of ours ground their grain in a "mill," *mel*, added "water," *wodor*, and "yeast," *yes*, to make a "dough," *dheigh*, which they would "bake," *bhog*, in an "oven," *uqno*, to make "bread," *pa* (Latin *panis*, hence English "pantry," the place where bread is kept).    13

All this we know from those old root words, which have come down to us in a score of languages. So have their numerals, which were: 1, *oinos*; 2, *duo*; 3, *treies*; 4, *qetwer*; 5, *penqe*; 6, *sweks*; 7, *septn*; 8, *okto*; 9, *newn*; 10, *dekm*.    14

## Where they lived

Where did these anchestors live? Since all Indo-European languages lack a common word for lion, tiger, elephant, or camel, the homeland could not have been far south.    15

Their old word *sneighw* (English "snow," Russian *sneig*, Greek *nipha*, Welsh *nyf*, Latin *nix*, French *neige*) might even push this homeland far northward.    16

Wild animals they knew were the "snake," *serp*, the "beaver," *bhebhru*, the bear, the goose, the rabbit, and the duck. They had a word for a "small stream," *strew*, and another for a "little pond," which came down into English as "marsh," "mire," and "moor," and into Latin as *mare* — hence English "mariner" and "maritime." But of vast salt oceans they probably knew nothing. When, fanning out, **migrating** branches of the tribe met the thunder of ocean surf, each gave this new marvel a separate name.    17

Of trees they knew the birch and the beech, and because, much later, the writings of northern Europe were scratched on smooth boards of "beech," *bok*, we get the English word "book."    18

All these animals and trees are natives of the temperate zone. Many other signs point to one possible location in central Europe. But gradually, pushed by overpopulation or invaders, the Indo-Europeans began to move.    19

Their wanderings lasted thousands of years and led them far afield. One branch was to push Slavic up to the **polar** sea, another was to bring Latin down to the Mediterranean, while still others were to carry Celtic into what is today Great Britain and France, and Germanic down to the right bank of the Rhine and up into the far northlands of Scandinavia.    20

On their wanderings they must have pondered the origins of things,    21
for the English word "God" has its root in *ghutom*, meaning "the Being
that is worshiped." To them, as to us, the syllable *sac* meant "sacred";
and from *prek* ("praying") down through Latin *precari* ("to pray") comes
our word "prayer."

The ideas **enshrined** in these words are not the least of the inheri-    22
tance from that long-forgotten tribe — an inheritance more ancient than
the walls of Troy and probably more enduring than the pyramids.

## COMPREHENSION CHECK

Answer the following items by circling the correct answer or filling in the
blanks.

1.  The phrase that best states the topic of this selection is:
    a. our common ancestors
    b. the evolution of language
    c. a common language root

2.  It is believed that these early peoples were not simply wanderers
    because:
    a. Their animals and trees were native to temperate zones.
    b. They had a word for "plow."
    c. They had domesticated the cow.

3.  Based on the words from which it was derived, the word *maritime* must
    have something to do with _____

4.  From this selection we can conclude that our early ancestors believed
    in some sort of superior being.
    a. true
    b. false

5. Using a dictionary if necessary, give three English derivatives formed from the following ancient roots:

a. *hydor* _____ _____ _____

b. *pater* _____ _____ _____

c. *mare* _____ _____ _____

d. *serp* _____ _____ _____

e. *sac* _____ _____ _____

## CHAPTER 2: PRACTICE IN PREVIEWING

### *Prereading Activity*: **Previewing**

Before reading, preview the selection by skimming and scanning for important information and completing the following chart.

1. Title _____

2. State the main idea of the introduction.

_____

3. List the headings and titles of the inserts.

_____

_____

_____

_____

_____

4. Explain the main idea of the chart on page 403.

   _____

   _____

5. List and define at least three important terms.

   a. _____

   b. _____

   c. _____

6. Define the words in boldface print.

   a. _____

   b. _____

   c. _____

7. Write a sentence stating what you think the selection is about.

   _____

   _____

---

## The Pace of Life

**BY ROBERT LEVINE**

*Most cities where people walk, talk and work the fastest also have the highest rates of heart disease. But what do the exceptions tell us?*

> "'Will you walk a little faster?'
>     said a whiting to a snail.
> 'There's a porpoise close behind us,
>     and he's treading on my tail.'"

If you live in a city where people keep treading on you, are you more    1
likely to have heart trouble? Our research says yes, generally speaking —
though other factors of culture and personality play a big part in determining individual susceptibility to life in the fast lane.

Our research team — graduate students Karen Lynch, Kuni Miyake,    2
Marty Lucia and six other volunteers — recently measured the tempo of
life in 36 American cities of various sizes in all parts of the country to
answer two questions: 1) How does the overall pace compare from one
city and region to another? 2) Is there any relation between an area's
pace of life and its residents' physical condition — specifically the **prevalence** of coronary heart disease (CHD)?

What makes these questions especially interesting right now is the    3
continuing controversy between researchers who think that a strong
sense of time urgency — the classic Type A struggle to make every second
count — is an important element in CHD, and those who believe a combination of anger and hostility is the only Type A characteristic that really
causes heart disease.

We studied three large (more than 1.8 million people), three medium-    4
sized (850,000–1.5 million) and three smaller (350,000–550,000) cities
in each of the four census-defined areas of the United States — Northeast,
Midwest, South and West. In each, we looked at how fast people walked,
talked and worked. (See "Measuring a City's Pace" [page 402] for more
details about the study.)

**The speedy Northeast**

As the chart [on page 403] indicates, the three fastest cities and seven    5
of the fastest nine are in the Northeast. Northeasterners generally walk
faster, give change faster, talk faster and are more likely to wear watches
than people in other areas.

Boston edges out Buffalo for first place, trailed by New York City,    6
everyone's prestudy favorite. Perhaps New Yorkers lose a couple of steps
stopping to watch the local festivities. Walter Murphy, who collected the
walking-speed data there, reported an improvised music concert, an attempted purse snatching, and an unsuccessful mugging during the hour
and a half he clocked pedestrians on one corner.

The West has the slowest pace overall, due mostly to particularly slow    7
walkers and bank tellers. Least hurried of all is America's symbol of sun,
fun and laid-back living. Los Angelenos are 24th in walking speed, next
to last in rapid speech and far, far behind people in every other city we
studied in money-counting speed. Their only concession to the clock is
to wear one — the city is 13th highest in watches worn.

## Measuring a City's Pace

To see if there is any relationship between a city's characteristic pace and its rate of CHD, we looked at four indicators.

**Walking speed:** We clocked how long it took pedestrians to move 60 feet along relatively uncrowded streets. To eliminate the effects of socializing, we timed only people walking alone. We also excluded children, pedestrians with large packages or obvious physical handicaps, and window shoppers.

**Working speed:** We timed how long bank clerks took either to give change, in set denominations, for two $20 bills or to give us two $20 bills in return for change.

**Talking speed:** In each city we tape-recorded how long it took postal clerks to explain the difference between regular mail, certified mail and insured mail. We then calculated their actual "**articulation**" rates by dividing the number of syllables in the response by the total time it took.

**The watch factor:** As a simple measure of concern with clock time, we counted the percentage of men and women who were wearing wristwatches.

Individually, each of these measures has its weaknesses: They all tap into special groups, not the city's general population; the second two are confounded by skill and efficiency; and the last is affected by fashion as well as concern with time. Taken together, though, they sample a wide range of people and activities and reflect many facets of a city's pace of life.

Finally, we created an index of the overall pace of life in each city by giving the four scores equal weight and adding them together. The chart [on page 403] shows how the cities ranked, from 1st to 36th, in each category.    —R.L.

The stopwatches we used weren't all that told us the West lives time differently from the East. We often learned as much from the process of data collection as from the data. To get the exact time of day in No. 1-ranked Boston, for example, we dialed "N-E-R-V-O-U-S." In my home town of Fresno (31st in time urgency), the number is "P-O-P-C-O-R-N."    8

# Fast Cities, Slow Cities: How They Rank

| | Overall Pace | Walking Speed | Bank Speed | Talking Speed | Watches Worn | CHD* |
|---|---|---|---|---|---|---|
| Boston, MA | 1 | 2 | 6 | 6 | 2 | 10 |
| Buffalo, NY | 2 | 5 | 7 | 15 | 4 | 2 |
| New York, NY | 3 | 11 | 11 | 28 | 1 | 1 |
| Salt Lake City, UT | 4 | 4 | 16 | 12 | 11 | 31 |
| Columbus, OH | 5 | 22 | 17 | 1 | 19 | 26 |
| Worcester, MA | 6 | 9 | 22 | 6 | 6 | 4 |
| Providence, RI | 7 | 7 | 9 | 9 | 19 | 3 |
| Springfield, MA | 8 | 1 | 15 | 20 | 22 | 7 |
| Rochester, NY | 9 | 20 | 2 | 26 | 7 | 14 |
| Kansas City, MO | 10 | 6 | 3 | 15 | 32 | 21 |
| St. Louis, MO | 11 | 15 | 20 | 9 | 15 | 8 |
| Houston, TX | 12 | 10 | 8 | 21 | 19 | 36 |
| Paterson, NJ | 13 | 17 | 4 | 11 | 31 | 4 |
| Bakersfield, CA | 14 | 28 | 13 | 5 | 17 | 20 |
| Atlanta, GA | 15 | 3 | 27 | 2 | 36 | 33 |
| Detroit, MI | 16 | 21 | 12 | 34 | 2 | 11 |
| Youngstown, OH | 17 | 13 | 18 | 3 | 30 | 6 |
| Indianapolis, IN | 18 | 18 | 23 | 8 | 24 | 22 |
| Chicago, IL | 19 | 12 | 31 | 3 | 27 | 13 |
| Philadelphia, PA | 20 | 30 | 5 | 22 | 11 | 16 |
| Louisville, KY | 21 | 16 | 21 | 29 | 15 | 18 |
| Canton, OH | 22 | 23 | 14 | 26 | 15 | 9 |
| Knoxville, TN | 23 | 25 | 24 | 30 | 11 | 17 |
| San Francisco, CA | 24 | 19 | 35 | 26 | 5 | 27 |
| Chattanooga, TN | 25 | 35 | 1 | 32 | 24 | 12 |
| Dallas, TX | 26 | 26 | 28 | 15 | 28 | 32 |
| Oxnard, CA | 27 | 30 | 30 | 23 | 7 | 34 |
| Nashville, TN | 28 | 8 | 26 | 24 | 33 | 14 |
| San Diego, CA | 29 | 27 | 34 | 18 | 9 | 24 |
| East Lansing, MI | 30 | 14 | 33 | 12 | 34 | 29 |
| Fresno, CA | 31 | 36 | 25 | 17 | 19 | 25 |
| Memphis, TN | 32 | 34 | 10 | 19 | 34 | 30 |
| San Jose, CA | 33 | 29 | 29 | 30 | 22 | 35 |
| Shreveport, LA | 34 | 32 | 19 | 33 | 28 | 19 |
| Sacramento, CA | 35 | 33 | 32 | 36 | 26 | 23 |
| Los Angeles, CA | 36 | 24 | 36 | 35 | 13 | 28 |

Lower numbers indicate faster speeds, more watches worn, higher CHD rates.
*Rates of coronary heart disease, adjusted for the median age in each city.

**Walking and talking**

There usually isn't much difference between one rank and the next.   9
But at the extremes, people march to very different drummers. In walking
speed, for example, the fastest pedestrians — in Springfield, MA — cover
60 feet in an average of 11.1 seconds, 3.6 seconds faster than they do in
Fresno, the slowest town. If they were walking a football field, the Massachusetts team would move the full 100 yards and cross the goal line at
about the same time their California opponents were still about 25 yards
short.

Differences in talking speed are even greater. The fastest-talking postal   10
clerks — in Columbus, OH — rattle out nearly 40% more syllables per
second than their colleagues in Los Angeles (3.9 compared to 2.8). If they
were reading the 6 o'clock news, it would take the California workers
until nearly 7:25 to report what the Ohio clerks finish at 7.

With these pace figures in hand, we compared them with rates of   11
death from CHD in each city to see if there is any association between the
two. Since age is a major factor in heart disease, we statistically adjusted
the CHD figures for the median age of each city's population.

**The pace of death**

Pace of life and CHD were highly related, as a whole, for both cities   12
and regions. In fact, this statistical relationship was even stronger than
the **correlation** researchers usually find between heart disease and Type
A personality measures such as hostility, aggression and competitiveness.
The speed of a person's environment seems to predict the likelihood of
heart disease as well as Type A personality test scores do. This turned out
to be true no matter how we corrected for age, or whether we took it into
account at all.

Why are people in Type A (fast-paced) environments more likely to   13
get heart disease? Largely, we suspect, it's because these environments
attract Type A people — who then do their best to keep the pace fast.
Social psychologist Timothy Smith of the University of Utah and his
colleagues have shown that Type As both seek and create time-urgent
surroundings. Thus the fastest cities in our study may represent both their
dearest dreams and their creations.

The combination of hard work and an urgent sense of time doesn't have to be lethal. This became clear several years ago when Ellen Wolff, Kathy Bartlett and I surveyed three indicators of the pace of life in 12 large and medium-sized cities in England, Indonesia, Italy, Japan, Taiwan and the United States. (See "Social Time: The Heartbeat of Culture," in the March 1985 issue of *Psychology Today*.)

The Japanese led on every measure — they walked the fastest, their postal clerks took the least time to sell us stamps and their public clocks were the most accurate. To our surprise, however, they had by far the lowest CHD death rates of the four countries for which we had statistics (there were none available for Taiwan or Indonesia). Japan's CHD mortality rates, in fact, were the lowest among the 27 industrialized countries compared in a recent report released by the World Health Organization.

How does a fast-charging Type A population avoid CHD? Cultural values appear to be one key. Researchers Michael Marmot and Leonard Syme found that Japanese-American men who did not have a traditional Japanese upbringing were 2 to 2.7 times more likely to have CHD than those who had been raised traditionally. This still held true even when all of the usual CHD risk factors — diet, smoking, cholesterol, blood pressure, triglycerides, obesity, glucose and age — were taken into account.

The Type A personality scale includes a series of questions about being hard-driving — competitive, short-tempered, impatient — as well as a series about being hard-working. For people in the United States, high scores on the first set of questions usually go hand-in-hand with high scores on the second — both are part of the same behavior pattern.

But in Japan, where social harmony may be the most highly respected social value, competition and aggression have little place. When Japanese take the Type A personality scale, being hard-driving has little to do with being hard-working.

Even translating the "hard-driving" Type A items is a problem. One frustrated researcher found that the best Japanese translation for the question "Do you like competition on your job?" was "Do you like impoliteness on your job?"

Competitive hostility and anger, it appears, play little part in the hard-working pace of the Japanese. In our own culture, though, there is often a fine line between speed/time urgency on the one hand and competition/hostility on the other — and the combination can be life-threatening.     —R.L.

Smith found that time pressure also initiates, maintains and exacer-    14
bates Type A-like behavior in Type Bs. They act more like As, while As
strive to push the beat even faster—all in an environment already filled
with coronary-prone personalities.

## COMPREHENSION CHECK

For the following items either circle the correct answer or fill in the blanks.

1. The title that would best infer the topic of this selection might be:
   a. The Speedy Americans
   b. Fast Lifestyles and Heart Disease
   c. American Versus Japanese Lifestyles

2. The sentence that best states the main idea of this selection is:
   a. American attitudes toward time vary greatly from place to place.
   b. Americans who live in fast-paced environments have a greater
      chance of contracting heart disease than those who live in slower-
      paced areas.
   c. The Japanese have a lower incidence of heart disease than Ameri-
      cans because they experience less hostility.

3. Researchers in this study found that the Northeastern states:
   a. contained the top ten fastest-paced states
   b. contained the top seven fastest-paced states
   c. contained the fastest bank tellers

4. Researchers in this study found that the fastest-paced cities in the
   world are in:
   a. the United States
   b. England
   c. Japan

5. The fastest talkers speak approximately:
   a. 1.1 syllables per second faster than the slowest talkers
   b. 3.6 syllables per second faster than the slowest talkers
   c. 3.9 syllables per second faster than the slowest talkers

6. From the chart on page 403, it appears that the second-fastest-paced area of the United States is:
   a. the Midwest
   b. the South
   c. the Northwest

7. From the chart on page 403, which of the top ten fastest-paced cities has the lowest incidence of heart disease? _____

8. Use the context of the sentence and your knowledge of prefixes and roots to define the word *correlation* in paragraph 12.

   _____

9. Why do you think talking speed was measured by an actual articulation rate rather than by the length of time of the response?

   _____

   _____

10. From this article you can conclude that:
    a. Type A personalities often choose to live in fast-paced areas.
    b. Type B personalities influence Type A personalities.
    c. Type A personalities are at a greater risk of heart disease than Type B personalities.

**CHAPTER 3: PRACTICE IN FINDING THE MAIN IDEA**

## *Prereading Activity*: **Finding the main idea**

Read the first paragraph of the selection "The Unwritten American Bargain" and write a sentence stating the main idea.

_____

_____

## The Unwritten American Bargain

### BY GEN. COLIN L. POWELL

I graduated from Morris High School on Boston Road in the Bronx when   1
I was 16. My parents expected me to go to college — they expected me to
do better than they had done. And I valued my parents' opinion so highly
that there was no question in my mind. I was going to college. And where
to go to college was not an issue either. I was accepted at New York
University and at the City College of New York. But NYU cost $750 a year,
and CCNY cost $10 — no contest for a poor boy from the South Bronx.

I didn't do exceptionally well at CCNY — or at least, I didn't think so   2
at the time. I passed with straight C's and graduated only because of my
superior grades in ROTC, the Reserve Officer Training Corps. It took me
four and one-half years, one summer session and a change of academic
major — plus straight A's in ROTC — but I did graduate.

My CCNY graduating class went off in a thousand and one directions,   3
as do all classes. Many people went the same way I did, into the Army.
The Army was exciting: It promised adventure, it was a way to serve
and most of all it was a job. For me, it turned out to be a maturing process also.

Between the ages of 16 and 33, something happened to me because   4
later, when I went to George Washington University and got my Master's
degree, I made an A in every course except one, in which I made a B. I
believe the difference was a matter of growing up, the sense of responsibility the Army had given me, a few years of war and perhaps a wife and
two children.

But I believe it was also the foundation I had gotten at CCNY. In fact,   5
soon after entering the Army, I discovered how important CCNY had
been. I was serving with West Pointers and with other ROTC graduates
who had the benefit of having attended some fairly **prestigious** universities. But I found out that the education my fellow ROTC cadets and I
had received at CCNY was a great one, notwithstanding my own failure
to drink as deeply from it as I might have. In terms of our ability to write,
to express ourselves, to reflect the skills and mental disciplines of a liberal
arts education, to be knowledgeable of our culture and our values, to
know our history, we were equal to our **contemporaries** from any

school in the nation. And for that I must thank the institution — the teachers and the faculty of the City College. And also the entire public school system of the City of New York — including Public Schools 20 and 39, Junior High School 52, and Morris High School.

My story is not very different from the stories of tens of thousands of   6
other CCNY graduates who received the benefits of a great, free public education. Most of those people fit the same mold I did — kids from working-class immigrant families. Their parents had dreams and ambitions for their children — if not always the means to fulfill those dreams. And we lived in a city that believed in its obligation to educate its youth and to be the dream-maker for those parents.

It was sort of an unwritten but intuitively understood three-way bar-   7
gain: a bargain among parents, kids and schools. The parents were aware of it. The kids weren't so much aware but just sensed it through their parents. The schools strove to hold to it. Entire neighborhoods were buoyed by it — how could they not be? Education was the way up.

Parents worked long hours, many of them at **menial** tasks. The kids   8
were often **latchkey** boys and girls. There were so many "minorities" that none of us really thought of ourselves as being in a minority. An implicit trust in "the bargain" and in one another, person to person and person to institution, was undefined but nonetheless powerful, strong and abiding. After all, it was America. And America meant progress. There simply was no disputing that — you could get a black eye if you tried.

Looking back, I guess if I had to say what was the most important   9
lesson I ever learned — and that's hard because there are several — my first inclination would be to say it is the **imperative** to drink very deeply at the fountain of knowledge wherever, whenever and in whatever guise that fountain might appear.

But looking more deeply, I believe there's a more vital thing to be   10
learned. It's the obligation we all have to keep the fountain flowing, now and for future generations. The lesson is not simply to get the most we possibly can out of every ounce of education we can get our hands on and never stop learning. That's very important, but there is more. We must ensure there is always a fountain to drink from and no obstacles to drinking.

We must ensure there is always some sort of bargain — a mutual 11
promise concerning education — among the parents, schools and children in our cities. This bargain is the single most important building block
of our future. It will determine what America will be like in the 21st
century. It will shape our future more dramatically than anything else
we do.

I believe it was Henry Adams who said that the purpose of education 12
is to increase the extent of our ignorance. That sounds a bit crazy until
you give it some long, hard thought. If Adams was right, maybe that's
why my teachers at CCNY and elsewhere knew someday I would be
sufficiently ignorant to look back and thank them. And sufficiently ignorant to want to protect the imperfect but beautiful process that made
me that way.

## COMPREHENSION CHECK

For the following items circle the correct answer or fill in the blanks.

1. The topic of this selection is:
   a. public education
   b. CCNY
   c. Colin Powell

2. The sentence that best states the main idea of this selection is:
   a. Colin Powell was a success because he studied and worked hard.
   b. Public higher education offers everyone the opportunity to receive a
      college education and hence a chance to succeed in America.
   c. Education is the way up for all people.

3. The topic sentence in paragraph 2 is:
   a. sentence 1
   b. sentence 2
   c. sentence 3

4. The topic sentence in paragraph 5 is:
   a. sentence 1
   b. sentence 2
   c. sentence 3

5. Write a sentence that states the main idea of paragraph 3.

   _____

   _____

6. Explain what Powell meant by the unwritten American bargain (paragraphs 7 and 8).

   _____

   _____

   _____

7. Powell did better when he went to George Washington University because _____

8 Use the context of paragraph 5 and your knowledge of prefixes and roots to define the word *contemporary*.

   _____

9. What does the author mean when he says "we must ensure there is always a fountain to drink from and no obstacles to drinking"?

   _____

   _____

   _____

10. What did Henry Adams mean by the statement, "The purpose of education is to increase the extent of our ignorance"?

   _____

   _____

   _____

**CHAPTER 4: PRACTICE IN METACOGNITIVE SKILLS**

## *Prereading Activity*: Developing questions

Begin by reading only the highlighted sentences in the selection. On the line above each sentence, write a question you think may be answered in the paragraph. Then skim for difficult vocabulary words and try to guess their meaning.

As you read the selection, paraphrase the important ideas in the margins.

## You Must Remember This

**BY BILL BRYSON**

*Why* _____

_____

**Here's a question for you. How is it that a man such as yourself—bright, ambitious, clean-thinking, big heart, good teeth—can go through life remembering the most utterly useless things, such as the theme song to the** *Howdy Doody* **show and the starting lineup for the 1967 Mets, yet cannot recall something as fundamental to happiness as where you put your car keys two minutes ago?**   1

No doubt you have asked yourself this question before. And   2 no doubt you have also noticed a certain **perverse** fact about your memory—that the things you seem to remember best (the names of the fifty state birds, the members of Woodrow Wilson's Cabinet) are the things no one wants to know, while the things that really are worth keeping in mind (your girlfriend's birthday, where you put the phone number of the man who offered you $15,000 for your old Austin-Healy Sprite) are the things you seem most unable to remember. If only you could reverse this situation. Then wouldn't life be sweet?

The difficulty is that no one knows for sure whether such a    3
feat is possible. It may be that your memory is infinitely expandable — indeed, some neurologists believe that with every new fact
you take aboard, your brain actually grows, physically expands,
to make room for the new data. On the other hand, it may simply
be that new facts are just slotted into any available spaces, very
possibly at the expense of old, little-used memories, which are
thus lost to you forever — a sort of continual spring-cleaning of
the brain. This would help to explain why we forget as much as
we do. But no one knows for sure.

The simple fact is that almost everything to do with your    4
memory — how it works, where it resides, why it is so madden-
ingly **quirky** and selective — has long **eluded** the explanations
of science. In the words of one of the field's leading researchers,
Dr. William T. Greenough of the Beckman Institute at the University of Illinois, "the more we study it, the more perplexing a lot of
it becomes." Even so, many scientists, including Greenough, believe we are at last on the brink of understanding the cellular basis
of memory — what makes it work. If they are right, it will be
one of the most important and exciting **neurological** break-
throughs of this century. It might even help you keep track of your
car keys.

*How or What*

**The first thing to bear in mind when considering your**    5
**memory is that it is already a pretty wondrous thing,**
**vastly more powerful and efficient than you probably**
**think it is.** Take your visual memory. You may be surprised to
know that it is nearly perfect. In a Canadian study, a researcher
showed subjects 10,000 random photographs and found that virtually every person in the test could remember every photo-
graph — that is, they could pick out the photos they had seen from
ones they had not seen, even after a time lag of many months.
And it can be done with astonishing speed. If I show you a picture
of someone and ask whether you recognize the face, it will take

you less than a second to make a search of all the tens of thousands of faces stored in your memory and decide whether this one is known to you. That is quite an achievement.

Add in all the nonvisual information at your command — the odd bits of history, literature, geography, science and so on, all the countless little details you need to know just to function as a human being — and it becomes evident that you have a vast storehouse of knowledge inside your head, a private Library of Congress, into which you can **delve** for any one of hundreds of millions of fragments of fact and experience. Just consider your vocabulary. In terms of speech alone, it has been estimated that if you are a reasonably intelligent adult (and you must be if you've read this far) you have a vocabulary of a quarter of a million or more items — words, names, abbreviations, snatches of foreign languages and so on. Yet if I say to you, "Do you like eating gribbles?" it will take you about a third of a second — the duration of an eye blink — to search through the **myriad** files in your mental **lexicon**, establish that no such word as "gribbles" exists and formulate a suitable reply. In normal conversation we repeat this process continuously, usually in less time than it takes the speaker to finish his statement.

6

*Why*
_____

_____

**So why is it that with all this mental firepower at your command you can't seem to remember a phone number for more than a few seconds, are forever forgetting where you put your tennis racquet and sometimes find that you can walk purposefully into a room and then have absolutely no idea why you are there**? The simple answer is that for all its whizbang speed and agility, your memory is also — by design — terrible. However much of an ace you are at retaining vast quantities of information, you aren't much good at absorbing new data. This is true of all of us. Even with fairly intense effort, the average person can retain only about seven new bits of infor-

7

mation at a time — a single phone number, say — and then only for a few seconds.

*How*

_____

_____

   **The reason for this is the way the mind organizes the**   8
**functions of memory and divides the labor between the**
**two main memory types: short-term and long-term.**
Short-term memory works as a filter; without it, your brain
would become too cluttered with **sensory detritus.** Most of
what you need to function — reading road signs, understanding a
conversation, comprehending this sentence — can be processed
and discarded in an instant. To manage this huge task of filtering,
short-term memory employs electrical impulses. These extremely
fast memory traces can begin to fade after just a few seconds.
Hence, that embarrassing tendency to instantly forget the name
of almost every person you are ever introduced to. (Don't feel too
bad. They forget you with equal **celerity.**)

*How or What*

_____

_____

   **Long-term memory, on the other hand, involves a**   9
**chemical change within the brain.** In some physical way
your brain fidgets and reorganizes itself with every new fact it
takes in. Scientists have long puzzled over exactly how this phenomenon happens — what allows our minds to snatch an experience that may be over in seconds and to make a record of it that
can last for decades. Now at last they believe they may find out.
"We are on the brink of understanding which molecules are involved in the regulation of memories," says Dr. Aryeh Routtenberg of Northwestern University. "This is terribly exciting."

*What*

---

---

   **Various scientists have suggested a variety of possible    10
agents—a protein called kinase C, a gene called c-fos, a
family of enzymes called glycoproteins.** If, as Routtenberg
believes, kinase C is the vital component, it could have incalcu-
lable benefits for people suffering from certain diseases involving
protein deficiency—notably Down's syndrome and Alzheimer's
disease. It is even possible that it could lead to successful memory
drugs, though scientists are widely split on this. Professor Steven
Rose of the Brain Research Group in Britain is skeptical. "Much
of my life is spent examining memory drugs—I have one involving fish oil in front of me now—and I have yet to see one that
even remotely lives up to its promise," he says.

*How or What*

---

---

   **Routtenberg, however, thinks a memory drug is a very    11
real possibility, and that its discovery might not be too far
away, though the results are unlikely to be dramatic.** You
probably wouldn't even be aware of the effects—just as when you
swallow a vitamin C capsule you don't suddenly feel healthier.
"By stimulating the production of kinase C," Routtenberg says,
"you might be able to retain for a couple of days a fact that you
would normally forget after a few minutes. You are not going to
be able to swallow the *Encyclopaedia Britannica*. It will never be
that simple. But you may be able to take a pill that will enhance
your ability to remember the *Encyclopaedia Britannica* when you
read it."

*What*

---

---

   **In the meantime, is there anything you can do to im-    12
prove your memory?** Well, yes, sort of. You can exercise it. In

an experiment reported in 1980, an American college student with an average memory was intensively trained until he was able to recall a string of numbers like this: 9230491212939498 573658375476362738475859483747584584859485734739485769854992398. Researchers were amazed. Then someone thought to try the student on a random string of letters. He could remember only six or seven — the same number as could an untrained person. The lesson to be drawn from this is that you can, with a lot of work, vastly improve your memory for certain types of information, but it won't apply to other areas of memory. By and large, all it will be is a kind of party trick. . . .

## COMPREHENSION CHECK

For the following items circle the correct answer or fill in the blanks.

1. The topic of the selection is:
   a. how to improve your memory
   b. why you can't remember
   c. how the memory works

2. State the main idea of the selection by explaining what the author is saying about the topic.

   _____

   _____

3. The main idea of paragraph 3 is found in:
   a. sentence 1
   b. sentence 2
   c. sentence 5

4. In your own words, state the main idea of paragraph 10.

   _____

   _____

5. Some scientists believe the brain is infinitely expandable while others believe:
   a. It has a limited number of slots for knowledge.
   b. Only certain parts of it are expandable.
   c. Only long-term memory is expandable.

6. Each of the following is true of memory except:
   a. It is extremely fast when drawing from facts stored in the long-term memory.
   b. Visual memory is extremely accurate.
   c. Short-term memory is of little use since it lasts only a few seconds.

7. Use the context of paragraph 6 to define the word *lexicon*.

   _____

8. The word *celerity* in paragraph 8 probably means:
   a. speed
   b. inaccuracy
   c. memory

9. The reason we cannot remember the name of a person who has just been introduced to us is:
   a. Short-term memory is designed to filter information and discard what is not needed.
   b. It is not important to us.
   c. A chemical change in the brain results in its being "dumped."

10. According to the selection, the author believes that a drug to improve memory is just around the corner.
    a. true
    b. false

11. From the selection you can conclude that:
    a. How we remember is a mysterious and complicated process.
    b. Visual memory is better than auditory memory.
    c. Long-term memory is more valuable than short-term memory.

```
CHAPTER 5: PRACTICE IN NOTE TAKING
```

### *Prereading Activity*: **Preparing to take notes**

To prepare for this reading, set up your note page as described in Chapter 5.

As your professor or a friend reads you the following selection, take notes using the format described in Chapter 5. Discuss the selection with your classmates, taking notes as described for discussion on page 148.

## Hate Speech on Campus

**BY JOSEPH S. TRUMAN**

Recent efforts by large public universities and colleges aimed at stemming   1
the tide of hate speech on campus have caused all of us in the academic community to carefully assess our position on this issue. Hate speech refers to written or spoken words directed towards a particular group (typically although not exclusively a minority group) with the purpose or effect of verbally harassing and harming them. In the educational setting, this can refer to language used both in and outside the classroom, by teacher or student, while still within the campus.

Schools such as the University of Michigan, the University of Wiscon-   2
sin, and the University of California have already written new regulations to restrict this form of speech, declaring that it disrupts the educational process and retards progress made in bringing equal opportunity and access to education for all.

Does hate speech harm the individual to whom it is addressed? I can   3
speak to this myself. My parents came to this country nearly four decades ago from the Middle East. I was born in Texas and later grew up in California's Central Valley. My early years were spent constantly trying to conform and avoid the appearance of being different. As a young person in public schools, I often heard comments, jokes and insults about my ethnicity and the place my parents had once called home. I can assure you that these comments hurt — and in a different way than they might if reversed against those in more populous numbers. If they caused me

some pain as a white male, I can only imagine what they must feel like when they are directed to those already burdened with discrimination in our society.

As an adult and an educator, however, today I see this from a different point of view, standing before the class instead of seated within the class. Consequently, I now find myself internally conflicted over this issue. I have always tried in my class to avoid promoting my own social and political agenda, believing instead that classroom discussions, within reasonable limits, should be open and accessible for all. This promotes participation from the broadest number of students, and enhances the learning process.    4

As a teacher, I thus look with unease at regulations which might restrict what can be said in the classroom. My discomfort is grounded in the fact that I am not certain that clear regulations prohibiting hate speech can be designed without also entangling other forms of speech — speech that may otherwise be protected by the First Amendment.    5

A wise undergraduate student in my own Free Speech class debated me on this point last year, declaring that those rules aren't so difficult. People know what kind of words and insults we're talking about, she said — and to illustrate her point, she promptly recited three different types of racist, sexist and homophobic slurs.    6

For me, however, her examples were the obvious ones. Yes, most people do know about bigoted, hurtful insults and slurs — but should we draft a rule that prohibits only the obvious choices? Many forms of racist and sexist speech, for example, are often times far more subtle, although their impact is no less devastating. How do we define rules prohibiting these? I assume we do this by making our restriction broader, but when we do so, how do we avoid prohibiting other speech which may not necessarily be hate speech?    7

This was the problem for Michigan, when a graduate student teacher challenged the University of Michigan's rules, arguing they were so broad that they forced him to remove parts of his lecture material for fear of offending some unknown members of his class. He didn't in fact know if the material would offend anyone or not — but the rule was so broad that he feared the risk of penalty if he guessed wrong. The federal court hearing the case declared Michigan's rules unconstitutional.    8

In spite of the pain of my own past experience, I find I cannot endorse   9
rules such as these, either. Hate speech is the expression of bigotry and
prejudice — and these in turn are the products of ignorance. I know no
better place to address ignorance than in our schools, and no better way
to do so than in exposing all of our ideas, good and bad, ugly and beautiful, to the light of scrutiny within our classes.


## COMPREHENSION CHECK

For the following items, using only your notes, circle the correct answer or
fill in the blanks.

  1. The topic of this selection is:
     a. free speech
     b. First Amendment rights
     c. hate speech

  2. In one sentence summarize the main idea of this selection.

    _____

    _____

  3. Define hate speech.

    _____

    _____

  4. Name at least one school that has recently written new regulations
    regarding this type of speech. _____

  5. What personal experience did the author have with the issue of hate
    speech?

    _____

    _____

6. What is the author's conflict as a college instructor?

_____

_____

7. What does the author fear will result from regulations that are too broad?

_____

_____

8. Which college is having its regulations on hate speech challenged in court? _____

9. Is the author in favor of broader regulations on hate speech? Explain.

_____

_____

10. Do you think it is permissible to joke about particular groups of people in derogatory ways? Why or why not?

_____

_____

## CHAPTER 6: PRACTICE IN PROBLEM AND SOLUTION

### *Prereading Activity*: **Examining the problem**

One of the greatest problems facing first-year college students is the psychological adjustment to greater personal and social freedom. Write a few paragraphs describing one problem you had adjusting to the social or academic freedom of college. _____

_____

_____

# Old Habits

BY DANIELLE LEWIS

It is so hard to break old habits! Ever since I can remember, I was trained    1
to do certain things at certain times. Like most others, the important
thing I learned was always to obey my parents even if I really didn't
want to.

My parents have always been there to guide my way. They had set    2
enough rules so that no matter which way I stepped, I was still out of
place. I worked so hard to live by all their rules and regulations. I strived
to perfect everything I did so I could hear their praises instead of a "How
To Do" lecture. But they would not let me fall, even as off-balanced as I
was at times, because they were right there to catch me. If I was too
wobbly though, they would straighten me up rather quickly. For the most
part, I was an obedient child, and I am grateful to my parents and society
for molding me into the person I am. I'm proud of myself for putting up
with so much and not rebelling by using drugs or alcohol, or by developing a bad attitude.

Now I'm an eighteen-year-old in college with more freedom than I    3
have ever had before, until I go home, and then I'm their little angel. You
know, the child they know they can count on to be honest. Well, one of
the rules my parents taught me was that all that was said in the family
was kept to the family and was not to leave the house. Since I have been
here, the rules have changed a bit. All that is said or done here is left here
when I go home. Sometimes it is so hard not to discuss school, friends,
and certain incidents with them.

This is when I resent the person I have become. I am not very creative    4
because I've always been judged on preciseness and not creativity. I went
through most of high school wearing a mask, until I was alone or with a
friend, and then I could be myself. There were even times when I had to
take a close look in the mirror to find out if I was really in there some-
where. Once I found myself, I felt secure until the mask fell on my face
again. Then that little insecure girl and all her fears were wound up in a
knot again.

I came to college so that I could escape my home life, spread my    5
wings, and discover who I am and what it is I really want in life — not
what to do and how to do it. I want to solve my own problems. I no
longer want to live in fear of hurting my self-image. I want to be treated
as an adult, but most of all, I want to be friends with my parents. I want
them to actually sit down and listen to what I have to say without
criticizing.

These are the goals I had hoped to fulfill my first year of college. Well,    6
most of the rules and regulations my parents had set for me are still in
effect. I feel as if I am betraying them if I choose a different method of
living. How do I break the habits they have instilled in me after all these
years without a feeling of betrayal? A compromise is in order, but it's hard
to straighten a warped record.

## COMPREHENSION CHECK

For items 1–7 circle the correct answer or fill in the blanks.

1.  The topic of the selection is
    a. accepting new ideas and values
    b. accepting the challenge of independent thinking
    c. breaking the rules

2.  The sentence that best states the main idea of the selection is:
    a. A first-year college student has trouble adjusting to the social de-
       mands of college life.
    b. A first-year college student describes an emotional struggle with her
       evolving independence.
    c. A first-year college student wants to be friends with her parents.

3.  Which sentence states the main idea of paragraph 2?
    a. sentence 1
    b. sentence 2
    c. sentence 4

4. Explain in your own words why the author feels that she is not creative.

_____

_____

_____

_____

5. True or false? This student was probably given choices when she was growing up.
   a. true
   b. false

6. This student was brought up to be honest.
   a. true
   b. false

7. Why do you think this student can't discuss her college experiences with her parents?

_____

_____

_____

_____

For items 8–10 either respond in essay form or discuss in small groups as assigned.

8. In your own words explain the dilemma or problem this student is facing. Do you think her problem is related to a "generation gap" between her and her parents or do you think the problem lies elsewhere?

9. Have you experienced anything similar to that which this student experienced and, if so, give examples to describe your own dilemma.

10. Following Anderson's five steps, create a plan to help this student (or yourself) become more independent.

**CHAPTER 7: PRACTICE IN UNDERLINING/ANNOTATING, OUTLINING, AND SUMMARIZING**

## *Prereading Activity*: Previewing to create questions

Carefully preview the reading selection. As you skim the selection, note that questions have been formulated for you in some of the sections. Underline these questions. As you read, write answers to these questions as well as important details in the margins.

## Interpersonal Influence

BY JAMES W. KALAT

### Conformity

Conformity is the tendency to do what others are doing. Sometimes    1
conformity is good. When professor and students all come to class at the
same time, they conform in a way that is mutually beneficial. Sometimes
conformity is neither good nor bad, as in people's tendency to dress alike.
Sometimes conformity is dangerous, as when someone uses drugs because "everyone else is doing it."

*A classic experiment on conformity*    Why do we conform? Do we con-    2
form in all situations or just some? S. E. Asch (1951) set out to demonstrate that people conform only in ambiguous situations. We might very
well conform to fashions in dress, for example, where there is no objective
right or wrong, or to the political views of other people, where right and
wrong tend to be uncertain. We are much less likely to conform, Asch
predicted, in situations where we *know* we are right and others are wrong.

Asch showed lines to college students in groups of eight. He told them    3
that the purpose of the experiment was to measure visual perception, and
that they were to decide which of the lines on the right was the same
length as the one on the left. The task was quite simple. To finish the
experiment as simply and quickly as possible, Asch asked the students to
give their answers aloud. The procedure was repeated for 18 sets of lines.

Only the student seated seventh in the circle was a true subject. Asch    4
had paid the others to pretend they were subjects. On the first and second
sets of lines, everyone gave the correct answer. But on 12 of the remaining
16 sets, the paid **confederates** all agreed on an incorrect answer. Would
the true subject go along with the crowd?

To Asch's surprise, 37 of 50 subjects conformed to the majority opin-    5
ion at least once, and 14 of them conformed on more than half the sets.
The mean was 3.8 conforming answers out of 12.

***Reactions of those who did or did not conform***    Those who did not    6
conform gave different reasons for their independence. Some were su-
premely self-confident: "I'm right and everyone else is wrong. Nothing
unusual — it happens all the time!" Others were so withdrawn and **introverted** that they apparently paid little attention to what the majority
thought. Still others, though nervous and full of self-doubts, dutifully
gave the answers that seemed right to them.

What about those who conformed? Some of them said that after they    7
heard everyone else give the same answer, they *saw* it that way too and
truly believed that the answer they gave was correct. Others said that they
saw the lines differently from what the others were reporting but decided
that they themselves must be wrong. ("Maybe I need to have my eyes
checked.") Still others knew they were giving the wrong answer when
they went along with the majority but said they did not want to call
attention to themselves by being different.

***Factors that influence conformity***    What factors influence the degree to    8
which people conform? One factor is the size of the majority. In later
experiments, a subject who was faced with one or two other people giving
incorrect answers seldom conformed to the incorrect view. But subjects
who were outnumbered at least 3-to-1 generally conformed. Beyond
three, the size of the majority made little difference. A 3-to-1 majority
induced as much conformity as a 7-to-1 majority.

(An episode on the TV show *Candid Camera* demonstrated the same    9
**phenomenon**. One unsuspecting person got on an elevator. Then various actors got on, *facing backward*. When only one or two faced backward, the first person ignored them. When three or more faced backward,
however, the first person generally turned and faced the rear.)

Another factor in Asch's experiments was having an "ally." Some    10
subjects faced six people who agreed on a wrong answer and one who
gave the correct answer. Only a few conformed to the majority opinions
under those conditions. Evidently it is hard to stand as a minority of one,
but not so hard to join one other person.

A third factor, uncovered in later experiments (Cohen, Bornstein, &    11
Sherman, 1973), is whether or not the situation is **ambiguous**. Contrary
to Asch's original hypothesis, subjects conformed *more* when there were
clear right and wrong answers than when the choices were pretty much
the same. Perhaps people assume the majority will be more willing to
tolerate their "**deviation**" when the decision is hard to make.

### Obedience to authority

When the Nazi concentration camps were exposed after the Second    12
World War, those who had committed the **atrocities** defended themselves by saying they were "only following orders." International courts
rejected that defense and people throughout the world told themselves,
"If I had been there, I would have refused to follow such orders," and, "It
couldn't happen here."

*Milgram's experiment on obedience to authority*    Perhaps so. But we    13
never know for sure what we might do in a situation we have never faced
before. Milgram (1974) set up a situation in which one person might
inflict harm on another by obeying the "authority" of a psychological
experimenter. Pairs of men, 20 to 50 years old, were told that the experiment was designed to find out what level of punishment is most effective
and whether punishment is more effective when some people impose it
than when others impose it. One member of the pair was to be the
"teacher" and the other was to be the "learner." Each drew a piece of
paper from a hat to determine which was to be which. The drawing was
**rigged**. Milgram had paid one man to play a particular role; that man
served as the "learner" for every "teacher."

After the drawing, the "teacher" watched the experimenter strap the    14
"learner" into a shock device. Milgram explained the procedure: The
teacher, sitting in another room, would read aloud a list of paired associate words, such as "yellow–corn." Then he would start at the beginning
of the list, read the first word, and offer four choices, "Yellow: (1) brick;

(2) corn; (3) fever; (4) river." The learner, listening over the intercom, was to press one of four levers to indicate his choice. If his answer was correct, the teacher would say "correct" and go on to the next question. If his answer was incorrect, the teacher would give the correct answer and flip a switch to deliver a shock.

The teacher was supposed to give a 15-volt shock for the learner's first   15 mistake, and then move to the next higher shock for each successive mistake. Shocks were marked in 15-volt intervals from 15 to 450. Printed over the various shock levels were the words "mild — moderate — strong — very strong — intense — extremely intense — severe — XXX." The point of the experiment was to see how strong a shock the teacher would administer in obedience to the experimenter. (The teacher did not, of course, know this.)

Although the learner never actually received shock, he acted as if he   16 had. He screamed and moaned, complained about a heart problem, insisted that he be allowed to quit the experiment, and kicked the wall. At some point each teacher asked who would take responsibility if anything went wrong; the experimenter replied that he would take responsibility, but that nothing would go wrong. ("While the shocks may be painful, they are not dangerous.") Beyond 315 volts the learner was silent, failing even to answer the questions. If the teacher asked what he should do, the experimenter told him to treat silence as an error, give the correct answer, and deliver the next shock.

Twenty-six of forty teachers continued to give shocks all the way to   17 450 volts. The results were about the same after the procedure had been modified: The experiment was conducted in a downtown office building instead of a university campus. A different man was recruited to play the role of the "learner." Women were used instead of men. In each case, about half of all the teachers went right on to the maximum shock.

*Reactions of those who thought they were shocking another person*   18
Many students who hear about this experiment react at once by saying, "There must have been something wrong with those people. Maybe they were **sadists**." They were not. The teachers were normal adults, representative of their community. Generally those with a history of military service were more likely than others to obey the orders; so were people with little education. But some people from all walks of life obeyed,

including blue-collar workers, white-collar workers, and professionals. All of them grew nervous during the experiment. They expressed concern for the learner's health. They asked the experimenter whether it might make sense to stop the experiment. And some did quit. The interesting and disturbing fact, however, is that so many normal people continued to give the shocks, despite their misgivings.

*Factors that influence obedience*   Several factors influenced the degree   19
of obedience exhibited. When the teachers were in the same room with the learner, more of them stopped giving the shocks. The same was true when the experimenter gave the directions and then left the teacher unsupervised. Obedience was almost complete, however, when the responsibility was divided. If one teacher read the words and a second teacher gave the shocks, 37 of 40 pairs continued all the way to 450 volts.

## COMPREHENSION CHECK

For the following items fill in the blanks or circle the correct answer.

1. The topic of the selection is:
   a. experiments in obedience
   b. conformity and obedience
   c. factors in conformity

2. State the main idea of the selection by explaining what the author is saying about the topic.

   _____

   _____

3. Which sentence is the topic sentence of paragraph 8?
   a. sentence 1
   b. sentence 2
   c. sentence 4

4. State the main idea of paragraph 18 in your own words.

_____

_____

5. The subjects who conformed in Asch's experiments gave all of the following reasons for their actions *except*:
   a. They were so nervous they didn't really know what they were answering.
   b. After they heard the other answers, they actually saw it that way.
   c. They saw it differently but figured maybe they needed glasses.
   d. They knew they were giving wrong answers but gave them anyway.

6. The more a person is outnumbered, the more likely he or she is to conform.
   a. true
   b. false

7. Use the context of the sentence and your knowledge of prefixes and roots to define the word *introverted* in paragraph 6.

8. The "Candid Camera" experiment indicates that:
   a. When the behavior is ambiguous, people are more apt to conform.
   b. If one has an ally, he or she is less likely to conform.
   c. The size of the majority influences conformity.

9. The Milgram experiment suggests that:
   a. People conform more when they are being supervised.
   b. The more educated a person, the more likely he or she is to conform.
   c. People feel no compunction about hurting others.

10. You can conclude from this selection that:
    a. Conformity is a bad thing.
    b. Most people tend to obey orders.
    c. People tend to conform rather than be different.

**COMPREHENSION EXERCISE 1** *Outlining*

Use the scrambled sentences below to complete the outline.

*Conformity*

I. _____

   A. *Asch's experiment involved perception of two sets of lines using confederate subjects.*

      1. _____

         a. *There were 3.8 conforming answers out of 12.*

      2. _____

         a. *Some were very self-confident individuals.*

         b. _____

         c. _____

      3. *What were the reasons for conforming?*

         a. _____

         b. _____

         c. _____

   B. _____

      1. *The size of the majority affected whether they conformed.*

      2. _____

      3. _____

II. _____

   A. *Milgram's experiment involved shocking a subject under orders from an authority figure.*

1. *Will people obey an authority figure who orders them to inflict harm on others?*

2. *About half of all subjects obeyed the authority figure to the maximum.*

3. _____

   a. _____

   b. _____

   c. _____

4. _____

   a. *They were nervous.*

   b. _____

   c. *They questioned the morality of what they were doing.*

5. _____

   a. *The distance between the victim and the subject affected conformity.*

   b. _____

   c. _____

Who were those who obeyed?

What factors influenced obedience?

They didn't want to call attention to themselves.

Conformity was greater when responsibility was divided.

What were the reasons for not conforming?

Many who conformed had a history of military service.

How did those who obeyed feel?

More conformed when the authority figure was present.

Conformity is a tendency to behave like others.

Fewer conform if they have an ally.

When the situation is clear-cut, more people will conform.

They tended to be less educated.

They were introverted individuals and unaware of the other answers.

Do people conform less in situations where they know there is a clear-cut right or wrong?

After they heard others, they saw it that way too.

What factors influence the degree to which people conform?

Generally, people were from all walks of life.

How far will people go in obedience to authority?

They were concerned for the welfare of those they were hurting.

Some figured they must be wrong and possibly in need of glasses.

Although full of doubts, some dutifully gave the right answer.


**COMPREHENSION EXERCISE 2** *Summarizing*

Write a summary of the selection "Interpersonal Influence" using only the outline you completed in Comprehension Exercise 1.


**CHAPTER 8: PRACTICE IN READING CHRONOLOGICAL ORDER**

### *Prereading Activity*: **Organizing a time line**

Scan the selection "Drug Abuse" for specific dates and time periods, writing them on the time line chart on page 438. As you read the selection, complete the rest of the time line.

# Drug Abuse

### BY RICHARD WARGA

Drugs have been known to humanity since antiquity. Marihuana, for   1
instance, has been traced back to 2700 B.C. Opium was known to the
Egyptians as long ago as 1500 B.C. Opium has been used consistently
as a painkiller since the eighteenth century. To the medical profession,
opium was almost a universal **panacea** and was at different times prescribed for pain of cancer, dysentery, gallstones, childbirth, and toothache.

The addictive properties of opium were not understood either by the   2
ancients or by more recent doctors. Not until two refined products of
opium — morphine and codeine — came into being in 1805 and 1832, respectively, were opium's addictive powers suspected. Strangely enough,
it took a third advance, the invention of the hypodermic needle, to clarify
the situation. During the Civil War, morphine and codeine were frequently injected. As a result, thousands of soldiers became addicted to
these opiates, which were sold everywhere. The most devastating opium
derivative, heroin, was **synthesized** in 1898. It too was available to
everyone. Opium was not the only dependency-producing drug in common use. Until approximately 1902, Coca Cola contained a small dose of
cocaine.

It might surprise you to learn that the levels of addiction today in no   3
way equal those present in 1914, when the nation finally recognized the
danger of opium and passed the Harrison Act to control it. At that time,
it was estimated that one out of every four hundred people in our country
was addicted. The estimate for 1965, in contrast, showed one in 3,300.

Several trends in drug use are quite disquieting. Before the 1940s,   4
most drug-dependent people were middle-aged or older and usually
were not from the lowest socioeconomic class. Most of them came to be
dependent through medical channels, although some artists also used
drugs. The picture changed after World War II, when a shift in use from
middle class to lower class occurred. This change also involved a shift to

use by ethnic and minority groups, particularly in large cities. . . . Another disturbing trend is the shift in drug use from the middle-aged and older to the young. From 1940 to 1962, there was a steady increase in the under-eighteen group and a decrease in the over-forty group. Today, drug abuse is spreading from the cities to the suburbs and is involving younger and younger people of all social classes. It is no longer an **affliction** of the poor in the slums.

Another trend has been the tendency among drug users to get away 5 from the use of a single drug, such as an opiate derivative. Speed, goofballs, glue sniffing, banana peels, and LSD — almost any substances that might create a reaction — have been used singly and in **tandem**.

A major social problem that did not exist earlier is the combining of 6 criminality and drug dependence. Although most addicts must steal and rob in order to support their habit, which often costs sixty or seventy dollars a day, some evidence shows that the excitement of performing a criminal act may be a part of the psychological life of a drug user. In some mysterious way, the outlaw feeling becomes important, so that lawlessness may not necessarily be a result of drug dependency; it may be part of a whole way of life.

## COMPREHENSION CHECK

For the following items circle the correct answer or fill in the blanks.

1. Which of the following might be a better title for the selection?
   a. The Changes in Drug Use in the United States
   b. The History of Drug Use
   c. The Effects of Drug Use

2. State the main idea of the selection in your own words.

_____

3. Coca Cola contains a small amount of cocaine.
   a. true
   b. false

4. Drugs:
   a. are more widely used today than in the early 1900s.
   b. are used by fewer people today than in the early 1900s.
   c. traditionally have been used by the lower class.

5. What invention advanced the use of opium-derivative drugs?

   _____

6. According to the selection, heroin is more dangerous than morphine.
   a. true
   b. false

7. Which of the following drugs is not an opium derivative?
   a. marihuana
   b. heroin
   c. codeine

8. Using the context of the sentence, write a synonym for the word *panacea* in paragraph 1.

9. The word *tandem* in paragraph 5 probably means:
   a. without
   b. together
   c. frequently

10. From the selection, you can conclude that drug use is increasing in the United States.
    a. true
    b. false

| Time Line: Drug Abuse | |
|---|---|
| *Dates* | *Events* |
| 2700–1500 B.C. | |
| 18th century | |
| 1805, 1832 | |
| Civil War | |
| 1898 | |
| 1902 | |
| 1914 | |
| 1940–1962 | |
| 1965 | |
| Pre–World War II | |
| Post–World War II | |
| Present | |

## CHAPTER 9: PRACTICE IN READING CAUSE AND EFFECT

### *Prereading Activity* : **Mapping cause-and-effect relationships**

Read the following sentences from the reading "Hard Facts About Nuclear Winter" and then map the cause-and-effect relationships being described by filling in the blanks.

1. The group, which soon became known as TTAPS (an acronym based on last names), discovered that the smoke could have a devastating effect on the Earth's climate.

*Cause*                           *Effect*

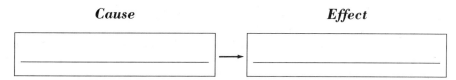

2. Their sweeping, controversial conclusion, later published in the same issue of *Science*, was that such a climatic catastrophe could "cause the extinction of a major fraction of the plant and animal species on the Earth." In that event, the possibility of the extinction of *Homo sapiens* cannot be excluded.

*Cause*                           *Effects*

# Hard Facts About Nuclear Winter

BY ANDREW C. REVKIN

Early in 1979, the Congressional Office of Technology Assessment (OTA)    1
completed a 151-page report called "The Effects of Nuclear War." The
first finding, set off in boldface, was *"The effects of a nuclear war that cannot
be calculated are at least as important as those for which calculations are attempted."* That has proved to be an unusually apt **caveat**.

Now, only a few years after the OTA report, and four decades after the    2
invention of nuclear weapons, the scientific and defense communities
have suddenly learned of an aspect of nuclear war, overlooked by OTA
and almost everyone else who had studied the subject, that could prove
to be more devastating than any of the other effects — including the blast
and radiation.

The forgotten factor? Smoke. Government scientists had been study-    3
ing the physical effects of nuclear explosions for decades, had produced
massive volumes full of detailed observations, had scrutinized accounts
of the blasts at Hiroshima and Nagasaki, the firestorms at Dresden, Ham-
burg and Tokyo. But no one had calculated the climatological effects of
the globe-spanning pall of dark smoke that could rise from the thousands
of fires ignited by a nuclear war. Indeed, with the exception of two neglected reports produced for the U.S. government in the 1960s, the word
*smoke* is hardly mentioned in the scientific literature.

A paper published in the Swedish journal *Ambio* in 1982 thus came    4
as a complete surprise, stunning scientists and defense experts alike with
its simple, **ominous** conclusion. Paul Crutzen, a Dutch atmospheric scientist, and John Birks, an American chemist, calculated in a rudimentary
but convincing way that smoke from a nuclear war — several hundred
million tons of it — "would strongly restrict the penetration of sunlight to
the Earth's surface and change the physical properties of the Earth's
atmosphere." And their calculations were based only on smoke from
burning forests. When another research team considered smoke from
burning *cities*, the forgotten factor took on even more significance.

Richard Turco, an atmospheric scientist at R & D Associates, in Marina     5
del Rey, California, had been working with three researchers at the NASA
Ames Research Center, two of whom were former students of Cornell
astronomer Carl Sagan, on the atmospheric effects of dust raised by nuclear explosions. When Turco read an advance copy of the *Ambio* study,
he immediately saw that smoke would be far more important than dust.

Turco reworked the *Ambio* calculations, adding in the smoke from     6
burning cities. Along with the NASA group — O. Brian Toon, Thomas
Ackerman and James Pollack — and Carl Sagan, he put together a comprehensive analysis, including computer models, of the "global consequences of multiple nuclear explosions." The group, which soon became
known as TTAPS (an acronym based on last names), discovered that the
smoke could have a devastating effect on the Earth's climate.

The findings were so dramatic, in fact, that in late April 1983, more     7
than 100 scientists were invited to a closed session at the American Academy of Arts and Sciences, in Cambridge, Massachusetts, to review the
study. The physical scientists met first, testing the assumptions, dissecting
the models, checking the data. Some adjustments and refinements were
made, but the basic conclusions held.

Then the biologists took a crack at it. They **extrapolated** from the     8
climatic effects to the impact on agriculture and **ecosystems**. The destruction wrought by nuclear war, they concluded, would be much
greater and more long-lived than anyone had previously conceived.

The results were announced to a capacity crowd at a conference in     9
Washington, D.C., on Halloween 1983 and were published in the December 23 issue of *Science*. The TTAPS group concluded that "a global nuclear
war could have a major impact on climate — manifested by significant
surface darkening over many weeks, subfreezing land temperatures per-
sisting for up to several months, large perturbations in global circulation
patterns, and dramatic changes in local weather and precipitation rates —
a harsh 'nuclear winter' in any season."

The biologists also presented their findings. Their sweeping, contro-     10
versial conclusion, later published in the same issue of *Science*, was that
such a climatic catastrophe could "cause the extinction of a major fraction
of the plant and animal species on the Earth. . . . In that event, the possibility of the extinction of ***Homo sapiens*** cannot be excluded."

## COMPREHENSION CHECK

Complete the following items by filling in or circling the best answer.

1. What was the "forgotten factor"?

   _____

2. What factor was Richard Turco studying when he became aware of this forgotten factor?

   _____

3. What conclusions did biologists reach after studying the effects of this forgotten factor on ecosystems?

   _____

   _____

4. The topic of this selection is:
   a. the smoke factor
   b. nuclear war
   c. nuclear winter
   d. ecology

5. The main idea of the selection is:
   a. Nuclear winter will occur as a result of atomic war.
   b. The effects of nuclear winter will be devastating.
   c. The factor of smoke added to the dust from a nuclear war make the possibility of humankind's extinction greater than heretofore believed.

6. Using the context of the sentence to help you, give a synonym for the word *ominous* in paragraph 4.

   _____

7. Using the context of the entire paragraph to help you, explain what *extrapolated* in paragraph 8 means.

   _____

8. Using the context of the entire paragraph, explain what the phrase *Homo sapiens* means (paragraph 10).

9. On a separate piece of paper map the chain reaction described in paragraphs 9 and 10 (you have already completed part of the map in previous activities).

10. Some people feel it is foolish to try to calculate the effects of nuclear war because once it occurs little can be done about the effects. On a separate piece of paper write one or two paragraphs giving your opinion on this. Do you agree?

## CHAPTER 10: PRACTICE IN READING COMPARISON AND CONTRAST

### *Prereading Activity*: **Previewing**

Preview the selection by reading the title, the first paragraph, and the dates and numbers. Then complete the following statement:

The author is comparing economic conditions in the United States before

## The Economic Escalator

**BY JACK LEVIN**

*Americans on Their Way Down*

The term "downward **mobility**" is being used to characterize the eco- 1
nomic plight of an entire generation of middle-class Americans who are
slipping and sliding their way down the **socioeconomic** ladder. Forget
about the short-term effects of **recession**. According to political analyst
Kevin Phillips, the culprit is an economic trend that began in the 1980s
and will likely continue indefinitely.

The rich really have been getting much richer . . . and doing so at the       2
expense of poor and middle-income Americans who have seen their
status evaporate. Through at least the last decade, the biggest losers have
been blacks, Hispanics, young men, female heads of households, farmers,
and steelworkers; but almost everyone else has also suffered to some
extent.

In a shift away from manufacturing and toward services, we have       3
been transformed into a post-industrial society. In 1959, production of
goods represented some 60 percent of all American employment, but by
1985, this figure had dropped to only 26 percent. The overwhelming
majority of Americans are now employed in the service sector of the
economy. During this **transitional** period, new jobs were created, but in
the main these were poorly paid and provided few opportunities for
upward mobility. Thus, large numbers of Americans were forced to take
a substantial drop in pay and, therefore, in their way of life.

According to Phillips, the widening gap between rich and poor may       4
have been encouraged by national economic policies of the 1980s — a
period which represented a strong **reversal** of almost four decades of
downward income redistribution. At the upper end of our class system,
the after-tax proportion of income for the wealthiest 1 percent of Americans climbed from 7 percent in 1977 to 11 percent in 1990. Even when
adjusted for inflation, the number of millionaires doubled between the
late seventies and the late eighties, resulting in a record one million
households reporting a net worth of at least $1 million.

For families on lower **rungs** of the socio-economic ladder, however,       5
living standards have deteriorated. Since 1977, the average after-tax family income of the bottom 10 percent of Americans declined 10.5 percent
in current dollars. According to a recent study by Professor Timothy
Smeeding, the percentage of U.S. children living in poverty rose from less
than 15 percent in 1978 to 20 percent today. Compared with seven other
industrial countries (Sweden, West Germany, Australia, Canada, Britain,
France, and the Netherlands), the United States has the dubious distinction of being the most unequal. That is, we have more poverty and fewer
people who are middle class.

Growing income inequality has already been linked with a worsening       6
of our most stubborn and perplexing social ailments. Professor Henry
Miller of the University of California notes that homelessness is a growing

problem in our major cities—a problem that is not susceptible to easy solutions.

He suggests that we were previously able as a society to assimilate    7
many of the homeless into the military or industry. In today's economy, however, those who lack education or marketable skills remain permanently unemployed or take dead-end jobs. What is more, in the process of converting inexpensive rooming houses into high-priced condominiums for the affluent, the **gentrification** of urban areas during the 1980s forced even more of the poverty-stricken onto the streets.

According to *American Demographics*, young adults have been particularly hard hit by downward mobility. As a result, they are taking longer    8
to finish school, living for a longer period of time with their parents or other relatives, and delaying their plans to marry. Young married couples are today less likely to own their own homes. Many return to live with their parents.

Comparing their worsening economic circumstances with those of    9
their parents, millions of young people have begun to question the validity of the American Dream and are less optimistic about the future. Called "selfish" "**passive**," and "ultra-conservative" by those who remember the **liberal activism** of the prosperous 1960s, many young adults are merely trying to maintain or improve their standard of living. In the face of an **erosion** in their incomes, they frequently regard tax increases as a burden which they cannot afford.

---

*Millions of young people have begun to question the validity of the American Dream.*

---

American business leaders are beginning to understand that America's economic problems have a long-term basis in reality. The Business    10
Council, whose members consist of 100 executives from America's largest companies, suggested recently that the current **recession** will be succeeded by a prolonged period of lean economic times. The public seems to agree: a recent *Business Week* survey determined that 64 percent of Americans predict that the economy of the United States will be dominated by foreign companies within ten years.

The continuing trends away from manufacturing and toward in-   11
equality between rich and poor are, of course, far from **inevitable**. But
a reversal would necessitate a major commitment on the part of political
leaders, business, and the public who recognize the urgency of finding a
solution. The **urban** underclass is now at least four times larger than it
was during the turbulent 1960s, when our major cities were burning.
Disturbances have already begun to erupt in some major cities. Some
predict that there will be riots of "earthquake" proportions within two to
three years in at least four major cities: New York, Chicago, Los Angeles,
and Miami. At that point, there will undoubtedly be widespread support
for making essential changes in our economy. The real question is one of
timing: will we be too late?

## COMPREHENSION CHECK

Complete the following items by circling the correct answer or filling in the
blanks.

1. The topic of this selection is:
   a. the changing economy in the United States
   b. the declining socio-economic status of Americans
   c. the effects of recession

2. State the main idea of the selection by explaining what the author is
   saying about the topic.

   _____

   _____

3. The best statement of the main idea of paragraph 3 would be:
   a. Many jobs were lost in the shift from an industrial to a service
      economy.
   b. The shift from an industrial to a service economy has resulted in a
      substantial decrease in economic status for many Americans.
   c. The United States has shifted from an industrial economy to a ser-
      vice economy.

4. The only segment of the population that is not increasing in numbers is:
   a. the poor
   b. the middle class
   c. the rich

5. The proportion of after-tax income for the wealthiest 1 percent of American households increased 7 percent from 1977 to 1990.
   a. true
   b. false

6. What are the two reasons the author gives for an increase in homelessness?

   a. _____

   b. _____

7. Using the context of the paragraph and your knowledge of prefixes and roots, define the word *transitional* in paragraph 3.

   _____

8. Each of the following is an effect of downward mobility *except*:
   a. Young people are becoming passive.
   b. Young adults are taking longer to finish school.
   c. Homelessness is increasing.

9. From this selection you can conclude that one of the main reasons for violence in our cities is poverty.
   a. true
   b. false

10. What part do you see education playing in this problem of downward mobility?

   _____

   _____

   _____

   _____

# COMPREHENSION EXERCISE *Comparing economic conditions*

Complete the following chart using the information given in the selection "The Economic Escalator."

| Socio-Economic Conditions Pre- and Post-1980 | | |
| --- | --- | --- |
| *Points of Comparison* | *Pre-1980s* | *Post-1980s* |
| Characteristics of economy | | |
| Income distribution | | |
| Housing | | |
| Young adult population | | |

# CHAPTER 11: PRACTICE IN READING ISSUE AND DEBATE

## *Prereading Activity*: Stating the issue

Before reading, preview the selection carefully. Then, using an interrogative sentence (question), state the issue that is being discussed in the selection.

# Back to the Chain Gang?

BY LARRY REIBSTEIN WITH GINNY CARROLL

AND CARROLL BOGERT

*Justice: In this fearful election season, politicians have found an irresistible target: prisons*

When the Mississippi legislature met in special session, it was supposed    1
to deal with prison overcrowding. But the get-together in August [1994]
quickly dissolved into a get-tough-on-criminals frenzy. . . . The lawmakers decided they were tired of "**coddling**" prison inmates. They voted to
yank individual television sets from prisoners, ban air conditioning, prohibit weightlifting equipment and — in the biggest throwback — dress inmates in striped uniforms with CONVICT stamped across the back. The
fact that none of these measures will likely deter crime was beside the
point. "We want a prisoner to look like a prisoner, to smell like a prisoner," said state Rep. Mack McInnis. "When you see one of these boogers
a-loose, you'll say, 'I didn't know we had zebras in Mississippi'."

Say hello to the new chain gang — and Mississippi isn't alone. From    2
Albany to Sacramento, lawmakers have discovered that bashing prison
inmates is . . . [the] easiest and most **disingenuous** way to exploit voters'
anti-crime sentiment. Ohio, Wisconsin and North Carolina, among others, have enacted or proposed bans on telephones, televisions, basketball,
boxing, wrestling and martial arts. California, eroding the Jerry Brown–
era "Prisoners' Bill of Rights," is charging inmates $3 to initiate court
actions and has banned R-rated movies. South Carolina has banned **conjugal** visits for minimum-security inmates, ending a 50-year tradition.
New Jersey is considering a "people's prison" where inmates would do
10 hours a day of hard labor, with no educational programs, no gyms, no
TVs. Congress has also struck a blow against crime, eliminating educational grants for federal prisoners. Says Jonathan Turley, director of the
Prison Law Project: "It's difficult to imagine a measure **draconian**
enough to satisfy the public desire for retribution."

. . . Some of the action is symbolic. Louisiana passed a law banning    3
**martial** arts in prison even though it offers none. Mississippi banned air
conditioners though few inmates have them. . . . Supporters insist that

**Rate of imprisonment**
Prisoners per 100,000 U.S. residents

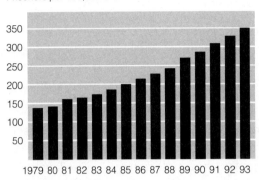

### A Growth Industry

The U.S. prison population set another new record last year, breaking 900,000 for the first time.

**What they did**
Federal inmates, by offense

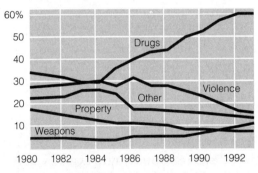

Source: U.S. Department of Justice, Bureau of Justice Statistics

making prisons harsher will somehow deter crime. "Knowing there's no televisions here, maybe they'll think twice before committing a crime," Sgt. Dan Smith of Clay County, Fla., suggested to The New York Times after the Sheriff's Office removed TVs from county jails. Others maintain that prison life has grown soft and too inviting for some down-and-out people. "We have too many benefits and too little punishment," says New York state Sen. Michael Nozzolio, who wants to revoke scholarships for prisoners. Although studies show education is one of the few programs that cuts **recidivism**, Nozzolio says: "We have lifers getting two and three master's degrees at taxpayer expense."

**Deterrent factor**: Critics say those arguments simply add up to   4 mindless retaliation. There's no evidence that something like banning TVs will give pause to someone contemplating, say, a drive-by shooting or a walk-by mugging. "Does anyone really believe that taking away a television is going to affect the crime rate?" asks David Rothman, a Columbia University historian of American prisons. How about barbells, which are a particularly popular target for get-tough lawmakers? Citing the 1993 riot in Lucasville, Ohio, where prisoners used barbells to smash a cinder-block wall, legislators argue that bulked-up inmates cause too many problems in and out of prison. Experts scoff at this contention. "We haven't seen any 98-pound weaklings bulked up into 210-pound **behemoths** who rob and rape people," says William Turner, a San Francisco lawyer who has won several suits forcing states to clean up their prison systems. And, inmates say, weight lifting acts as a tension-reliever. As one parolee in Wisconsin explains: "People that lift iron have a fixation with themselves. They just sit there and lift, and they don't cause no problems. They're so big, no one wants to mess with them."

With most prisons already dangerously overcrowded, wardens and experts worry that **idle** inmates are dangerous, first to other convicts, but also to prison staff. Prisoners are "like kids who need an electronic baby-sitter," says New York state correctional spokesman James Flateau. Just ask Harvey Garlotte, 36, who is serving a life sentence for murder in the South Mississippi Correctional Facility. He says that last week guards began confiscating private TVs. Most of the individual TVs are in death row, psychiatric wards and isolation quarters, leaving only **communal** areas where dozens of inmates can gather to view one set. Claims Garlotte: "If they're going to take the TVs and all, things are going to blow apart." 5

**Changing conditions**: Do barbells and TVs really amount to coddling? To a prisoner in the 19th century, complaints the likes of Garlotte's would sound pretty farfetched. Then, prisoners had a cell and a Bible and not much more. But the definition of acceptable conditions has changed with the times. In the early 1900s leg shackles came off and athletics were allowed as part of "normalizing" the prison. After World War II rehabilitation was the buzzword, and by the end of the 1960s the Surpeme Court established certain minimum rights for prisoners, like the right to worship, hold property and contact lawyers. But since the 1970s the notion of rehabilitation has lost ground. While for some inmates prison is a shelter from urban streets, a place where they can get three square meals and clean clothes, few people who have studied prisons would contend 6 that even the nicest ones are pleasure domes. Says Turley, "We no longer pretend to have a prison policy other than **retribution**, no philosophy other than warehousing." And after the new laws, a pretty bare warehouse at that.

## COMPREHENSION CHECK

Complete the following items by filling in the blanks or circling the correct answer.

1. The topic of the selection is:
   a. overcrowded prisons
   b. prisoners' rights
   c. prison conditions

2. State the main idea of the selection by explaining what the author is saying about the topic.

   _____

3. The main idea of paragraph 2 is found in:
   a. sentence 1
   b. sentence 2
   c. sentence 8

4. According to the defenders of weight lifting in prison, prisoners build themselves up in order to keep other prisoners away, rather than to threaten other inmates.
   a. true
   b. false

5. Which of the following has actually been shown to rehabilitate prisoners?
   a. education programs
   b. weight lifting
   c. athletic programs

6. Using the context of the paragraph, define the word *coddling* in paragraph 1.

   _____

7. Using the context of the sentence, give a synonym for the word *behemoth* in paragraph 4.

   _____

8. Which of the following measures would be most likely to reduce idleness in the prisons?
   a. 10 hours a day of hard labor
   b. removing TVs and barbells
   c. eliminating education programs

9. You can infer from this article that some people may commit crimes in order to have a place to live.
   a. true
   b. false

10. From this article you can conclude that people have become more interested in:
   a. revenge than retribution
   b. retribution than rehabilitation
   c. prison overcrowdedness than retribution

**COMPREHENSION EXERCISE**  *Mapping and essay writing*

Using the outline below, map the arguments in the article "Back to the Chain Gang?". Then write an essay giving your own opinion on the issue.

### *"Back to the Chain Gang?"*

A. State the issue in the form of a question.

   _____

B.  Describe the background by listing the proposals.

_____

_____

_____

_____

C.  Possible positions

Yes  _____          No  _____

*Supporting Arguments*

1.  _____          1.  _____

2.  _____          2.  _____

3.  _____          3.  _____

4.  _____          4.  _____

## CHAPTER 12: PRACTICE IN READING RESEARCH AND STATISTICAL DATA

### *Prereading Activity*: **Previewing the research**

The following selection is excerpted from a book about raising children. This particular section of the book discusses a study concerning sex-role stereotyping. Before reading, preview the selection carefully. Pay special attention to headings, quotations, and italicized words. What method of research was used in the study described?

_____

# Growing Up Free: Raising Your Child in the 80's

BY LETTY COTTIN POGREBIN

## The preschool child

Because children have to decode two sex roles — the one to play and the one to avoid — each sex must be familiar with the approved "norms" for the other sex.   1

This is an acquired talent. Before age two, there is little evidence of sex-typed awareness or **preferences**, but by two-and-a-half or three, both girls and boys know which toys "belong" to each sex and which tools, appliances, clothing, and activities go with mommies or daddies.   2

Between infancy and early adolescence, research shows that more boys than girls feel heavily pressured by sex role standards. For example, to protect their "masculine" image, tiny little boys will assiduously deny themselves a highly attractive "feminine" toy and choose to play with an unappealing sex-neutral toy instead, whereas girls feel free to pick the "opposite" sex toy if it is more attractive, and they don't give the boring neutral toy a second glance.   3

In nursery school, boys who cross the sex line to play with dolls, dress-up clothes, kitchen toys, or art materials are criticized by their classmates six times as often as other children, while girls who try out such "masculine" activities as blocks, hammers, transportation toys, or sandbox play may be ignored by their peers but are not criticized.   4

Kids don't just know sex linkages, they have a pretty clear picture of the power differences involved. A child between about three and five knows enough to say, "Mommy never really has things belong to her." Or "He's the daddy so it's his but he shares nice with the mommy."   5

Preschoolers' ideas about adult occupations are already **ossified** stereotypes. I often tell the story of a friend who took a childrearing leave of absence from her job as a newspaper reporter. One day, when her three-year-old, Sarah, expressed interest in a TV story about a crime reporter, my friend decided to explain her own career: "Before you were born, I used to have a job like that," the mother said, building to a simple but exciting description of journalism. "I went to fires or to the police station and the stories I wrote were printed in the newspaper with my name on them."   6

After listening attentively, Sarah asked, "Mommy, when you had this    7
job before I was born, did you used to be a man?"

What necessitated the magical thinking that turned her mother into    8
a man was Sarah's inability to associate the exciting job of a newspaper
reporter with the female sex.

Seventy Wisconsin children, ages three to five, had much the same    9
problem. When asked "What do you want to be when you grow up?"
the boys mentioned fourteen occupations: fireman, policeman, father/
husband, older person, digger, dentist, astronaut, cowboy, truck-driver,
engineer, baseball player, doctor, Superman, and the Six-Million-Dollar
Man. Girls named eleven categories: mother/sister, nurse, ballerina, older
person, dentist, teacher, babysitter, baton-twirler, iceskater, princess, and
cowgirl.

Next, the children were polled on their more realistic expectations:    10
"What do you think you *really* will be?" they were asked. The girls altered
their choices toward even more traditional roles — changing from ballerina, nurse, and dentist, to mother — while the boys changed to *more*
active, adventurous futures — for instance, from husband to fireman.

Pittsburgh children of the same ages were asked "What do you want    11
to be when you grow up?" followed by "If you were a boy (girl), what
would you be when you grow up?" For the first question, most chose
stereotyped careers: policeman, sports star, cowboy, and one "aspiring
spy" for the boys; nursing and the like for the girls. To the second — what
they would be if they were the "opposite" sex — the children answered
with stereotyped other-sex occupations as well. But their *reactions* to that
second question were striking: The boys were shocked at the very *idea* of
being a girl. Most had never thought of it before, some refused to think
about it, and one "put his hands to his head and sighed. 'Oh, if I were a
girl I'd have to grow up to be nothing.'"

The girls, on the other hand, obviously had thought about the ques-    12
tion a great deal. Most had an answer ready. "Several girls mentioned
that this other-sex occupational ambition was their *true* ambition, but
one that could not be realized because of their sex." More **poignantly**,
the gender barrier had become so formidable that it even blocked out
fantasies and dreams. "Thus, one blond moppet confided that what she
really wanted to do when she grew up was fly like a bird. 'But I'll never
do it,' she sighed, 'because I'm not a boy.'"

### Stereotypes according to five- to eleven-year-olds

When kindergarten children were asked to imagine a typical day in 13
their futures, the girls talked about getting up to clean house and feed the
baby; the boys talked about performing an operation and being on a
space ship.

To find out whether children increase their knowledge of sex stereo- 14
types between kindergarten and fourth grade, researchers showed children pictures of a man and a woman and asked which one would match
a range of behaviors or characteristics. For example, "One of these people
is a bully. They are always pushing people around and getting into fights.
Which person gets into fights?" Or, "One of these people is emotional.
They cry when something good happens as well as when everything goes
wrong. Which is the emotional person?"

Additional questions elicited information about which person day- 15
dreams, owns a store, talks a lot, says bad words, is confident, and so on.
Comparing the age groups, examiners found an increase in the number
of items stereotyped between kindergarten and second grade, but no
change between second and fourth grade — which suggests that with
the basic stereotypes under their belts, children need little additional
elaboration.

One more intriguing result: *Both girls and boys learn the male stereotype* 16
*earlier than the female one. The male ideal obviously demands greater attention.*

By age five or six, almost all children claim (in their own vocabularies, 17
of course) that every male is more powerful, invulnerable, **punitive**,
aggressive, fearless, and competent than every female.

Eight- to eleven-year-old boys say that adult men need to make de- 18
cisions, protect women and children in emergencies, do hard labor and
dirty work, fix things, support their families, get along with their wives,
and teach their children right from wrong. Men are the boss, control the
money, get the most comfortable chair and the daily papers, get mad a lot
but laugh and make jokes more than women do and are more fun to be
with.

The boys say that female adults are indecisive, afraid of many things,   19
get tired a lot, need help often, stay home most of the time, are **squeamish**, don't like adventure, are helpless in emergencies, do things the
wrong way, and are not very intelligent. Women always "have to keep
things neat and tidy, take the pep out of things, easily become jealous and
envy their husbands, feel sad more often than men, and are pests to have
along on an adventure."

Eight- to eleven-year-old girls have similar stereotypes in their   20
repertoire: child care, the interior of the house, clothes and food are
"feminine"; manipulation of the physical environment, machines, transportation, the structure of the house, most recreation, and most occupations are "masculine."

Primary school children also classify being good at games as "mas-   21
culine," being quiet as "feminine." Trucks, cars, and **boisterous** self-
assertion are "masculine"; jump ropes, dolls, cuddling, and dependency
are "feminine." Arithmetic and athletic, spatial and mechanical skills are
"masculine"; reading and artistic and social skills are "feminine." School
objects, such as a blackboard and a book, are "feminine"; chess is
"masculine."

### Stereotypes according to twelve- to seventeen-year-olds

Many of the tensions of adolescence are attributable to one unfortu-   22
nate misconception, which begins here and persists into maturity: *the
confusion of sex role standards with sexual competence.*

Lack of experience and a frame of reference for their developing sex-   23
uality lead teenagers to equate extremes of "femininity" and "masculinity" with the ultimate in sexiness. They are anxious about everything:
their physical appearance, hormonal changes, popularity, desirability as
a romantic and sexual partner, academic standing, and destiny in life.
Understandably, many adolescents therefore seek an identity within the
clearcut outlines of stereotype. At this age, digressions from the "norm"
are imagined to bring social **ostracism** and worse.

Sex-typed interests peak for girls at thirteen and for boys at sixteen,   24
years that roughly correspond to the peak transformations of puberty.
Take, for example, the **montages** created from magazine pictures by
some eighth-graders. The boys were asked to express "Boys' Ideas of

Their Maleness"; the girls "Girls' Ideas of Their Femaleness"; and then each group did "opposite" sex evaluations.

One group of boys plastered a large number 2 on their montage about   25
femaleness and a number 1 on their maleness poster. Seeing this, the girls' group immediately pasted a big zero on their "Girls" Ideas of Maleness" montage. In later discussions, the girls poured out their resentment of men and boys: "They think they're superior because they bring home all the money; boys are inferior and always in trouble; they are lazy; they act like animals."

Verbally, the boys characterized girls and women as being bossy, nosy,   26
self-centered, talkative, and interested in their looks, breasts, menstruation, birth control, getting married, and having babies.

The "Girls' Ideas of Their Femaleness" montage concentrated on   27
beauty, marriage, love, sex, make-up, cooking, money, dieting, cleanliness, perfume, jewelry, clothes, and skin. Yet the girls objected to the boys' idea of their femaleness because "all it is is sex, sex, sex, sex, making love, bust developers, work, cooking, children and cleaning. They think we're their slaves."

On their own maleness montages, the thirteen- and fourteen-year-   28
old boys pictured sports, hunting, cars, cycles, muscle development, military service, careers, and work. In some posters, family scenes appeared minimally; in others not at all.

These posters, and their creators, depict two different worlds and the   29
brand of male-female **alienation** that is all too familiar among adults.

As the plot thickens on the adolescent social scene, an **aboutface** is   30
happening in the intellectual sphere: Children stop stereotyping school achievement as "feminine" and start stereotyping the whole academic package as "masculine." To test this finding, I asked some thirteen-year-old girls which gender label they would put on mathematics:

"Math is a girl's thing because all the girls are better at it."

"No, it's a boy's thing when you think of how boys need it when they grow up."

"Women need it too — for adding up prices and budgets."

"Yeah, maybe if you think of arithmetic, it's female. But when you think of a mathematician, it's male."

Sex role standards for achievement become more definite and ex-    31
treme with age. By the time they are seventeen, both sexes almost unan-
imously stereotype athletics and arithmetic as male, and reading and
social skills as female.

High school seniors are also relentlessly judgmental about what is    32
inappropriate for adults. In one national survey, 30 percent of them said
a woman's place is in the home and 4 percent think women are totally
incapable of working outside the home.

## COMPREHENSION CHECK

Complete the following items by filling in the blanks or circling the correct
answer.

1. The topic of the selection is:
    a. stereotyping
    b. raising children
    c. sex roles

2. State the main idea of the selection by explaining what the author is
    saying about the topic.

    _____

3. Which of the following organizational structure is used most frequently
    throughout the selection?
    a. comparison and contrast
    b. simple listing
    c. chronological order

4. According to this selection there is more pressure on boys than on girls
    to fit into their sex roles in the early years.
    a. true
    b. false

5. Generally speaking, both boys and girls view males as more powerful than females.
   a. true
   b. false

6. Use the context of the paragraph to define the word *ossified* in paragraph 6.

   _____

7. Use the context of the paragraph to define the word *montages* in paragraph 24.

   _____

8. Why do you think that school achievement suddenly becomes stereotyped as a "masculine" endeavor in adolescence, whereas in the younger years it was viewed as "feminine"?

   _____

   _____

9. You can conclude from the selection that sex roles are innate.
   a. true
   b. false

10. What does the author mean when she states in paragraph 29 that the montages depict "the brand of male-female alienation that is all too familiar among adults"?

   _____

   _____

   _____

**COMPREHENSION EXERCISE**   *Designing a research study*

This study shows that children have very rigid ideas about and perceptions of their sex roles. It does not attempt to examine the reasons for these perceptions. Based on your answers to the following questions, design a study that would examine possible reasons for these learned behaviors and perceptions.

1. What hypothesis would you attempt to prove?

   _____

2. What method of research would you use?

   _____

3. How would you gather your data?

   _____

   _____

4. What problems might you have in arriving at valid conclusions?

   _____

   _____

   _____

**aberrant** (*adj.*) deviating from what is true, normal, or typical.

**abjectly** (*adv.*) miserably; wretchedly.

**abolitionist** (*n.*) one who favors the utter destruction or annulment of something.

**aboutface** (*n.*) 1. a turning or facing in the opposite direction. 2. a reversal of attitude.

**absolute** (*n.*) 1. perfect. 2. complete, whole. 3. not mixed, pure. 4. not limited; unrestricted. 5. positive; certain. 6. actual, real.

**absolutist** (*n.*) one who believes in the absolute certainty of a particular position.

**academician** (*n.*) a member of a school, college, or academic community.

**activism** (*n.*) the policy of taking direct action, especially for political or social ends.

**affliction** (*n.*) anything causing pain or distress; calamity.

**aggregation** (*n.*) a gathering of people together in one place.

**alienation** (*n.*) state of being estranged or alone.

**ambiguous** (*adj.*) having two or more possible meanings.

**analogue** (*n.*) a thing or part that is the same or comparable in certain respects.

**anarchy** (*n.*) 1. the complete absence of government and law. 2. disorder in any sphere of activity.

**annul** (*v.*) to do away with; to cancel.

**anomaly** (*n.*) departure from the regular arrangement or usual method; abnormality.

**anonymity** (*n.*) the quality or state of being anonymous or unknown.

**anonymous** (*adj.*) 1. with no name known or acknowledged. 2. given or written by a person whose name is withheld or unknown.

**anorexia** (*n.*) an abnormal lack of appetite that can result in serious illness or death.

**anthropologist** (*n.*) one who studies the races, physical and mental characteristics, distribution, customs, etc. of mankind.

**appraisal** (*n.*) an estimation of quantity or quality.

**arbiter** (*n.*) 1. a person selected to judge a dispute. 2. a person fully authorized to judge or decide.

**arbitrary** (*adj.*) based on one's preference, notion, or whim.

**articulation** (*n.*) the act of speaking in distinct syllables or words or of expressing oneself clearly.

**assumption** (*n.*) anything taken for granted or presumed.

**atrocity** (*n.*) atrocious behavior; brutality.

**audacity** (*n.*) 1. bold courage; daring. 2. insolence; impudence.

**behemoth** (*n.*) a huge animal.

**bent** (*n.*) 1. an inclining or tendency. 2. mental leaning; propensity, as in "a *bent* for music."

**bias** (*n.*) a slanting or leaning; partiality; prejudice.

**biochemical** (*adj.*) pertaining to the branch of science that deals with plants and animals and their life processes.

**boisterous** (*adj.*) loud and exuberant.

**brood** (*n.*) the children in a family; offspring.

**buffer** (*n.*) any person or thing that lessens shock.

**bulimia** (*n.*) an abnormal craving for food that leads to heavy eating and then intentional vomiting.

**bull** (*n.*) an official document or decree from the Pope.

**cachet** (*n.*) 1. a distinguishing mark, as a quality. 2. a mark stamped or imprinted on mail.

**capricious** (*adj.*) subject to whim or impulse; erratic; flighty; unpredictable.

**caveat** (*n.*) 1. a warning. 2. *in law*, a notice that an interested party files with the proper officers directing them to stop an action until he or she can be heard.

**celerity** (*n.*) quickness; speed.

**censorship** (*n.*) the practice of supervising public morals by the removal or prohibition of materials considered unsuitable.

**charlatan** (*n.*) one who pretends to have knowledge or ability that he or she does not have.

**chicanery** (*n.*) trickery.

**chronic** (*adj.*) 1. lasting a long time; recurring. 2. perpetual, habitual; constant.

**circadian** (*adj.*) having to do with the day or daily.

**coddling** (*n.*) gentle treatment; pampering.

**cognitive** (*adj.*) pertaining to the activity of knowing or the mental processes by which knowledge is acquired.

**cohort** (*n.*) a group or band; an associate or colleague.

**communal** (*adj.*) belonging to a community; public.

**compulsive** (*adj.*) that which is compelling or cannot be avoided.

**condoned** (*v.*) forgiven or overlooked.

**confederates** (*n.*) allies; those united in an alliance.

**conjecture** (*n.*) guesswork; inferring, theorizing or predicting from incomplete evidence. (*v.*) to guess, arrive at, or predict by conjecture.

**conjugal** (*adj.*) of marriage or the relationship between husband and wife.

**contemporaries** (*n.*) persons or things of about the same age or date of origin.

**correlation** (*n.*) a close or mutual relation.

**corroborate** (*v.*) to strengthen; confirm; support.

**decapitation** (*n.*) the act of severing the head from the body.

**delirium tremens** (*n.*) a violent delirium resulting from excessive drinking of alcohol.

**delve** (*v.*) to make an investigation; to search for the facts.

**desultory** (*adj.*) jumping from one thing to another; disconnected; not methodical.

**deterrence** (*n.*) a thing or factor that keeps one from doing something through fear or anxiety.

**detoxification** (*n.*) process wherein the body is weaned of alcohol.

**detritus** (*n.*) debris.

**devastating** (*adj.*) disastrous.

**deviation** (*n.*) a turning aside from the standard or norm.

**discriminatory** (*adj.*) showing a favoritism or bias.

**disgruntled** (*adj.*) to be peevishly discontented or disappointed.

**disingenuous** (*adj.*) not straightforward; insincere.

**disparity** (*n.*) inequality or difference, as in rank, quality, etc.

**distilled spirits** (*n.*) alcoholic beverages.

**docile** (*adj.*) 1. easy to teach; teachable. 2. easy to discipline; obedient.

**draconian** (*adj.*) harsh, severe, cruel.

**dysfunction** (*n.*) not functioning or working properly.

**ecosystem** (*n.*) forests, deserts, ponds, oceans, or any set of plants and animals interacting with one another and with their nonliving environment.

**effeminate** (*adj.*) having or showing qualities generally attributed to women, as weakness, delicacy, etc.; unmanly.

**elude** (*v.*) to avoid or escape from by quickness or cunning.

**embody** (*v.*) 1. to give bodily form to. 2. to give definite or visible form to.

**embolden** (*v.*) to give courage to; cause to be bold or bolder.

**endocrine** (*adj.*) of any gland that secretes hormones to different parts of the body, directly affecting target tissue or stimulating the secretion of another hormone.

**enshrined** (*adj.*) held sacred; preserved.

**enslavement** (*n.*) a state of slavery, domination, or subjugation.

**entity** (*n.*) being, existence; a thing that has real and individual existence in reality or in the mind.

**erosion** (*n.*) a gradual wearing away.

**erratic** (*adj.*) 1. having no fixed course; irregular; wandering. 2. eccentric; queer.

**escalate** (*v.*) 1. to rise. 2. to expand.

**exobiologist** (*n.*) a scientist who studies life on other planets.

**extrapolate** (*v.*) to estimate (a value, quantity, etc. beyond the known range) on the basis of certain known variables.

**felony** (*n.*) a major crime, as murder, arson, rape, etc., for which statute provides greater punishment than for a misdemeanor.

**fermentation** (*n.*) 1. the breakdown of complex molecules in organic compounds, caused by the influence of a ferment. 2. excitement or agitation.

**gentrification** (*n.*) the act of becoming upper-class.

**hallucination** (*n.*) 1. the apparent perception of sights, sounds, etc. that are not actually present. 2. the imaginary things apparently seen, heard, etc.

**heinous** (*adj.*) hateful; odious; very wicked; outrageous.

**heritage** (*n.*) 1. property that is or can be inherited. 2. something handed down from one's ancestors or the past, as a culture, tradition etc.; birthright.

**homeostasis** (*n.*) a state of internal stability or balance.

***Homo sapiens*** (*n.*) man; human being; the only living species of the genus *Homo*.

**horticultural** (*adj.*) pertaining to growing fruits, vegetables, and flowers.

**hyperrational** (*adj.*) able to reason beyond the obvious.

**hypothesis** (*n.*) an unproved theory, proposition, etc. tentatively accepted to explain certain facts or to provide a basis for further investigation, argument, or study.

**hypothetical** (*adj.*) assumed or supposed.

**ideogram** (*n.*) 1. a graphic symbol representing an object or idea without expressing the sounds that form its name. 2. a symbol representing an idea rather than a word.

**idle** (*adj.*) 1. worthless, useless. 2. unemployed; not busy.

**illusion** (*n.*) 1. a false idea or conception. 2. an unreal or misleading appearance or image. 3. a false perception or conception of what one sees, where one is, etc.

**immersion** (*n.*) the state of being absorbed or deeply involved.

**immunity** (*n.*) 1. resistance to a specified disease or toxic substance. 2. exemption from taxes, military service, etc.

**immutable** (*adj.*) never changing or varying; unchangeable.

**imperative** (*n.*) a necessity.

**impervious** (*adj.*) 1. incapable of being penetrated. 2. not affected or influenced by.

**inanimate** (*adj.*) not living.

**incarcerated** (*adj.*) imprisoned.

**incessantly** (*adv.*) continually or repeatedly, without interruption; constantly.

**indulgently** (*adv.*) to act in an indulgent manner.

**inevitable** (*adj.*) certain to happen, unavoidable.

**inflict** (*v.*) to wound or impose punishment.

**inherent** (*adj.*) existing naturally within someone or something; inborn.

**innocuous** (*adj.*) that which cannot injure or harm; harmless.

**interstellar** (*adj.*) between or among the stars.

**intoxication** (*n.*) 1. making or becoming drunk. 2. great excitement.

**intricate** (*adj.*) perplexing, complicated, involved, hard to follow.

**introverted** (*adj.*) concentrated or directed on oneself.

**irrational** (*adj.*) 1. not rational; lacking the power to reason.
2. senseless; unreasonable; absurd.

**latchkey** (*adj.*) expression to describe children who go home to unoccupied homes.

**lethal** (*adj.*) 1. causing death; fatal; deadly. 2. of or suggestive of death.

**lexicon** (*n.*) a dictionary; especially of an ancient language.

**liberal** (*adj.*) broad-minded; favoring reform or progress.

**liberate** (*v.*) to free.

**linguist** (*n.*) a specialist in language.

**lofty** (*adj.*) 1. very high. 2. elevated; noble, grand. 3. haughty, overproud; arrogant.

**magnitude** (*n.*) greatness of size or influence.

**manacle** (*n.*) 1. a device for confining the hands, usually consisting of two metal rings that are fastened about the wrists and joined by a metal chain; a handcuff. 2. anything that confines or restrains.

**mandatory** (*adj.*) required.

**martial** (*adj.*) pertaining to or suitable for war.

**mediocre** (*adj.*) of middle quality, neither very good nor very bad.

**meditation** (*n.*) deep thought.

**menial** (*adj.*) low; task of little worth.

**metacognition** (*n.*) one's knowledge about cognition and the regulation of cognitive experiences.

**metamemory** (*n.*) one's knowledge of memory and memory processes.

**microcosmically** (*adv.*) participating within a little world that is a miniature of the world in general.

**micro-environment** (*n.*) specific conditions and circumstances that constitute an individual's life experiences.

**migrating** (*adj.*) moving from one place to another.

**mishmash** (*n.*) a hodgepodge or a jumbled mixture; mess.

**misnomer** (*n.*) a name or epithet wrongly applied.

**mitigating** (*v.*) to make less severe.

**mobility** (*n.*) having the capacity to be moved.

**montage** (*n.*) the art of making a composite picture of a number of different pictures.

**mundane** (*adj.*) of the world; wordly, as distinguished from heavenly.

**myopic** (*adj.*) having to do with nearsightedness.

**myriad** (*n.*) an extremely large number.

**neurological** (*adj.*) having to do with the nervous system.

**nocturnal** (*adj.*) 1. of the night. 2. functioning at night. 3. done or happening in the night.

**nomads** (*n.*) people having no permanent home.

**ominous** (*adj.*) of or serving as an evil omen; threatening; sinister.

**oracle** (*n.*) 1. in ancient Greece and Rome, the place where or medium by which deities were consulted. 2. the revelation of a medium or priest. 3. any person or agency believed to be in communication with a deity.

**ossified** (*adj.*) rigidly fixed or hardened.

**ostracism** (*n.*) an exclusion or alienation by general consent.

**panacea** (*n.*) a cure-all.

**passive** (*adj.*) 1. inactive but acted upon. 2. offering no resistance; submissive; patient. 3. taking no part; inactive; inert.

**pedigree** (*n.*) 1. descent; lineage. 2. known line of descent.

**per se** (*adv.*) itself, inherently.

**perverse** (*adj.*) deviating from what is considered right or acceptable.

**pessimism** (*n.*) the tendency to expect the worst outcome in any circumstances; a looking on the dark side of things.

**phenomenon** (*n.*) any fact or event that is apparent to the senses and can be scientifically described.

**philologist** (*n.*) one who studies the authenticity and meaning of literary texts.

**pictograph** (*n.*) 1. a picture representing an idea; hieroglyph. 2. writing of this kind.

**pique** (*v.*) 1. to arouse resentment in by slighting or offending. 2. to arouse or excite.

**poignant** (*adj.*) 1. sharply painful to the feelings. 2. touching.

**polar** (*adj.*) of or near the North or South Poles.

**pragmatic** (*adj.*) busy, active, practical.

**preclude** (*v.*) to shut out; hinder; make impossible, especially in advance.

**preference** (*n.*) the giving of advantages to one person or group.

**prefix** (*n.*) a part attached at the beginning of a word that serves to produce another form of the word.

**premise** (*n.*) a previous statement serving as the basis for an argument.

**prerequisite** (*adj.*) required beforehand, especially as a necessary condition for something following. (*n.*) something prerequisite.

**prestigious** (*adj.*) having a reputation of high renown.

**prevalence** (*n.*) being widely practiced, occurring, or accepted.

**primate** (*n*) any member of the most highly developed order of mammals, composed of humans, apes, and so on.

**primeval** (*adj.*) of the first age or ages; primitive.

**prohibition** (*n.*) 1. the forbidding by law of the manufacture or sale of alcoholic liquors; specifically, in the U.S. the period (1920–1933) of prohibition by federal law. 2. an order or law that forbids.

**proliferate** (*v.*) to reproduce in quick succession.

**prolific** (*adj.*) 1. producing many young or fruit. 2. creating many products of the mind. 3. fruitful; abounding.

**punitive** (*adj.*) inflicting punishment or concerned with punishment.

**quirky** (*adj.*) peculiar or unpredictable.

**razzed** (*v.*) teased, ridiculed, derided, etc.

**recession** (*n.*) 1. to go backwards. 2. *in economics,* a temporary falling off of business.

**recidivism** (*n.*) the falling back into or return to (crime).

**relevant** (*adj.*) pertaining to; related to.

**resynchronize** (*v.*) to return to a state of synchronization.

**retention** (*n.*) 1. to get back, recover. 2. to restore; revive.

**retribution** (*n.*) deserved punishment or reward.

**reversal** (*n.*) a turning back or around.

**revulsion** (*n.*) a sudden, complete, and violent change of feeling; abrupt, strong reaction; especially, disgust.

**rigged** (*adj.*) 1. equipped or outfitted. 2. prearranged.

**rungs** (*n.*) steps on a ladder.

**sadist** (*n.*) one who receives pleasure from mistreating others.

**scrutiny** (*n.*) a close examination; careful, lengthy look.

**sedentary** (*adj.*) characterized by sitting.

**sensory** (*adj.*) having to do with the senses.

**shoddy** (*adj.*) having less worth than apparent; inferior or lacking in required or claimed quality.

**sibling** (*n.*) one of two or more persons born at different times of the same parents; brother or sister.

**skepticism** (*n.*) skeptical or doubting attitude or state of mind.

**smug** (*adv.*) 1. originally, trimly and neatly. 2. in a manner that is fatuously content with one's own accomplishments; self-satisfied.

**snuff** (*n.*) 1. a preparation of powdered tobacco taken up into the nose by sniffing or applied to the gums. 2. the act or sound of snuffing.

**socio-economic** (*adj.*) relating to a combination of social and economic conditions.

**sociologist** (*n.*) one who studies the development, organization, and problems of society and social groups.

**sodomize** (*v.*) to engage in abnormal intercourse, as with a person of the same sex or between a person and an animal.

**spew** (*v.*) to throw up from; vomit; eject.

**squeamish** (*adj.*) 1. easily nauseated; queasy. 2. easily shocked.

**stability** (*n.*) being stable or steadfast; permanence.

**stimulus** (*n.*) 1. something that incites to action or increased action; incentive. 2. *in psychology or physiology*, any action or agent that causes or changes an activity in an organism.

**subtly** (*adv.*) 1. cleverly, skillfully. 2. with subtle thought; with fine distinctions. 3. elusively.

**suggestible** (*adj.*) possible to be influenced by suggestion.

**syllabic** (*adj.*) of a syllable or syllables.

**synthesized** (*v.*) the combination of parts or elements so that a whole is formed.

**tandem** (*adv.*) one behind the other; in single file.

**temperance** (*n.*) 1. total abstinence from alcoholic liquors. 2. self-restraining in conduct, expression, indulgence of the appetite, etc. 3. moderation in drinking alcoholic liquors.

**tenable** (*adj.*) capable of being held, maintained, or defended.

**transcend** (*v.*) 1. to go beyond the limits of; exceed. 2. to be superior to; surpass; excel.

**transitional** (*adj.*) a linking of two things; connecting.

**transparent** (*adj.*) 1. capable of being seen through. 2. easily understood, recognized, or detected.

**triarchic** (*adj.*) a division of three distinct groups, each under its own ruler.

**unique** (*adj.*) 1. one and only. 2. unusual. 3. having no equal.

**urban** (*adj.*) of, in, or constituting a city.

**utilitarian** (*adj.*) of or having to do with usefulness.

**valedictorian** (*n.*) in schools and colleges the student, usually the one ranking highest in scholarship, who delivers the farewell speech at graduation.

**variability** (*n.*) a condition of changeability or inconsistency.

**variants** (*n.*) that which is different in some way from others of the same kind.

**vile** (*adj.*) 1. morally base or evil; wicked. 2. repulsive, disgusting. 3. degrading, lowly. 4. of poor quality; very inferior; bad.

**villainy** (*n.*) the fact or state of being wicked or evil.

**vitals** (*n.*) the vital organs, such as the heart, brain, etc.

**vouch** (*v.*) 1. to attest; affirm or guarantee. 2. to cite a source. 3. to serve as evidence or give assurance.

**wantonly** (*adv.*) 1. acting with reckless disregard for justice, decency, etc. 2. acting without restraint.

**warrant** (*n.*) 1. authorization by law. 2. justification for some act, belief, and so on.

## EXERCISE 2

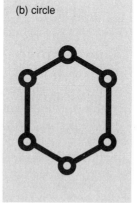

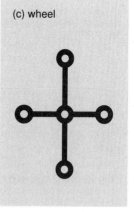

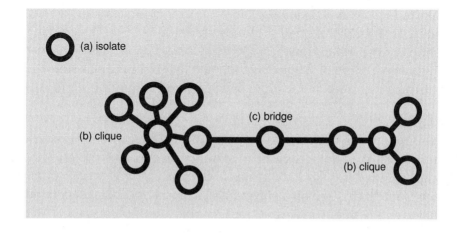

The following three excerpts are taken from the chapter "Group Communication" in the textbook *The New Communications* by Frederick Williams.

## Communication on the Group Level

You have doubtless already spent many hours of your life in face-to-face communication that involves more than two persons, a situation that can properly be called **group communication**. However, the number of people involved is not so important as the patterns of communication and how they relate to the structure or maintenance of the group. Again, as in the study of interpersonal communication, we will see an association between communication and the development of social structures among people.

### Groups large and small

We often make a distinction between small-group communication, which involves approximately three to twenty-five people, and large-group communication, which may involve more than twenty-five people. In small-group communication, there are few enough people so that everybody has a chance to participate in the give-and-take. With larger groups, we are usually dealing with one or a few people communicating to an "audience." A discussion around the dinner table about the day's events is an example of small-group communication. So is a committee meeting of ten people. However, a college lecture delivered to a class of sixty students, some of whom may become involved in discussion with the instructor, is more on the order of large-group communication.

### Types of groups

Groups are fundamental to human existence. We are, for example, born into what sociologists call a **primary group**. As we grow old enough to leave this primary group from time to time, we join other groups, such as children on a playground, a preschool class, other family groups, and eventually regular groups of other children in school. All of these additional groups and ones continuing through adulthood are called **secondary groups**.

In adult life, we also carry out significant amounts of our communication in secondary groups. We socialize with friends and join sports groups, study groups, church groups, school groups, or work groups, to name a few. One mark of adulthood is that we greatly expand the type and complexity of the groups within which we communicate.

***Common types of groups*** As you will see in the following list, groups can have quite different sizes and characteristics. But most have some qualities in common. We will spend the bulk of this chapter discussing these qualities.

*learning group*: a college class or seminar, for example

*living group*: one or several roommates; a cluster of individuals who live near you; or individuals in a dormitory, sorority, or fraternity

*organizational group*: a collection of individuals who represent some formal part of a business, institution, or organization, such as the people in the accounting office, the receptionist, the "marketing" group

*committee*: people who come together to accomplish some specific goal, either members of an organization or individuals assembled only because they are needed to solve a particular problem

*social group*: individuals who are together for purposes of mutual pleasure or enjoyment, such as those invited to a party, a mixer

*therapeutic group*: individuals who are using the group experience in order to help one another work out personal problems, to stimulate one another, or to engage in any other type of personal growth; "encounter," "assertiveness training," "consciousness raising," or "growth" groups

*ritual group*: typically a collection of individuals who come together to celebrate certain ideas or feelings or to go through certain prescribed actions that are meaningful to them, for example, a religious service or a traditional, formal meeting of a business group, where the main purpose is to come together and to participate in certain rituals

*circumstantial group*: a collection of individuals brought together by some course of events, often accidental or circumstantial, as a group of individuals who find themselves waiting in line at the bank or who are traveling together in a section of an airplane

*event, ceremony, or public communication group*: individuals who come together to attend a presentation or performance of some type, for example, a motion picture audience, the audience for a public speech, people attending a concert

*rally, riot, mob, public gathering*: usually a large group of people who come together for some cause in which they have some immediate, on-the-spot interests, to which the assemblage gives momentum and strength, as in the case of a protest group

## The media of group communication

Typically, we consider group communication to be face-to-face, with speech and nonverbal communication as the main media. But as with interpersonal communication, there are media alternatives for group communication. Technology has expanded these alternatives.

For example, telephone conference calling has been available for many years. The operator simply connects multiple parties at an appointed time. Although group communication by telephone can be quite successful, the loss of visual feedback makes it somewhat frustrating, because you cannot see the immediate reactions of others to what you say. A two-way video teleconference provides at least a partial visual channel for group interaction. But, as you can imagine, it is expensive to set up such groups. At one time, the Bell Telephone operating companies offered a Picturephone Meeting Service. Now it has been replaced with a variety of video communications services, some available through the new regional telephone companies and some from new vendors.

Another medium for group interaction is the computer teleconference. This involves the exchange of keyboarded messages that are sent and received by computer terminals linked by telephone lines to a central computer. The computer stores the messages as a record of the group interaction and also makes them available to individuals who are communicating with the group during "off" times. You can join the group at any hour you wish, no matter whether anybody else is participating at the time. You can look at the proceedings, add your comments, and sign off. This is called an asynchronous computer conference.

## A Group's Life Cycle

Although groups vary in how they occur, most follow a cycle of birth, life, and death, or, in group terms, an "establishment–maintenance–termination" cycle of their own. This cycle is most evident in task groups that are formed to solve a particular problem. For example, five individuals in an accounting firm are asked to form an ad hoc committee to select two new accountants from among several dozen applications. The group is formed only to perform that function. It will be maintained while they carry out the review and selection process and will be dissolved upon completion and presentation of its report. The life cycle of a group such as this will be relatively clear if you are a member or an observer of it. In this particular case, the individuals probably know one another well, so it is not difficult for them to come together, do their job, and then get on with their other work.

The life cycles of groups often become a bit more complex when individuals who do not know one another come together to form a group, particularly a task group of some type. Suppose, for example, that you have been selected as one of fifty students, drawn from different colleges and universities around the nation, to come to Chicago for a two-day meeting; the task is to come up with ideas on how to get students to register to vote. If you were participating in this group, you would probably experience phases reflecting both formal and informal aspects of group life cycles. All involve specific types of communication. These phases are:

### Birth

1. Invitation: You are invited and agree subsequently to attend. You accept the understanding of your purpose in attending this meeting.

2. Agenda: You arrive and are given a plan for action that you and the group may follow. It may also remind you what you are to achieve.

3. Beginning of activities: You attend an opening session where you begin to carry out the schedule of the group. You are now actively involved in the proceedings.

*Maintenance*

1. Role assignment: You establish the roles you wish to take as the group "comes to life."

2. Role adjustment: You personally interpret what you wish to make of your role; for example, you are a follower who wants to assert more of a leadership position.

3. Conflict arousal: Not everybody, including you, is likely to be in initial agreement as the group operates. You encounter differences of opinion, personal interpretations, and motives.

4. Conflict resolution: If the group is to be reasonably successful, there will have to be an agreement to resolve differences of opinion sufficiently to get the job done. You will have to be willing to make compromises between your personal goals and those of the group.

5. Problem–solution sequence: This is mixed with all of the other aspects of birth, maintenance, and even conclusion of the group. You will usually participate in the following general sequence:

   a. goal definition

   b. clarification of the goals in terms of importance and implications

   c. identification and evaluation of goals or values or motives against which possible solutions will be evaluated

   d. identification of a range of alternative means for accomplishing the goals or solving the problem

   e. evaluation of alternatives to the values, goals, or motives discussed earlier

   f. selection of the desired alternative, course of action, or solution

   g. consideration of requirements to implement the action or solution

*Termination*

1. Commitment: You are asked to agree that a decision or a sensible alternative has been reached and to make a commitment to support this solution.

2. Acknowledgment of completion: You participate in the recognition that the group's job has been completed and the crediting of members with the job they have accomplished.

3. Formal dissolution: The group is dissolved but sometimes with an agreement on how it might be reassembled if necessary.

Of course, some groups never seem to come to an end. Some of this is by design, as in the permanent committees of an organization, long-lived family groups, or an institution (such as a university, church, club) that has no intention of concluding activities. However, if you do not already, sooner or later in your life you will find yourself participating in groups that really have no continuing significance, other than their own existence. These are, for example, the committees one runs across in businesses and universities that accomplish nothing more than simply meeting. They may meet because it is useful for the organization to show to its public that it exists. If you participate in many of these groups, you will very soon notice that they have gone beyond a natural or productive life cycle. Nothing could be more efficient than their dissolution.

## Group Leadership

Who runs the group? If you are like most people, you might say, right off, "the leader." The problem is that upon closer examination, we find that leadership operates in a variety of ways. The stereotype of a conscientious, assertive, and even compassionate leader moving everybody toward the group's objectives seldom really exists exactly in this way. Leadership may vary all the way from an absolute dictatorship to styles of democracy that would impress even our founding fathers. Also, there are many situations where leadership, whether or not the role is defined, really does not exist. A group simply wanders in whatever direction the discussion drifts. Usually we call these three leadership types the *authoritarian, group-centered,* and *hands-off* styles of leadership, respectively.

## The authoritarian leader

Every Monday morning sharply at 6:30, Dr. B meets with the resident physicians on the staff of the local hospital. The meeting lasts exactly 20 minutes. Almost to the second, the first 15 minutes is spent in reviewing the status of the staff for the week, any special financial considerations that may have arisen, and the schedule of events. The last 5 minutes, with almost absolute certainty, are devoted to Dr. B's near "sermon" on the need to uphold standards, image, and profitability of the hospital. Questions are not invited, and, for as long as most people can remember, no member of the group ever made a significant statement at a meeting. It is Dr. B's meeting. When he is unavailable, the group does not meet.

Authoritarian leadership is sometimes called "leader-centered" because what occurs is almost totally under the control of the leader. No participation other than dutiful listening and compliance is invited in the meeting. Communication is mainly one-way from leader to participants. Leader communication in such situations is often impersonal, meaning that the persons attending the meeting are seen more in terms of the roles they are fulfilling than in terms of individuals. Despite the one-way direction of Dr. B's meeting style, the physicians attending it do not necessarily feel that the time is wasted. After all, they do gain a knowledge of what is going on in the hospital, particularly what Dr. B thinks is going on. Also, the meeting gives the resident physicians a chance to mingle sociably for coffee after the meeting, although Dr. B seldom stays long enough to join them.

## Group-centered leadership

The university's Linguistic Circle meets monthly. It is made up of university faculty in the foreign language, linguistic, and language arts departments and a few of the more advanced graduate students. Although Linguistic Circle is a relatively formal occasion — that is, it isn't a party, and there are certain unwritten rules of behavior — it is a relatively warm and social affair, but primarily an intellectual one. The main program for each meeting is the presentation of a scholarly paper on a topic in linguistics, followed by group discussion of it. Although Professor Z has been the recognized chairman of the Linguistic Circle for as long as anybody can remember, he is mainly a coordinator. Different faculty are invited to sponsor a session, and the group as a whole generally participates equally in deciding any special business of the Circle. Last year, Professor Z was out ill for an entire semester. Although the members of the Circle missed his participation in intellectual discussion, leadership of the group was not perceptibly affected.

Group-centered leadership is sometimes called "democratic" in that all members are invited to participate fully in the decisions and actions of the group. The leader takes on a responsibility more of coordination than of direction. Because the program schedule is chosen by individual members, nearly everybody gets something on the program that is of personal and professional interest. A group-centered style of leadership may create a situation that is not as efficient as the authoritarian-led group, but at the same time it is less dependent on any single individual being present as a leader.

## Hands-off leadership

The Imagineering organization does research, development, and design for the Walt Disney organization. The most critical of the group structures within this organization are "project" teams that include writers, artists, engineers, and an occasional musician and that develop large-scale exhibits. Although each project has a "leader," who usually has a business background, that person's main task is to see that the projects stay on budget and schedule. Because the individuals in this organization are long-time professionals, once they are assembled as a project team, there really is little need for daily or even weekly monitoring by the project leader. These professionals can get the job done mostly on their own. Recently, one of the project leaders left to take a job with another company, and one of the most important projects in the Imagineering organization continued to progress well, although the leader has not yet been replaced.

This hands-off, or as it is sometimes called, *laissez-faire*, type of leadership does not necessarily mean the absolute absence of a leader. Instead, it means that often there is a leader available for handling problems should they arise or that somebody has been designated as having the overall responsibility. However, there is little direct contact or need for this leader on a day-by-day basis. Whereas authoritarian or group-centered leaders may be in very active contact with members of their groups, the laissez-faire leader is relatively inactive unless called upon for advice or assistance. Of course, this is a positive view of hands-off leadership. We are all aware of situations where hands-off leadership has resulted in a group that gets absolutely nothing accomplished. The success of hands-off leadership depends upon having group members who are self-directing and a task that does not require a high degree of central control.

Magazines and journals that are published at set intervals throughout the year are called **periodicals**. These periodicals may be of a **general** nature, covering topics of general interest to the public. Magazines such as *Newsweek, Life, Glamour, Field and Stream, Good Housekeeping*, and *National Geographic* would be considered general periodicals.

Of greater interest to students, however, are periodicals that publish **specialized, technical** material. These journals regularly report the results of research and cater to the interests of scholars in a variety of scientific, technical, and professional areas. *Accounting Review, American Journal of Nursing, Business Review, Developmental Psychology, Justice Quarterly*, and *Social Research* are just a few examples of the hundreds that are published each year.

**Indexes**, which contain references to articles written within certain time periods, serve as efficient guides to the existence and location of specific information. Most indexes are printed in new editions each year, with updated supplements covering the most recent months. Many indexes today are also on microfilm or computerized data bases.

General interest periodicals are listed in the *Reader's Guide to Periodical Literature*. This index contains references to more than 100 popular magazines and journals and is updated with soft-covered supplements every two weeks. Although the magazines indexed in the *Reader's Guide* do not cover technical research information, the guide may be useful in the initial stages of research, to determine the breadth of a particular topic or to evaluate the practical and social implications of research findings.

Academic and professional periodicals, which publish research information and related reports, are listed in specialized indexes. Depending on the size of your library, you may find any number of specialized indexes covering myriad academic and professional disciplines. A few commonly available indexes include *Applied Science and Technology Index, Biological Abstracts, Business Periodicals Index, Cumulative Index to Nursing and Allied Health Literature, Current Law Index, Education Index, Humanities Index, Psychological Abstracts*, and *Social Sciences Index*.

## How to use periodical and technical indexes

Indexes do not contain research information per se, but they enable you to locate the specific sources of such information. Most indexes classify articles in two ways: subject headings and author's last name. *See* and *See also* references as well as subheadings suggest other possible listings for your topic. Because individual indexes have different classification systems, it is important to acquaint yourself with the abbreviations and coding system described at the front or back of each index. An example of a typical index entry appears on page 485.

subject heading ——→ SEXUAL ABUSE

Sexual assault—the nurse's role (Smith LS)
AD NURSE 1987 Mar-Apr; 2(2): 24-8 (9 ref)

cross reference ——→ Sexual Abuse, Child
*see CHILD ABUSE, SEXUAL*

SEXUAL COUNSELING

Sexual counseling of the patient following
myocardial infarction (Cohen JA) (CEU, exam
questions) CRIT CARE NURSE 1986 Nov-Dec; ←———————— journal
6(6): 18-9, 22-4, 26-9 (27 bib)

Nursing's role in the sexual counseling of critical
care patients (Cardin S) (editorial) DCCN 1987
Mar-Apr; 6(2); 67-8

SEXUAL HARASSMENT

What's the best way to handle a sexually
aggressive patient? (Jordheim AE) (survey) J
PRACT NURS 1986 Dec; 36(4): 30-3

Sexual harassment: legal implications—nursing
*part 2* (Creighton H) NURS MANAGE 1987 Jul;
18(7): 16, 18 (13 ref)

Effective responses to sexual harassment
(Heinrich KT) NURS OUTLOOK 1987 Mar-Apr;
35(2): 70-2 (5 ref)

Ain't misbehaving? . . . nurses suffer sexual
harassment (Orr J) NURS TIMES 1987 Mar 4-10;
83(9): 25                                          ——————— author's name
Sexual harassment on the job (Gibbs P) WASH
NURSE 1986 Nov-Dec; 16(9): 22

subheading ———————→ LEGISLATION AND JURISPRUDENCE—
UNITED STATES

Sexual harassment: legal implications—nursing
*part 2* (Creighton H) NURS MANAGE 1987 Jul;
18(7): 16, 18 (13 ref)

Sexual harassment: legal implications *part 1*
(Creighton H) NURS MANAGE 1987 Jun; 18(6): 18,
20, 22 (22 ref)

SEXUALITY

Sexual knowledge of nephrology personnel
(Ulrich BT) (research, tables/charts) ANNA J
1987 Jun; 14(3): 179-83, 230 (11 ref)

Sexual dysfunction in the female ESRD patient
*part 1* (Rickus MA) (CEU, exam questions) ANNA
J 1987 Jun; 14(3): 184-8 (13 ref)

Example from *Cumulative Index to Nursing and Allied Health Literature*

# CREDITS

(Numbers in parentheses indicate pages on which material appears in this book.)

## Chapter 1

"Every Saturday Night," an excerpt from R. C. Anderson, R. E. Reynolds, D. L. Schellert, and G. T. Goetz, "Frameworks for Comprehending Discourse," *American Educational Research Journal*, 14, 1977, pp. 367–381. **(9)**

Tony Randall, "How to Improve Your Vocabulary," from the *Power of the Printed Word* Series, 1985. Used with permission of International Paper, Purchase, New York. **(15–18)**

Don Lago, "Symbols of Humankind," *Science Digest*, March 1981. **(22–24)**

Russell Baker, "Don't Talk Dirty to Me," originally titled "Vile as Smoke," *The New York Times*, January 6, 1988. © 1988 by The New York Times Company. Used with permission of The New York Times Company. **(27–29)**

## Chapter 2

Wayne Weiten, "Hypnosis: Altered Consciousness or Role Playing?" *Psychology: Themes and Variations*, pp. 169–172. © 1989 by Wadsworth, Inc. Used with permission of Brooks/Cole Publishing Company. **(35–37)**

"Ants: The Oldest Farm in the World," from *Newsweek*, December 19, 1994. © 1994 Newsweek, Inc. All rights reserved. Reprinted by permission. **(42)**

William John Watkins, "Chronobiology: Finding Your Peak Time of Day," *Passages*, October 1982. Used with permission of William John Watkins, Ocean NJ. **(45–49)**

Wayne Weiten, "Hypnosis: Altered Consciousness or Role Playing?" *Psychology: Themes and Variations*, pp. 156–158. © 1989 by Wadsworth, Inc. Used with permission of Brooks/Cole Publishing Company. **(53–57)**

Madeline Drexler, "All Work and Not Enough Play," reprinted from *The Boston Globe* by permission of the author. **(63–65)**

## Chapter 3

Madeline Drexler, "Get Smart," *The Boston Globe*, May 28, 1989. Used with permission of Madeline Drexler, Watertown MA. **(83–86)**

Jack Levin, "Better Late Than Never," *Bostonia*, May/June 1989. Used with permission of Jack Levin, Boston MA. **(89–91)**

Isaac Asimov, "What Is Intelligence, Anyway?" Used with permission of Janet Asimov, New York City NY **(94–95)**

Paul Chance, "When Teaching Hurts," *Psychology Today*, April 1988. ©1988 Sussex Publishers, Inc. Used with permission of Sussex Publishers, Inc. **(99)**

## Chapter 4

David Shaffer, "Development of Metamemory," *Developmental Psychology*, 2nd ed., pp. 339–340. © 1989 by Wadsworth, Inc. Used with permission of Brooks/Cole Publishing Company. (**118–123**)

Beth Levine, "How to Improve Your . . . Oh, Yeah, Memory," *Seventeen*, January 1989. Used with permission of Beth Levine, Irvington NY. (**126–133**)

Richard Wright, "The Library Card" from *Black Boy*, Copyright 1937, 1942, 1944, 1945 by Richard Wright. Copyright renewed 1973 by Ellen Wright. Reprinted by permission of HarperCollins Publishers, Inc. (**135–140**)

## Chapter 5

Diane White, "Can We Talk?" *The Boston Globe*, March 3, 1992. Used with permission of *The Boston Globe*. (**158–159**)

## Chapter 6

"Questions and Answers" ("A Cure for Nail Biting"), *Psychology Today*, April 1989. © 1989 Sussex Publishers, Inc. Used with permission of Sussex Publishers, Inc. (**169**)

Five steps for solving problems adapted from Barry F. Anderson, *The Complete Thinker*, © 1980, Section B of Table 1, p. 15. Used with permission of Barry Anderson. (**172**)

M. R. Levy, M. Dignan, and J. Shirreffs, "Stress and Its Management," *Essentials of Life and Health*, 5th ed., 1988, pp. 47, 57–60. Used with permission of McGraw-Hill Publishing Company. (**174–177**)

Wayne Weiten, "Reappraisal: Ellis's Rational Thinking," *Psychology: Themes and Variations*, pp. 503–505. ©1989 by Wadsworth, Inc. Used with permission of Brooks/Cole Publishing Company. (**181–184**)

Suzanne Ouellette Kobasa, "How Much Stress Can You Survive?" *American Health Magazine*, September 1984. Used with permission of the publisher. (**188–190**)

M. Scott Peck, "Problems and Pain," *The Road Less Traveled*. © 1978 by M. Scott Peck, M.D. Used with permission of Simon & Schuster, Inc. (**192–193**)

## Chapter 7

Photo of a group. © Cathy Ferris 1992. (**198**)

Two short passages defining groups in Exercise 1 and 2, from Judson R. Landis, *Sociology*, 7th ed., pp. 106–107. © 1989 by Wadsworth, Inc. Used by permission of the publisher. (**201–203**)

Judson R. Landis, "Types of Groups," *Sociology*, 7th ed., pp. 108–109. © 1989 by Wadsworth, Inc. Used by permission of the publisher. (**205–206**)

Judson R. Landis, "Collective Behavior," *Sociology*, 7th ed., pp. 360–363. © 1989 by Wadsworth, Inc. Used by permission of the publisher. (**208–211**)

David Gelman with Peter McKillop, "Going 'Wilding' in the City," *Newsweek*, May 8, 1989. © 1989 Newsweek, Inc. All rights reserved. Used by permission of Newsweek, Inc. (**214–216**)

Roger Rosenblatt, "The Male Response to Rape," *Time*, April 18, 1983. © 1983 Time Warner, Inc. Used with permission of Time. (**219–222**)

## Chapter 8

Five short passages on narcotics illustrating chronology and narration from "Cry for Us and Our Children," *The Boston Globe*, Special Section, November 9, 1986. Used with permission of *The Boston Globe*. (**225, 226, 227–228, 230, 231**)

Linda Brannon and Jess Feist, "Using Alcohol and Drugs," *Health Psychology*, 2nd ed., pp. 352–355. © 1992 by Wadsworth, Inc. Used by permission of the publisher. (**233–237**)